This is a most valuable and absorbing reflection upon a rich lifetime in teaching. The author draws deeply upon that experience, well documented through diaries and relevant papers, to draw lessons about the very nature of teaching (and thus about the training of new teachers) which, not to be forgotten, is always affected by the wider social and political context. This book deserves an international audience because the issues raised and problems met are universal. Furthermore, the book is very clearly written, and excellently illustrated with examples, stories and critical reflections. **Richard Pring**, *Emeritus Professor at the Department of Education, and Emeritus Fellow of Green Templeton College, University of Oxford.*

The remarkable life of a principled Tanzanian educator and activist told with an eye for historical accuracy but also with emotion and humor. Essential reading for anyone interested in the history of Tanzania's Ujamaa period. **Peter Lawrence**, *Professor Emeritus of Development Economics, Keele University UK, and Lecturer in Economics, University of Dar es Salaam, 1970-72.*

Through his account of four decades of teaching experience at different levels in varied contexts in post-colonial Tanzania, Karim Hirji provides us with a timely reminder of the ways in which education generally plays the role of consolidating existing structures of power – whether this be of colonialists, or bureaucratic, corrupt party hacks, or the neoliberal state and its private sector partners. As he remarks, educators face a choice, now as ever: "serve the *status quo* or educate in ways that will promote equality and social justice". **Dr Anne Harley**, *Paulo Freire Project, Centre for Adult Education, University of KwaZulu Natal, South Africa.*

THE TRAVAILS OF A
TANZANIAN TEACHER

THE TRAVAILS OF A TANZANIAN TEACHER

KARIM HIRJI

Daraja Press

Published by
https://darajapress.com
© Karim Hirji 2018
All Rights Reserved
Editorial Management: Firoze Manji
Cover design: Catherine McDonnell
Cover Photo: William Warby

Library and Archives Canada Cataloguing in Publication
Hirji, Karim F., author
The travails of a Tanzanian teacher / Karim F. Hirji.
Includes bibliographical references.
Issued in print and electronic formats.
ISBN 978-1-988832-09-8 (softcover).–ISBN 978-1-988832-10-4 (ebook)

1. Hirji, Karim F. 2. College teachers–Tanzania–Biography. 3. Education, Higher–Tanzania. 4. Tanzania–Politics and government–1964-. 5. Tanzania–Economic conditions–1964-. 6. Autobiographies. I. Title.

LA2388.T342H57 2018   370.92   C2018-901189-0

C2018-901190-4

To
Symonds Akivaga, EA Moshi, FS Swai, FM Materu,
IM Dewji, George Hadjivayanis, Munene Njagi,
Jenerali Ulimwengu, Naijuka Kasihwaki, J Shengena,
Henry Mapolu, Andrew Chenge, Ramesh Chauhan,
Joe Kanywanyi, Andrew Lyall, Kighoma Malima,
AJ Temu, Marjorie Mbiliny, Kassim Guruli
And
All Other Student, Staff and Worker Activists of
the July 1971 Pro-Democracy Uprising
at the University of Dar es Salaam

+ + + + + +

What a teacher writes
On the blackboard of life
Can never be erased
Unknown Author

+ + + + + +

Contents

PREFACE		xiii
ACRONYMS		xvii
1.	VOLUNTEER TEACHER	1
2.	TRAINEE TEACHER	13
3.	TUTORIAL ASSISTANT	33
4.	A VISIT TO ZANZIBAR	41
5.	A PRO-DEMOCRACY UPRISING	55
6.	ASSISTANT LECTURER	79
7.	PLANNING OFFICER	89
8.	SENIOR INSTRUCTOR	117
9.	THE ACADEMY TODAY	149
10.	FUNDAMENTALS OF TEACHING	165
11.	THE BLACKBOARD SAGA	171
APPENDIX A AKIVAGA CRISIS TIMELINE		177
APPENDIX B AKIVAGA CRISIS IN HISTORY		179
APPENDIX C DEMOCRACY AND EDUCATION		201
APPENDIX D PHOTOS		209
ACKNOWLEDGMENTS		217
REFERENCES AND READINGS		219
AUTHOR PROFILE		227

PREFACE

No one gets rich teaching
But one lives a richer life
Unknown Author

+ + + + + + +

TEACHING HAS BEEN A VERITABLE LOVE OF MY LIFE. I joined this noble profession in April 1971, and officially ceased my ingrained routine of facing the blackboard in July 2012. During this period of slightly over four decades, I taught mathematics and statistics, first in a university mathematics department, then in a transport related educational institute, and finally, and for the most part, in university level public health and medical departments.

My teaching career fell into two phases: The first phase started in April 1971 when I was hired as a tutorial assistant (TA) at the Department of Mathematics of the University of Dar es Salaam (UDSM). A year later, I became an Assistant Lecturer. In March 1974, this promising line of work terminated abruptly. Through political machinations of the university administration, I was sent to a remote region of Tanzania. From lecturing linear algebra, I was transformed into a paper shuffling mid-level bureaucrat. My job title was Planning Officer. But planning for development was the least of what I did.

Fortunately, I was able to return to teaching a year and a half later when in October 1975 I was hired by the just founded National Institute of Transport (NIT) in Dar es Salaam as an Instructor in Transport Statistics. Because it was the first institution of its kind in sub-Saharan Africa, I faced challenges of the type I had never dreamed I would face. For five years, I immersed myself into this job. My colleagues and I faced numerous hurdles, practical, academic and societal. Some seemed insurmountable. Yet, by the end of 1980, a fully functional institute conferring certificates and diplomas reflecting a high academic standard in varied areas related to transportation was in operation.

At the end of 1980, I left NIT to study at Harvard University in the USA. My aim was a doctoral degree in Biostatistics. That was my entry into the second phase of my teaching career that was to last three decades. I worked in the health and bio-medical arena, teaching theory based and applied subjects related to medical research methods at universities in USA, Tanzania and Norway. I also conducted research in a specialized area of Biostatistics and took part in research projects on a variety of health issues. This research frequently led to publishing papers in statistical and medical journals, and writing a book and book chapters.

While the two phases have a unifying theme, they are distinct in terms of substance, style, audience and societal import. The focus of this book is on the first phase, that is, on the first decade of my work as a teacher. The pedagogic essence, episodes, societal context and outcomes of this phase are sufficiently extensive to justify a book of its own. The second phase will be presented in a forthcoming work.

METHOD

This book takes off from my two previous memoirs. In *Growing Up With Tanzania: Memory, Math and Musings*, I covered my childhood and schooling until I was ready to join the university. In *Cheche: Reminiscences of a Radical Magazine*, my comrades and I wrote on aspects of student life at UDSM. From here on I refer to these books as *GUWTZ* and *Cheche*, respectively. They show some aspects of my teaching life but in a limited manner. Here I present the full picture.

This book is not just about teaching. A teacher is also a human encumbered with the complexities, pleasures and impediments that come with life. They affect his work, attitude and relations with his students, fellow teachers and other people. Accordingly, at numerous time points in this narrative, I am drawn to reflect on the ongoing currents flowing in my personal and social lives.

But that is not it. What teachers teach and how they do it is affected in a significant manner by the broader social and economic context, by history, by the political trends of the day, and by the position of the teaching profession in the social order. In deference to this sociological reality, I devote due space to relevant contextual factors and events surrounding my teaching life. Two chapters deal entirely with two separate, barely week-long episodes that occurred at the place I was teaching. They were connected to academics but their significance transcended the lecture room. I also devote a chapter to my deeds during the time I was banished from teaching.

I consider myself a social activist and a teacher. To me, these roles complement each other. Activism does not necessarily distract a person from doing his or her job, or doing it well. If pursued in a diligent and ethical manner, it on the contrary enhances academic effectiveness and enriches one's relationships with colleagues and students. That is what I experienced throughout my teaching career. Thus, in this book, I integrate the basic elements and actualities of my activism where it is appropriate. I adhere to the maxim that primarily, a teacher is a social being, with weighty social responsibilities.

CONTENTS

I was not drawn into teaching overnight. It was a process that unfolded over time. My first contact with a teacher was a disastrous one. Teaching in a harsh way, she punished her students painfully for the slightest error. However, from then on, I had the good fortune of encountering a series of magnificent teachers (see *GUWTZ.*) They in a way drew me into their profession. Because I excelled in mathematics, I began tutoring fellow students in an informal manner from an early age. I thereby deem it fitting to begin this book with a chapter on the voluntary type of teaching work I have done over the years. Starting with tutoring schoolmates, it is one of the few places in this book where I venture into the second phase of my teaching life. After this, I delve into the three years of teacher training, at theoretical and practical levels, I received at UDSM.

The next four chapters cover my time at UDSM, first as a tutorial assistant and then, an assistant lecturer. Next comes a chapter on my eighteen months as a do-nothing bureaucrat in rural Tanzania. It is followed up by my involvement in the task of setting up an educational institution from scratch and teaching there. Chapter 9 compares the state of university level teaching today with that in early years. Then, after giving the main tenets of good teaching I have distilled from my personal experience, I end with an atypical of experience with which I ended my teaching career.

Appendices A, B and C expand on the material contained in Chapter 5 and Chapter 8. Appendix D has photos related to the events described in the book.

SOURCES

While our memory has valuable characteristics, it also has major drawbacks. It is eminently fragile, capable not just of forgetting key life events, but also of distorting them to an unrecognized extent. Often, it invents events that never occurred. It is thereby foolhardy to write a work like this based on memory alone. Luckily I have preserved a large bank of personal and general documents about places, people and general situation related to what I write on. At critical junctions, I maintained a diary of happenings of the day. All these have supplemented my memory.

In addition, I found documents from that era which helped me fill in the gaps in my own material. Importantly, I contacted friends and colleagues from those days, some I had not connected with for ages. I detail my contacts, sources and other material in the Acknowledgments section at the back of this book. Adopting a conversational style in a memoir enhances its readability and appeal. Yet exact conversations are hard to recall. The conversations in this book reflect, as accurately as I can make it, the essence of what went on. Finally, note that the spelling in this book follows US English.

Karim F Hirji
February 2018

ACRONYMS

ARPO	Assistant Regional Planning Officer
ASP	Afro Shirazi Party
ASPYL	Afro Shirazi Party Youth League
DS	Development Studies
DSM	Dar es Salaam
DUSO	Dar es Salaam University Student Organization
ESR	Education for Self-Reliance
FFU	Field Force Unit
GUWTZ	Growing Up With Tanzania
HSPH	Harvard School of Public Health
LSE	London School of Economics
MUCHS	Muhimbili University College of Health Sciences
MUHAS	Muhimbili University of Health and Allied Sciences
NGO	Non-Governmental Organization
NIT	National Institute of Transport
NITSO	NIT Student Organization
NTC	National Transport Corporation
PMO	Prime Minister's Office

RDD	Regional Development Director
RPO	Regional Planning Officer
TA	Tutorial Assistant
TANU	Tanganyika African National Union
TSh	Tanzania Shillings
TYL	TANU Youth League
UCLA	University of California, Los Angeles
UDSM	University of Dar es Salaam
USARF	University Students' African Revolutionary Front
VC	Vice Chancellor

I

VOLUNTEER TEACHER

*If you have knowledge
Let others light their candles at it*
Margaret Fuller

+ + + + + + +

LIKE ALL CHILDREN, I yearned for friendship and popularity. I was a shy kid of lean stature from a low income family, with lack luster ability in sports and games. One thing rescued me. From primary school days, I excelled in mathematics while many floundered in the subject. As they sought my help and I unhesitatingly obliged, my popularity rating rose several notches. This peer-tutoring habit developed in earnest in upper primary school, increased at my secondary school, and persisted into high school, undergraduate and even post-graduate pursuits.

In the year 1960, and the seventh grade of the Agakhan Boys School in Dar es Salaam, I was a new arrival from a remote southern region of Tanzania. My odd attire and quiet demeanor marked me out as a country bumpkin (derisively labeled in Kutchi as *bhar jo bhotho*). As I was praised by my teachers for my mathematical ability, even the elitist fellows in the class approached me in a friendly fashion for the answer to a tough homework question.

At my secondary-technical school, the Dar es Salaam Technical College, I found that my classmates had attended underfunded colonial schools and hence had a poor background in mathematics. I, on the other hand, came from schools that had given me very little exposure to Swahili. A mutually beneficial arrangement ensued. I helped them in mathematics while they enabled me to wade through the terminology, grammar and idiom of Swahili.

In my final year, I added a subject for my certificate examination, namely Additional Mathematics. It was normally done over a two-year period, and was not taught at my college. So not only did I have to cover all the material within a single year, but also had to do it on my own. Two other students a grade below me,

Abdulkarim Mohamed and Abdallah Madenge, were keen on it as well. Luckily, the needed books were available in the college library.

We teamed up and met three times a week to tackle a topic after another. Having read through the material beforehand, I effectively became the tutor. I passed the subject, though not at the grade level I had desired. In the following two years, I went to a boarding school, the Kibaha Secondary School, where I did my Form V and Form VI studies. The place lay twenty six miles from Dar es Salaam. On the weekends I was in Dar es Salaam to visit my parents, I often went to the College to help Abdulkarim and Abdallah prepare for their Additional Mathematics final exam. These interactions led to life-long friendships, a prize more valuable than any.

By high school, assisting fellow students in numeracy was but second nature to me. I recall tackling calculus and mechanics problems with Elias Kisamo, Titus Kamulali and Shiraz Kassam. I joined the Chess Club, became the school champion and taught chess to my friends in the city. I retain fond memories of chess games played with Navroz Lakhani. We sat on a cool cement bench in the elegant garden of the Upanga Jamatkhana (prayer house), staring for hours at a time at the quixotic pieces on the 8×8 board.

I confess that there was one covert reason why, especially at that juncture in my life, I helped out with mathematics; it narrowed my proximity to lovely members of the fair sex. My reserved personality prevented me from approaching or talking to girls my age on a one to one basis. Yet, now and then a pretty girl would come to me with a request to tackle a mathematical equation. A usual corollary of the task was that it yielded at least an approximate solution to my emotional non-linear differential equation.

AT UDSM

I started my BSc degree studies at the University of Dar es Salaam (UDSM) in July 1968. My two major subjects were Pure Mathematics and Applied Mathematics, and the minor was Education. I was being trained as a secondary school teacher of mathematics. The subject combination was not of my own choosing. I had wanted to pursue Pure Mathematics, Applied Mathematics and Philosophy at Makerere University in Uganda. But a bureaucrat in the Ministry of Education decided otherwise.

Only one other student was enrolled in the Pure and Applied Mathematics stream. And, sadly, he dropped it after the first year. Normally, students took mathematics as a single subject, combining it with Physics, Chemistry or Economics. Slated to be secondary school teachers, most of them had education as the minor subject.

Of my teachers at UDSM, the two who impressed me most were Professor

Ted Phythian and Mr (now Professor) Ralph Masenge. The latter gave me my very first lecture at UDSM. The course, Basic Analysis, was unlike any I had encountered earlier. Filled with abstract definitions and esoteric symbolism, it for the first time conveyed to me the crucial lesson that in mathematics, the logicality of each and every step you take, however small, matters. Nothing can be taken for granted, even a supposedly self-evident thing like $2 + 2 = 4$. The abstract nature of the topics notwithstanding, he conveyed them in an understandable fashion. His friendly demeanor, there being only two students in the class, and the multitude of examples he gave went a long way towards making his courses an educational experience of the first order. In my second year, he taught numerical analysis, his specialty, in a similar style. This course was taken by the other mathematics students too.

Professor Phythian taught courses in applied mathematics and computer science. He had the habit of laughing loudly at any provocation. He would write a formula on the board, look at it for a few seconds in a semi-puzzled fashion, and break out into a rippling laugh.

Karim, don't you realize what a majestic expression it is? Haa ha haa ha ha!

Being the sole student in the class, I would be at a loss to respond. It was like an unfathomable jumble to me. Then, in a step by step way, he would derive it from basic principles. By the end of the hour, I had to agree with his initial take on the formula. The course I recall best was Special Functions of Mathematical Physics. It was from him that I came to appreciate that even quite arcane topics in mathematics have concrete, at times indispensable, applications in the various branches of the natural sciences.

Dr David Cappitt and Dr Terry Heaps taught the advanced courses like Functional Analysis and Algebraic Topology. I could see that they had mastered their subjects, lecturing off the top of their head but in a systematic manner. But, three quarters of the time, I was lost. The approach was strictly formal, rarely went back and forth to connect up issues, and had but a few examples, and, which moreover, were not of the most illuminating kind. Only at the time of intense study for the end of the year exams did I begin to make head or tail of just a part of what they had taught.

In the few common mathematical courses I was required to take with others, I was always at the top of my class. No wonder, a number of them lined up outside my dorm room for help.

It was during this time that life imparted a most singular lesson onto me, a lesson that would reappear later on: That assisting others can at times have undesirable consequences. It happened like this: A friend I call HM, also a first year science student, was doing very well in Physics. But in some tough topics in mathematics, he came to me for help, particularly when the final exams were close by.

A week after the end of the first year final exams, Dr Masenge, and the head of the Department of Mathematics, Professor Phythian, told me that my performance had been excellent. In their opinion, I had stood above any other present and previous first year science student. It then came as a surprise, at least to me, that I was not given the annual prize for the best first year student in the Faculty of Science. The award went to HM. When this was announced at the start of the next academic year, the professor gently beckoned me to his office. In an apologetic tone, he told me:

> *Karim, there is no question in my mind that you deserved this prize. You are surely the best student this department has had thus far. Your overall exam score was way above that of all the first year science students. In the Faculty Board meeting, I strongly recommended you for the prize but was overruled by Professor Osborne.*

Professor Dennis Osborne was the Dean of the Faculty of Science and Head of the Department of Physics. I inquired:

> *But why?*

> *Well, in each of the past two years, the prize has gone to a double-mathematics student. Professor Osborne claimed that this was not fair to students from other departments. I held that the best should always get the prize, no matter what department he or she was in. In your case, I said that you were the best of the best. The majority of the academic staff, however, sided with Osborne. Karim, I am sorry to say that you lost out.*

There was also a hidden reason why I lost the prize. Professor Phythian knew it but did not say so at this time. It stemmed from a book I had read. Of the title *The Human Use of Human Beings*, it was the work of a leading American mathematician, Norbert Weiner. A best seller in the US, Canada and Europe, I had purchased it from the university bookstore at what today sounds like an absurd price of seven shillings and twenty five cents, the equivalent of a tad more than one US dollar.

Weiner was one the originators of the then emerging discipline of computerized automation and control, or robotics as it is called now. His book reflected on the beneficial and harmful consequences of the wide utilization of this technology. Distinctly impressed, I wrote a short piece about its main points. Mechanisms of automatic control (homeostatic processes) were, according to him, commonly found in the natural environment, biological organisms and society, and were the basis of numerous human technologies at well. Two examples are the pressure control valve in a steam engine, and the intricate system to control the blood pressure in human beings. Their actual mechanisms are vastly different, but the underlying principle is the same. A key implication of his theory is that to explain the marvelous, self-sustaining phenomena of nature, a resort to an external force or super being is not called for. Automatic regulation is intrinsic to matter. And human psychology exhibits that tendency as well.

Many complex issues are addressed in this small but dense book. But in a short article written for the student magazine, *The Echo*, I had focused on this particular point. Its title was *God and Golem, Inc.*, borrowed from the title of another book of Weiner. My article had appeared about a month before the first year exams. Professor Osborne had, in private, expressed displeasure towards it no small measure. A devout Christian who played a lead role in the campus church activities, he thought that my reflections were akin to nonsensical blasphemy.

I know this because he told that to Professor Phythian, who in turn warned me to not offend the Faculty Dean. Professor Phythian was also a good Christian. But, fortunately, he did not have a narrow outlook. His warning was given in a fatherly tone, more to protect me than for any other reason. This incident, I believe, played a role in why I missed out on the best student prize. But none of us referred to it.

This episode has wider societal implications. For those were the high-point years of the era of socialism in Tanzania. A common argument heard at the time was that socialism was an intolerant system that suppressed differing viewpoints. Well, here was an instance of a top-level scientist from the capitalist West exercising a form of control on ideas through covertly retaliating against the airing of views that, after all, came from a bestseller in the US, Canada, UK and Europe. It was not published in a communist nation. Nor was it written by a person espousing that ideology. The author was a prominent scientist at a top university in the US. It seemed as if we in Africa were not mature enough to discuss the ideas presented in such books.

Later in my life, I spent nearly fifteen years teaching at a major university in the US. I learned that over the years of the Cold War and beyond, thousands of US and external academics, including scientists, had faced sanctions, at times dismissal and loss of tenure, for espousing anti-corporate or anti-establishment views. I also witnessed it firsthand. Such sanctions were rarely exercised directly or openly but operated through subtle means like delayed promotion, heavy work load, loss of research funds, etc. The declared reasons for these acts were extraneous to the actual issues, but the message was loud and clear. If you do not control what you say and write, there will be consequences. Since it operates with subtlety and behind a curtain, censorship under capitalism is far more effective than George Orwell ever envisioned. The victim is under the illusion that he or she lives in a free society, unaware the he or she is being subtly influenced by multiple forces, or even being watched and censored.

ADULT EDUCATION

One major plank of the national education policy at the time I was at UDSM was the promotion of adult literacy. The aim was to ensure that every Tanzanian adult knew how to read and write in Kiswahili, and accurately perform basic arithmetic operations like counting, addition, subtraction, multiplication and division. The UDSM student union and several smaller student organizations were also involved in this nationwide undertaking.

On the assigned day and time, ten or so members of a group would go to a village or urban locality near the main campus to teach the adults gathered there. It was either a primary school, or a small room with a blackboard. In a few places, you sat with your wards under a large, shady tree where chairs and desks had been placed.

There was no set curriculum or textbook. There was no prior plan of action. If you were lucky, there would be a couple of books for the group to share. You assessed the level of your students, and proceeded from there. You made them practice what they had been taught earlier, or exposed them to new material. The class composition varied from week to week. Usually more women than men attended. If it was raining, the class was canceled. At planting and harvest times, only a few dedicated souls were in attendance.

I began taking part in this program from the second term of the first academic year. Except in the couple of weeks around the final exams, I was always present. The class met for about two hours at a time. My group taught in the *darajani* area in a village adjacent to the eastern entrance of the campus. The sessions were attended well, our adult students eager to learn. And, their humility was striking. They did not address us by name but always as *mwalimu* (teacher), and in a respectful manner.

I focused on arithmetic, and taught one to three students on a one-to-one basis. I continued taking part in this program throughout my undergraduate years and also into the years I was a member of the academic staff of the university. After my marriage in August 1973, my wife Farida joined the program as a volunteer teacher.

In those days, participation in such programs was not deemed as anything out of ordinary. No material incentive was involved, not even a cup of tea. You went to and fro at your own cost; there was no certificate of participation; and you did not secure any public recognition either. There was no compulsion or pressure; you went of your own accord, and could end your participation whenever you felt like it. Yet, tens of thousands of students and educated adults in the nation took part in that laudable drive to help all Tanzanians gain basic literacy skills.

Your most precious reward was the smile on the face of your trainee when, after weeks of effort and frustration, he or she could write his or her own name, or do basic sums. In the current era of lavish NGO funding, when people attending a meeting to plan a voluntary activity expect at least a meal and transport allowance, what took place in the 60s and 70s sounds as if it happened on an alien planet.

AT LSE

From September 1971 to July 1972, I did my master's degree in Operations Research (a branch of applied mathematics) at the London School of Economics. I describe my studies and other activities in Chapter 3. Here I note only one thing.

In the ten months I was in London, I recall only one occasion when I engaged in tutoring. In the first week of my arrival in the metropolis, I had the company of Issa Shivji who had just completed his master's degree in law. When we went to visit Abdulla Dharamsy, a friend from Dar es Salaam now settled in the UK, we found him in a state of anxiety. His professional certification exams in accountancy were on the horizon. He was prepared for all the subjects except Statistics. Needless to say, I spent hours guiding him through the required material. Later, I was happy to learn that he passed the exam. I am glad that he remains thankful to this day for the assistance I gave him.

AT HARVARD

Tutoring fellow students took a novel turn when I went for my doctoral studies in Biostatistics at the Harvard School of Public Health (HSPH). It was 1981. Boston was freezing cold and awash with snow, it being my first time to observe a totally white landscape. The foreign students, many with families, were housed at the HSPH owned International House. About 300 meters from the school, its three buildings were interconnected at the basement level. Most of us were at a loss in the not so welcoming US cultural and social environment. This place, with large areas for social activities and TV viewing, computer terminals connected to the main HSPH computer, exercise area, facilities and programs for children and weekly social events, provided a place where we could shut out the external world, and create a community of our own.

Basic Biostatistics was a required subject for most students at HSPH. Almost 90% of the first year students were thereby in one of the two such introductory classes. The most popular was taught by Professor Marge Drollett, an award winning lecturer. However, due to their poor background in numeric disciplines, many international students struggled with the subject.

Invariably, one, two, three, four and more of them began to approach me, in the school cafeteria, the residential common room and even at my door, for help with a homework problem. I was happy to oblige, but I also had a full program of studies, and it began to take up too much of my time. Not inclined to help this friend but not the other one, I devised a novel solution to the problem. I asked our residence manager if, for one evening of the week, the common room could be reserved for a teaching session. Chairs would have to be arranged and a blackboard and chalk secured. He was most cooperative; the arrangements were efficiently done; and a notice to the effect was put up.

My free tutoring sessions, lasting for ninety minutes, were held every Thursday at 7:30 p.m. There were between thirty to forty attendees, most from the International House, but a few outsiders came too. I went over the material they had covered in their Biostatistics class, and answered the questions posed. The attendees were immensely grateful for my assistance. In the process, I befriended students from Ghana, Nigeria, Kenya, Sudan, India, Pakistan, Taiwan, Beirut, Mexico, Egypt, the UK, Denmark and Norway.

There was also an indirect monetary reward. Farida and Rosa, my daughter, were with me. My scholarship stipend barely made ends meet. Desirous of pursuing further studies in management at the North Eastern University on a part-time basis, Farida took up the task of typing the HSPH student reports. It was the era before the PC and word processing. We purchased a fine electronic typewriter for the job, and she charged a dollar per page.

Initially, she did not have many clients. But my free tutoring led to contacts through which she secured more work. A fast and accurate typist, she raised enough funds over a two year period to obtain the AA (Associate in Arts) degree in management. She needed two more years of study to get the bachelor's degree. But instead of doing that, she switched to nursing studies at the Santa Monica College, qualified as a Registered Nurse, and successfully practiced this demanding profession for nearly two decades, in the US and in Tanzania.

AT UCLA

While a professor at the UCLA School of Medicine, I had a voluntary teaching experience of the most unique kind. It was 1991. A notice on a board near the main cafeteria caught my attention. A student organization concerned with the wellbeing of incarcerated juveniles was seeking volunteers. My interest piqued, I went to their meeting the next evening. Their main activity was to teach basic subjects to kids living behind bars. I immediately signed up.

The following week on, we drove every Tuesday to the Los Angeles County Juvenile Detention Center, situated some thirty miles from the UCLA campus. Two vans, provided by the University, were at our disposal. We had ten or so volunteers per van, all of them UCLA undergraduate students. I was the only professor in the group. The students welcomed my participation, though here I was like any other volunteer. I was the designated driver for one van. Our trip started at 5 p.m., and depending on the traffic, it took twenty to thirty minutes.

The first day was an eye opener. We were first addressed by the Director of the Center, a man with a broad smile on his face, but otherwise exuding a strict military aura. He had a message for us:

> The boys you will teach are between twelve and seventeen years in age. They will be friendly, even charming. But do not be taken in. This facility houses kids who have been convicted for serious crimes like gang violence, armed robbery, house breaking, grievous assault, and even rape and murder. You will not know who has done what, but be aware of who you are dealing with.

That was our introduction to the job. Then we were taken to a large hall where twenty five desks with two to three chairs per desk were arranged. As each of us took up a desk, our wards marched in, and were assigned to us on a random basis. At times I had one trainee, at times, two. Tutoring was done on a one to one basis with each session lasting for two hours. Pens and notepads were provided. The first time we did not have any books, but from the next week on, each of us was allowed to bring up to two books.

Though armed guards discretely sat in two corners, the atmosphere was jovial, and our wards were most friendly. The boys with a female tutor had the widest smiles on their faces. They would remain with that tutor for about three and a half months. We spent the first session introducing ourselves, asking about their educational background and interests, and devising a semester long program of instruction. The focus was on reading, writing and basic mathematics. Our trainees were school drop outs or had done badly in school. No one had successfully completed secondary schooling.

The jailed kids were eager to learn, full of questions. They normally did the work we assigned to them. I spent half the time going through a novel, and the other half on elementary geometry and algebra. The first novel I chose for my two boys was *Alice in Wonderland* by Lewis Carroll, which they enjoyed more than the mathematics part.

I participated in this program for two academic years (four semesters). And it was a revealing experience. The total of seven boys I taught were, in our interactions, no different from typical boys. Besides the setting, nothing was out of ordinary. Three of them were fast learners. They grasped difficult ideas with ease, asked probing questions, and wanted additional material. They had dreams of one day attending a university like UCLA.

During this period I read a host of books, journal papers, and news reports on the US system of justice. It was shocking to learn that the nation which claims to be a standard bearer of democratic governance in the world not only had the highest incarceration rate in the world, but that the administration of justice was inundated with injustice. Penalties were harsher for street crime as compared to white collar crime, though the latter exacted a greater financial and human toll.

The media and politicians created sustained public hysteria over a case or two of armed bank hold-ups but the bankers who shamelessly scooped billions received transient, milder opprobrium. Unlike for street crime, there was no nationwide system of keeping data on white collar crime.

The poor, mainly from African American, Latino and Native American communities were targeted unfairly and dealt with more harshly at each and every stage of the justice system. Consequently, the jails and prisons housed a higher, both in absolute and relative terms, number of individuals from socially disadvantaged and discriminated communities. In fact, the inmates taught by our UCLA group were all Latino. We were told that African American and Latino inmates were kept separate due to the ongoing internecine turf war between rival gangs from these two communities.

Each time we drove away after a training session, I could not but think about the tremendous loss to society and their own lives resulting from the avoidable lock up of so many young ones. True, their harsh acts had traumatized many families. Yet, that they too were victims of a society characterized by corporate control of vital societal sectors including all the branches of the government, a huge gap between the rich and the poor, and firm, institutionalized racism in education, housing, health care, transport, bank services, employment, and environmental pollution. Growing up in these deleterious circumstances had compromised their prospects in education and obtaining well paid jobs.

An issue of interest to me was the motivation of the students who participated in this education exercise. The four group leaders (two in each academic year) and a couple of other students were obviously dedicated to the cause. In addition to the tutoring work, they were involved in raising public awareness about the nature of the US justice system and promoting reform. But the most likely reason why the majority of our group, all undergraduate students from varied disciplines, took part in this voluntary effort was of a different kind. They desired to pursue studies at prestigious graduate universities like Harvard, Stanford, UC Berkeley and UCLA. Admission to these elite institutions was competitive in the extreme. Most of the applicants had top level academic grades and applicants far exceeded the available places. What often tipped the scale in favor of entry was the applicant's personal statement. Involvement in extracurricular activities of this type was taken as an item of special value in that statement.

My two and a half decades of experience at US universities impressed upon me voluntary work was an integral aspect of that system of going up the ladder. It added a sparkle to your record, and marked you out as responsible citizen. Most students did voluntary work because it enhanced their chances in further study, scholarship, study abroad and landing a well-paid job. You did it because others did it.

The contrast with why, in the 1960s and 1970s, Tanzanian students from different backgrounds had volunteered for the adult education and self-help programs was striking. At that earlier time, a genuine spirit of nation building and solidarity with fellow humans permeated the air. The interactions between those being served and the volunteers, and among the volunteers, reflected that spirit. We sang and talked about issues affecting the nation all in a comradely way. In the incarcerated youth project, on the other hand, we had formal interactions. When I ran into a fellow participant a few months down, I often saw that he or she had lost interest in the matter.

Yet, it is not a matter of nationality, genes or culture. It is a question of economics, pure and simple. Capitalism promotes self-promoting behavior. Tanzania currently is under the reign of capitalism of the neo-liberal variety. The get-rich-quickly tendency drives the day. College and university students and staff are ensnared by it too. On the surface, hundreds of groups exist to help people in distress or need — the Albinos, handicapped, rural girls, homeless kids, HIV infected persons, you name it. Their activities, however, do not stem from a genuine spirit of human bondage. The ubiquitous NGO culture has transformed the act of assisting fellow humans into a ritualized process that holds the prospects of material gain for the activist. Funds are dissipated through such events, of which a lower than desired portion reaches the target population. Their gain is transient, not lasting. On top of that, despite the handsome reward, and while the printed report looks glossy and impressive, the work of the activist is usually pathetic and sub-standard. And it is a self-perpetuating exercise.

LESSONS

Tutoring fellow students and others taught me several lessons. First, your grasp of a subject is gauged by how well you can explain it to a complete beginner. The person can raise unexpected questions which can lead you to a new perspective on the issue. Second, it made me appreciate the variation in the pace of learning, providing me a useful foundation of my work as a full time teacher. Third and more valuable, many of the instances of personal tutoring laid the basis for endearing and enduring friendships.

2

TRAINEE TEACHER

To teach is to learn twice
Joseph Joubert

+ + + + + + +

THE FORTNIGHT PRECEDING the first year university exams was a grueling time for me. It was the sole occasion in my life that I lived for and by mathematics and only mathematics. From early morning to near midnight, I was holed up in an isolated corner of the university library. My task: To decipher the arcane concepts of pure mathematics and decode the mind boggling formulas of applied mathematics. This single minded pursuit was interrupted by three short jaunts to the cafeteria, and a few hours of snooze. Even to close compatriots, I was totally incommunicado.

Not that I was miserable. Quite the opposite. It was an experience to relish, a time of enchanting discovery. Ideas I had but faintly grasped finally made sense. Concepts presumed disparate turned out to have subtle linkages. The outlines of the sublime thread linking the branches of the science of numbers began to emerge. This intense plunge into the abstract arena fostered a feeling of inner joy. To put it in spiritual terms, I attained a numerical nirvana of sorts.

The effort paid off handsomely. I swiftly breezed through the exams, as indicated in the last chapter. My frail physical self, however, did not emerge unscathed from the extended sleep depriving ordeal. In the final days, a sense of unease gnawed me, but I ignored it. Once the last paper was done, it could not be wished away. A sizable boil in a sensitive part of my anatomy confined me to bed with pain and fever. When a course of antibiotics failed to provide relief, a surgical procedure at the University Health Center was in order. Done expeditiously under local anesthesia, the outcome was swift and dramatic. Within a day, the fever had abated and the intense pain was history. The wound being dressed for three days, I was a free bird. It was my luck that the exams were over when the bio-devil reared its ugly head.

The last exam heralded a three month period of bliss for the students: no lecture, seminar or essay. From April to June, they engaged in pursuits of their own choice. One group, however, did not have it as good. For the BSc or BA with Education students, a divisive equation applied. Our vacation was a disjoint interval with the initial and final segments intersected by five weeks of teaching practice at assigned secondary schools.

POPATLAL SCHOOL

No sooner was I up and about from my surgery, I found myself on a day long bus trip. Hurtling at a perilous speed on a slippery, bumpy, rain soaked road, it felt like gliding on a sine curve. Was I uneasy? Hardly. Nazir Nensi, Shiraz Ramji and Zubeda Vellani, close buddies and fellow first year UDSM students, sat close by. Their chattiness made time flow fast. We were headed to Tanga for our teaching practice. Rain or shine, we were in ebullient spirits.

We put up at a homely boarding house, some half a mile from the central business area of Tanga. Our landlady doted on us like a mother, serving ample, hot, tasty breakfast, lunch and dinner each day. Sunday lunch was special: meat *pilau* with marinated salad and *madafu* (coconut water). We found four other boarders in residence. All primary school children, their friendliness made it feel like a home away from home. An expansive garden enlivened by hibiscus, rose, papaya, lemon plants and sugar cane clusters encircled the house. A thorny sisal plant in the middle lorded over the flora. On weekends, we played catch ball with or read to the kids in its grassy area.

Popatlal Secondary School, our allotted school, was a twenty minute brisk walk. Traversing a lush, semi-forested area over run by coconut palm, we arrived in time. On the way back, it was a leisurely stroll, the expanse of greenery mercifully shielding us from the blazing rays of the tropical sun.

The semi-private school, opened three years back, was run by the Hindu community. In the colonial era, the students would have been exclusively Asian. In 1969, about half were Asian, the rest African. At the entrance, we found Mr Kulwant Chaudry, the headmaster. It was the norm for him to eye his wards trickle in. Our first impression: A man with a genial demeanor. In practice, though, he was a strict, no-nonsense administrator.

He welcomed us warmly. Both sides would benefit, he frankly told us. We would acquire essential skills and his overworked staff would get some relief. While not spending as many hours in the classroom as a regular teacher, we were to abide by the same rules applying to them. Timely attendance was essential. Our main responsibility was to ensure that our students did not lag behind in the subjects we would teach.

After the pep talk, he took us around, introduced us to the teachers, and showed us the staff room and other facilities. An overview of the extra-curricular activities at the school preceded an invitation to take part in any of interest to us. Should we have any concerns, we were free to approach him directly. It was an edifying start for the edgy first-time teachers.

FIRST CLASS

I was to teach mathematics to Form IA and Form IIB. There was but a day to prepare. We had to make a list of topics with corresponding lesson plans. Beside guiding our classwork, the plans would be inspected by our UDSM supervisor.

On the fateful day, I was escorted into the classroom by the Form I teacher I was temporarily replacing. He had briefed me on the topics he had covered, and those I had to cover in the next five weeks. A brief introduction, and he left me to my own devices. Though not jittery, I was not too assured either. It being my first time to stand in such a role in front of a skeptical bunch of thirteen year old faces, I was not sure how it would go. Tongue tied momentarily, I hid it by rearranging my papers. How to begin? After a deep breath, my first word popped out:

Hamjambo?

After the briefest of a pause, they responded:

Hatujambo, mwalimu.

And then in English:

How are you?

Now the response was faster and louder:

We are fine, sir.

And then, with a typical Asian accent, I asked in Gujarati:

Kem Cho?

The class responded with chuckles and the ice was broken. After writing my name on the black board and saying a few words about myself, I stated my goals for the class. A stony silence prevailed.

My first question, whose answer I knew, was: what was topic of the last class? A chorus of voices said:

Linear equation in one unknown.

After briefly going over this topic, in an authoritative tone, I declared,

Now we advance to linear equations with two unknowns.

I started by writing on the blackboard:

$$2x + 5y = 19$$
$$3x + 2y = 12$$

I repeated the equations in words and declared x and y to be the unknown quantities whose values we needed to find. This was done by equalizing the coefficients of one variable in both equations. To make the coefficients of x equal, we multiply the first equation by 3 and the second, by 2 to get

$$6x + 15y = 57$$
$$6x + 4y = 24$$

Subtracting the second equation from the first gives

$$11y = 33 \quad \text{or} \quad y = 3$$

Finally, we substitute this value of y in any of the original equations and find that $x = 2$.

I demonstrated this procedure in a step by step manner for two other sets of equations. Setting three sets of equations to solve on their own, I went around checking their work. At the end, I assigned the homework. The next class covered a variation of this method called the method of eliminating one variable. The graphical method, which better illustrated with the idea of a variable and pictured the solution, followed.

I began in similar way in Form IIB where the topic was from geometry. In a few days, I had settled down into a decent routine with both the classes. I strove to balance chalk with talk, classwork with homework, and queries with instruction. Preparing for class was not an issue; I knew the subject like the back of my hand. What took up a lot of my free time was grading homework. At the end of our stay, it was gratifying to see most students scoring well. Only a handful remained stuck in dire numerical straits.

That is the low key manner in which what was to turn out to be a momentous and exhilarating saga of numerical pedagogy began. I was more than satisfied with what I had accomplished at Popatlal. But after several years of full time teaching, it dawned upon me that my approach had been tainted with a fundamental flaw. I deal with it at the end of this chapter.

SUPERVISION

Waiting for our supervisor was like waiting for Godot. She was expected any day, but it never seemed to come. Just as we were to enter the final week, Ms Elizabeth Connelly, an instructor in education at UDSM, landed in our midst to assess our work.

Though quite personable, she was all business from the first instance. First there was a group meeting where we outlined what we had done. We were told to hand in our lesson plans and informed that she would observe us in class over the next four days. Each person should expect at least two visits but who would be visited when was not spelled out.

There she was, in my classroom, the very next day, sitting in subdued silence in a corner as I entered. After a curt hello, I was told to proceed as I normally would. I was shaken but not sufficiently to lose my balance. When the hour was over, I felt it had gone rather well. She, however, did not think so. According to her, there were several problems. My pace was uneven; at times too slow and at times too fast. I needed to interact with the class as a whole, not just a few students. My grade for this session was a majestic C. I was not pleased.

The day after, she was back. Her report, reproduced below in full, says it all.

24-4-69, Mr. Hirji, Popatlal S. S., Maths – 1A

A much better lesson. The preliminary work — individuals doing problems on the board, got almost the whole class involved — hence the noise. They were really paying attention. Can you think of a way of retaining their interest without the noise? I still think you helped the pupils too much "That is wrong, correct it" instead of "Is that right?" But you definitely had much more class participation in working out the problems than before.

There was a nice balance between class work and individual work. The pupils were helping each other in the latter part of the lesson, which is very valuable as you can't see everyone at once & I think they understand each others' mistakes.

Some finished earlier than others. What can you do about this?

E M Connelly

Despite the laudatory remarks, my new grade was just a tad better: C+/B-. Some instructors are impossible to please, groaned I.

Truth be told, in the past four weeks, not only had I become eminently predisposed towards teaching but had formed an elevated opinion of my teaching ability as well. I felt that the performance of my students in the national exams would be as good as if they had been taught by an experienced teacher. I enjoyed their company. The queries they posed made me view mathematical ideas at a fresh angle. The staff were pleasant and helpful. The atmosphere was conservative, but it reflected the society at large. I covered the set topics on time, and conducted a review session. On the last test, most students met my expectations. I patted myself on the back, supervisor or no supervisor.

REVOLUTIONARY *SHAMBA*

In the year 1967, Tanzania adopted socialism and self-reliance as the guiding policy for national social and economic development (TANU 1967). The component of SSR dealing with educational matters was spelled out in the document *Education for Self-Reliance* (ESR) released around that time (Nyerere 1967).

During the colonial era, education for the broad masses was severely restricted, both in quality and quantity. The entire system was structured by race. A Form IV certificate was a passport to better living, but only a few had the chance to acquire it. Villagers and town people were hungry for education for their children. Soon after *Uhuru*, our nation thereby witnessed a vast expansion of primary and secondary schooling. Yet, all was not well. A decade into nationhood, the educational pyramid remained an unfair one. A small portion of primary school leavers entered secondary school and a smaller portion of secondary school graduates entered a college or university. Those not able to climb the educational ladder were in a quandary: the skills they had acquired qualified them for clerical jobs in the public and private sectors. But such jobs were too few and the number of applicants was rising fast. An education system of that mode could hardly facilitate genuine socio-economic development for the nation.

ESR aimed to rectify this state of affairs through introduction of activities that would impart practical skills at all levels of the system. Each school, primary or higher, had to have a farm, dairy or poultry project, wood workshop, sewing project or a similar project. In addition to taking part in these activities, the students would be involved in keeping the school compound and classrooms clean and organized.

It was hypothesized that the students would benefit on four fronts: (i) They would learn the elements of skills that could enable them to engage in income generating activities; (ii) Their attitude towards manual work would become more favorable; (iii) The advantages of working in a cooperative setting would become apparent to them; and (iv) They would come to value socialistic cooperation as a way of life. A youth ingrained with such an orientation would enable the nation to confidently embark on the path of genuine socio-economic development based on mutual cooperation. That, at least, was the grand theory.

Like other schools, Popatlal had received a directive from the Ministry of Education on setting up ESR activities. The policy document laid down the basic philosophy, not practical steps. The ministerial directive lacked detailed instructions. What projects to undertake and how to implement them was left to the school administration.

It so happened that two members from our group had a keen interest in ESR: Shiraz, a physics student, and I. Being members of a radical student group, the University Students African Revolutionary Front (USARF), we were committed to the promotion, through practical and educational activities, of the ideas and ideals of African liberation, Pan-Africanism and Socialism. USARF worked hand in hand with the UDSM branch of the youth wing, TANU Youth League (TYL), of the ruling party, TANU.

The headmaster told us that the school ran a two acre *shamba* (farm). On the second day, we first had a talk with the teacher in charge of the school TYL branch. Upon getting a lukewarm reception from him, we took matters in our own hands. We visited the area to find a cleared location, but with minimal and not too systematic planting. It was a random distribution of cassava, pineapple and papaya plants. A few sugar cane clusters stood in two corners, but not much else.

Even to our agriculturally stunted brains, it was not a pretty sight. What could be done? The school maintenance worker came to our rescue. Hamisi said that the soil was fertile and the rains were sufficient. If student labor was utilized as required, a productive farm with a variety of crops could be set up. But his views had fallen on deaf ears. Finding us receptive, he showered onto us a ton of suggestions on setting up a viable *shamba*.

On the first teaching day, as school was to end, Shiraz and I went to the headmaster's office. Though surprised, he had a sympathetic demeanor:

Ramji, Hirji, already having problems?

No sir, our classes have started well. We want to ask you about the school shamba.

Our unexpected reply puzzled him:

Oh, that. What about it?

We outlined our proposal on developing the school *shamba*. Would he permit us to take our student to work on it two days of the week? Not all of them, only the willing ones. While others played soccer, basketball, etc., our group would dig, clear, plant and water, two hours at a stretch. We outlined our cultivation plan but did not disclose then that, word by word, it reflected the advice we had got from Hamisi. To this day, I recall the expression on his face: delight mixed with astonishment. Without hesitation, he blurted out:

> *Sure, sure, you have my permission.*

The school was just three years old. The staff had many things to take care of, he said. Hence, the farm had not received the attention it needed. In a hushed tone, he went on:

> *I will be frank with you. Our teachers do not like ESR. The students and parents hate it. They prefer volleyball or soccer to shamba work. But politics is politics; it has to be done even if it will lower educational standards. The district officer is not pleased at the state of our shamba. I feel ill at ease when I have to show it to visitors. So, if you can improve it, you will do Popatlal a major favor. We have the farming equipment in the store, and I will give you all the help you need*

He conversed with us in the spirit of a conservative educator. A nice farm, though, conferred political advantage. His words had a racial tinge too; he talked to us as an Asian would to other Asians. It was implied that when Africans took over any project, they mixed it with politics and ruined it. We disagreed with that view but kept quiet. Our priority was to secure his cooperation in order to enable us to do what we wanted to do. I doubt he would have been as direct if an African was present.

That was the genesis of what soon came to be known as the *Mapinduzi Shamba* (Revolutionary Farm). Twelve students from Shiraz's classes and twelve from my classes had volunteered for *shamba* work. For two days a week, and two hours at a time, we and the students became *wakulima* (farmers). When our students saw that we did not just stand and issue orders, but jumped into the trenches with them, their spirits rose remarkably. At the end, our brows were as sweaty, our clothes as soiled, and our hearts as content as theirs.

Indeed, *shamba* work became a fun activity. Loud chatter, jokes and laughter abounded. Those who handled the hoe, rake or spade awkwardly were teased but gently. And work got done; lots of it. Boys worked hard to impress the girls. Shiraz and I recalled our adventures in the National Service a year ago (see *GUWTZ*).

With a corner reserved for us, a fair amount of the area was cleared. Cassava, sweet potato, tomato, beans and pumpkin were planted and watered. Two students brought kidney bean, small red bean and pumpkin seeds from home. They were planted but to what effect, we do not know. To set up a viable farm with a suitable crop mix needs at least two years of attention and effort. But our stay here was for five weeks only.

Our last afternoon at the school was spent at the *shamba*. The students were sad to see us leave. Some had brought in their autograph books. For one, I wrote:

> *Live the life of a candle that consumes itself while radiating light and love to all around it.*

And for another:

> *This world produces 4 times the food it needs yet one half of its population goes hungry. Should we not try our best to change this awful situation?*

As we bade farewell to each other, I wondered which teacher would continue what we had started? Would the farm bloom into an oasis of nutritious vegetables? Not being an era of easy communication, we unfortunately do not know if our efforts bore decent fruits or not.

We told the headmaster about the fine assistance given to us by Mr Hamisi and requested that he get a *zawadi* (present). Mr Chaudry told us not to worry. He would get the sum of twenty shillings for his contribution.

PAN-AFRICANIST QUIZ

Besides the *shamba* work, the other progressive activity we undertook at Popatlal was to hold a school-wide written quiz competition. The quiz had forty questions on science, world affairs, African liberation and national socio-political issues. There was a book prize for the three highest scorers. We had got them in advance from the UDSM bookstore. They were: Frantz Fanon's *The Wretched of the Earth*, Sembene Ousmane's *God's Bits of Wood*, and Robert Tressel's *The Ragged Trousered Philanthropists*. These works promoted liberation of Africa, socio-political interests of workers and peasants and socialism. We had estimated that a secondary school student of above average caliber would understand them. Looking back, I see we had miscalculated with respect to Fanon. He is a demanding read. Possibly, they appreciated the gist of his militant stance.

To our surprise, the headmaster was enthusiastic about the quiz. He may have felt that it concerned *siasa* (politics). Since political education was accorded a high priority in those days, it would enhance the school's standing with the district authorities. We did not tell him that some of the questions would challenge the ruling party's dogmatic approach to political education.

Our request for stencils and reams of paper met with his swift approval. Shiraz and I set the quiz and the secretary typed it onto the stencils. Five hours of work on the cyclostyling press on a hot afternoon enabled us to produce and bind about 100 copies. They were locked away in a cabinet in her office until the day of the quiz.

I recall about eighty students, mostly from Form III and Form IV, turning up. The questions were mostly multiple choice, pairing answers and filling in the blank type of questions. Five questions required a one sentence answer. One entire weekend was spent marking the papers and selecting the winners. We also wrote an answer scheme and placed it on two noticeboards. A typical question was:

> *Connect the freedom fighters with their nations: (A) Nelson Mandela (B) Amilcar Cabral (C) Agostinho Neto (D) Eduardo Mondlane (E) Malcolm X and (a) USA (b) Mozambique (c) Guinea Bissau (d) Azania (e) Angola.*

The top scorer had 50% of the answers correct telling us that socialistic education for the youth had a long road ahead. The prizes were given out in a school assembly during our final week. The head took the opportunity to thank Shiraz and myself for our efforts on the *shamba* and the quiz, and praised the students who had volunteered for farm work. But when he asked other teachers to follow our footsteps, I do not think it went down well. Some of them had said that we were ruling party stooges spreading political propaganda. Had they told us that directly, we would have countered that propaganda comes in two forms, the capitalist form and the socialist form. In modern society, the former is drummed into people's heads from childhood; we were balancing the picture by showing that on the other side lay a humanistic vision of society whose aim was to remedy the harsh reality faced by the common folk in Africa through cooperative effort and firm resistance to external economic domination.

Did the students gain from our projects? The time was too short for gaining a lasting impression. Yet, I feel they were impressed with our dedication, our respect for their views, and the fact that we struggled with the soil as hard as they did. Did they acquire a degree of respect for manual labor, and begin to appreciate the value of joint effort? We hoped so. The *shamba* was run in a democratic way. Open talk about what to do and how to do it was the norm. As we labored, we discussed global and local issues. They were keen to learn about life at the university. I wonder if we managed to convince them that one could be, in Chairman Mao's words, both red and expert? That a doctor or a mathematician can at the same time be an activist dedicated to the struggle for the rights and dignity of the downtrodden? That politics did not always signify opportunism? Perhaps we did or perhaps we did not.

For us, it was a class in agriculture. Students from farming families educated us about plants that should be placed in proximity and those that should be apart; watering schedules for different crops; and improvisation when what you need is hard to find. We came to know them close up. We learned what was overlooked in the educational psychology lectures at UDSM. Above all, we worked like a family; they respected us, but as elder brothers, and not as aloof authority figures.

RACE AND RACISM

Like other nations in East Africa, our recent colonial past was structured on racial separation, inequality and prejudice. Some strides had been made in confronting racial barriers in education but many areas of society were still plagued by them. The Asian community, comprising 1% of the population, still occupied a privileged position in the social and economic hierarchy. From the colonial days, and with justification, popular opinion in Tanzania held that it was an inward looking, money minded community.

To our students, we formed a counter example. They saw two Asians who, in flesh and blood, punctured that typical image. I hope it made our students learn to judge people not from the color of their skin but from their behavior and actions. One thing I was pleased to note was that by the end of our stay, our students interacted with us as fellow Tanzanians rather than in terms of race.

Yet, we remained mired within racial boundaries. There were six UDSM students in teaching practice at Popatlal, three Asian and three African. Though we interacted well in school, the Asians traveled and lived separately from the Africans. Sadly, those divisions persist to this day (see *GUWTZ*).

A ROMANTIC TRIANGLE

We were young, energetic. Our hopes and dreams stretched beyond infinity. But it was not just socialism and teaching that fired our spirits. A fragrance of romance floated in the air as well.

From our days in the national service, Shiraz and I had been friendly with Zubeda. She was in the Biology and Chemistry with Education stream at UDSM, and good happenstance for us, her school for teaching practice was the same as ours.

We were ecstatic. Her petite, well-formed figure, sparkling eyes and irresistible smile ruled our inner thoughts. For the two grandly smitten fellows, to talk to her daily was a dream come true. While on one front, Shiraz and I were comrades in arms, on this front, we were irreconcilable rivals. It was an unspoken rivalry. The European hippie radicals of the day promoted free love. We did not share that outlook. For now she was amiable to us both. But ultimately, it had to be either him or me, and nothing in between.

Yet, what a majestic illusion it was. After we returned to DSM, we saw her only sporadically. Two months on, as the new academic year began, a stupefying sight awaited us. Zubeda walked hand in hand with another guy. She still favored us with a smile but the two of them were as inseparable as we were inconsolable. In no time, it became a solid bond. They got married upon graduation from UDSM and migrated to Canada to live happily ever after.

The budding proponents of scientific socialism had their heads in the clouds. We did not appreciate that there was a key sticking point between her and us. She was devoutly religious, going daily to the prayer house. Our secular, humanistic stand had placed a different set of priorities on our plates. She asked us now and then: Why do you just talk about politics?

Instead of taking her to the Amboni caves or the ocean front or the cinema during the weekends, we marked the quiz or did other school work. Perhaps our efforts reflected a desire to impress her. If they did, they served a good purpose. Should we have toned down our ideals to comply with her wishes? If one comes short in the days of youthful idealism, what can the future augur?

We just had to nurse our loss. Humming sentimental songs from Hindi movies helped. We did not talk about it, but I guess Shiraz was mired in a similar mood. Gladly, our comradeship and activism did not abate one iota. Had one of our students sent us this saucy vision of algebra, it surely would have consoled us.

Dear Algebra:
Stop asking us to find your X
She is not coming back

Uknown Author

Despite our versatility in the discipline of quantification, the margin of error in our romantic calculations was spectacular. Our emotional equations did not fathom that matters of the heart do not operate on a planar world where simple rules of Euclidean geometry prevail. They unfold on a wobbly spherical surface, where what is just ahead of you disappears on the horizon without warning. On a plane, the angles of a triangle sum to 180 degrees. On a sphere, they can add up to 270 degrees. The additional degrees of freedom converted our simple binary projections into a maze of implausible outcomes. We had mistaken wild dreams as representations of objective reality; a hazy mirage, an oasis of sweet date palm; an enchanting smile, a sign of true love. It was too late when we realized that in the emotional arena, the Darwinian law turned from the survival of the fittest to that of the flirty-est.

AZANIA SCHOOL

My second teaching practice was a low key affair. Lasting two weeks in September

1970, it was at the Azania Secondary School in DSM. I taught mathematics to Form 3A and Form 3B. This time my supervisor was Mr SR Nkonoki, a lecturer from the Department of Education of UDSM. He observed my teaching on two occasions.

His longer reports first noted my strong points: (i) I knew the subject well; (ii) Each time I began with a review of the last session; and (iii) My blackboard writing was clear and to the point. On the negative side, he noted that: (i) I did not beforehand ensure that chalk was at hand: (ii) I did not give enough time for the class to copy the material on the board; (iii) I talked too much: (iv) I did not go over issues that had not been understood well; (v) I rushed the class; (vi) I did not have a detailed lesson plan; (vii) More pupil activity was needed; and so on and so forth.

His grades are not stated on his reports, but I gathered that they were on the low side. A `good potential mathematics teacher,' that was his verdict. It was clearly implied that reaching that potential would require time and effort, and even then, the desired outcome was not guaranteed

But that is not how I saw it. By the end of the two weeks, I felt I had done well with my class. As they say, when the man has spoken, he has spoken.

Azania School was a short walk from my house. My good high school friend Elias Kisamo was posted there at the same time. He taught physics. We spent breaks together over a cup of tea or soda and roasted ground nuts. I did not take up any extracurricular activity of the sort I had done at Popatlal. Not that my socialistic activism was on the wane. At this time, my priority was to work on an upcoming issue of *Cheche,* the USARF magazine. As its principal editor, I spent many hours after school and during weekends at the UDSM campus on this unpaid job.

Cheche gave space to prominent activists to air their views on burning social, economic and political issues of the day. It took the ruling party to task for its half-hearted implementation of socialism. It did not come as a complete surprise that two months later it was banned by the government of Tanzania (see *Cheche* for details).

REFLECTIONS ON TEACHER TRAINING

My undergraduate lectures on education at UDSM covered varied courses like child development, educational psychology, sociology of education, philosophy of education, curriculum development and teaching methods. Yet apart from Pavlov's experiments with dogs and some of John Dewey's ideas on pedagogy, there was hardly anything I retained from these courses. The presentations were too general and the material bore little relevance to the concrete conditions of Africa. Much of it looked as if it was lifted straight out of American textbooks and sources.

I found the education courses unattractive in the extreme. With their shallow ideas, the lecturers did not inspire. Their basic concepts projected and rationalized the tenets and values of capitalism. Usually, a couple of lectures into a course, I would develop an adversarial relationship with the main instructor. My class essays often contradicted his or her views. Even though they were better researched and longer than the essays of most students, all except one instructor marked them down. In the mathematics courses, I was at the top. In the education courses, I was lucky to get a passing grade.

My teaching practice reinforced my stand: these courses had not prepared us to teach, let alone to do it well. What I found most lacking was a subject oriented approach to teacher training. There are admittedly common issues and skills each teacher, whatever his focal area, must imbibe. But that is not the whole story. Teaching chemistry has challenges distinct from those encountered in teaching literature; teaching history is a far cry from teaching mathematics. Apart from being deficient in the basics of teaching, my training implied that in the deep, hazardous waters of mathematics instruction, I would have to swim on my own and without any life support.

Students typically regard a teacher as a monster out to make them sweat, whether they like it or not. The first barrier a teacher has to overcome is to impress upon them that she is not of that mold, that she is a sympathetic, friendly companion on a common journey. If that is accomplished without compromising her position of authority, she has gone a long way towards enhancing the receptivity of her words.

But that is half the story. A typical student also regards a subject like mathematics a monstrous entity. Hence, it is as critical to convey to the students that the subject she is teaching is as worthy of attention as say the music of the latest pop star or antics of their favorite soccer hero. I do not exaggerate. Her second primary task is to make them love the subject she teaches, be it history, English or mathematics. If at least a few of them continue to take a keen interest in it long after she has left the scene, she could not have asked for a bigger prize. She has ignited mental flames that will blaze on for decades.

The mind is not a vessel to be filled
But a fire to be ignited
Plutarch

This is especially apropos for mathematics. In Tanzania, as in nations across the world, it is the subject with the worst scores in the national exams. Moreover, it is a subject openly detested by a majority of the students. When of adult age, most of them are not in the least embarrassed to declare: I flunked mathematics, or I despise mathematics.

This is less related to what it is taught but more to the pernicious manner in which it is taught, the topics taught, and crucially, topics left out. As I have discussed these issues at some length in *GUWTZ* and *Cheche*, I refer you to these and other texts for elaboration. Suffice to say that my training to be a teacher was more in line with suppressing youthful fires, and producing robots who manipulated mathematics symbols effectively so to get good scores in the exams. And even in that regard, it did a poor job.

Whatever I learned about how to teach well, I did it on the job, through trial and error, and by learning from at times quite serious mistakes.

My teaching practice supervisors were smart, friendly, devoted, knowledgeable individuals. Sympathetic to the socialistic policies of the nation, they sought to raise the standards of instruction in schools. But both were locked into a traditionalist, standardized approach to teaching, and especially, teaching mathematics.

Their comments dealt with minutiae, mostly minor matters relating to style. What they stressed teachers generally acquire from experience. They took the contents as given. I was to stick to the syllabus. Details were discussed but big issues like what to teach, relevance and basic approach. were not broached. How can I make my students enjoy and love mathematics? That essential question was not on the horizon.

To gain positively from experience, one has to start with a sturdy base. Lacking that, we pursue the try-angle for too long, and stagger from error to error. A beginner finds herself demoralized in no time as her frustrations pile up. The litany of errors begin to fray the bonds that tie her to the students. Teaching turns into a series of routine motions one needs to perform to get the pay check. When an avenue opens up, she abandons teaching altogether. In the setting of abominable pass rates, the teachers of mathematics who persist are those who have nowhere else to go. They do not strive for academic excellence.

And the numbers say it. Mathematics teaching and performance in Tanzania today are at levels worse than was the case in the 1960s and 1970s. Fewer than 20% of the candidates sitting for the national Form IV examination tend to get a pass level grade in mathematics.

Assessing teaching ability through a couple of short classroom visits is dicey at best. While one can weed out the truly incompetent fellows from those doing a satisfactory job, further gradation is not of much value. Good teaching comes in many forms. Uneven progress, noisy classrooms, students staring into the air are not necessarily signs of ineffective teaching. Gauging teaching ability requires dwelling into the longer term bond the teacher forms with her students and the inner sense of respect they develop towards her.

The guidance provided by my supervisors was of lackluster quality. They were more attuned to nit-picking than to giving advice that would impel you to become a life-long, competent molder of young minds. When I today go over the outline of a model lesson plan given to me by Mr Nkonoki, I am aghast. Even then, I did not follow it. It was too rigid and excessively detailed. A teacher was made into an actor who has to memorize every word she will utter at specific times in the lesson.

I would not recommend such a plan to any would be teacher. I favor planning but abhor rigidity. Improvisation, flexibility, changing contents according to the mood and response of the class, and going backward when called for are essential tools of successful instruction. The path can vary but the key thing is that at the end of the day, you land where you had planned to land, and with most students beside you. These key precepts apply whether you are teaching at the primary level or the university level.

MODERN MATHEMATICS

A discussion of the teaching of mathematics in Tanzania needs to include the introduction of Modern Mathematics (or Modern Math in the American parlance) that occurred in the late 1960s.

Modern Math originated from the work of the School Mathematics Study Group led by mathematician Edward Begel in the USA. Under the sponsorship of the US government, from 1958 to 1972 it produced school textbooks and training material relating to the teaching of mathematics in schools. The group was highly influential in its heyday affecting mathematical curricula and retraining thousands of teachers across the nation (Phillips 2015).

One key reason why this group gained such wide traction was that it promoted its work as a central pillar in the urgent task of overtaking the perceived technological and scientific advantage gained by the Soviet Union. This Cold War rationale not only raised its popularity and funding but also shielded it from initial critical scrutiny (Phillips 2015; Sawyer 2001).

Achieving a balance between rote learning (drill) and conceptual understanding (explication of general ideas), between facts (specifics) and ideas (theory), between the concrete (intuitive) and the abstract (logical) is an important issue in the teaching of any subject. While attainment of conceptual understanding and ability to apply it to a broad set of specific conditions is an ultimate goal, the path towards this is not a straightforward one. This issue is especially germane to the teaching of mathematics in elementary and secondary schools.

A principal justification for the development of Modern Math was that traditionally, the teaching of mathematics had too heavily relied on drill, intuition and specifics. Modern Math remedied that deficiency by placing general and abstract concepts right at the beginning. Ideas like sets, relations and functions were placed ahead of exercises in arithmetic, algebra and geometry. It was claimed that the conceptual understanding gained at the outset would make it easier for students to grasp the more concrete topics introduced subsequently.

The tension between the two poles of the discipline was a reflection of the tension between the professionals and the educators:

> *A good mathematician feels that teachers continually distort the subject, and a good teacher feels that mathematicians continually obscure the subject.*
> Sawyer (1962)

But the outcome of introducing Modern Math turned out to be the opposite of the hypothesized one. In practice, it could not deliver the goods, as one teacher after next discovered. In stressing the abstract, it had gone to the other unworkable extreme. Despite the initial ballyhoo and wide adoption in the USA, Modern Math had died a natural death in that nation by the mid-1970s. While some of its topics persisted in mathematics curricula, as a basic philosophy of teaching the subject, it became an object of derision and humor.

Unfortunately, though not surprisingly, as Modern Math was on the wane in its country of origin, it was being introduced in Africa. With funding from the US Agency for International Development, the Department of Mathematics and the Institute of Education of UDSM spearheaded the acceptance and dissemination of the subject in Tanzania. Textbooks which were virtual copies of their American counterparts were printed, curricula hastily written but hardly any teacher retraining was done. My education lectures at UDSM did not dwell into why this transformation was needed here. The older experienced mathematics teachers as well as the new ones were essentially left on their own to deal with the strange expressions on the faces of their students as they expounded the abstract concepts of sets and one-to-one and onto functions.

Even as the US was recovering from this Cold War inspired disaster, mathematics education in Tanzania was plunging into a deep ravine from which it has not as yet escaped.

Today it is fashionable to lay most of the blame for the woes of the education sector in Tanzania onto the socialist policies of the past. This ideologically driven charge misses two key points. In the case of mathematics, a significant part of the blame lies in the uncritical adoption of a deeply flawed approach from the citadel of global capitalism.

Furthermore, it overlooks the paradoxical character of the `socialist' policy of that era. While the ruling party document championed education for self-reliance, our experts and the Ministry of Education were going in the opposite direction. As long as plenty of funds were at hand, they had no qualms in letting the external funding agencies call the tune.

Such contradictory features so extensively affected all the sectors of the economy and society in those days that calling Mwalimu Nyerere's policy a policy of socialism and self-reliance is akin to calling a lion a giraffe. In critical areas, it was a muddled policy of state capitalism based on dependency on the entities from the capitalist world to formulate, fund and implement most of the projects undertaken. I further discuss the policy of Education for Self-reliance in Chapter 6 and dwell on the character of these pseudo-socialist policies in several other chapters.

TEACHING MATHEMATICS

Teaching mathematics in ways that effectively instill its basic concepts into the developing mind on a long term basis requires starting from the concrete plane, ascending gradually to the conceptual plane followed by a return to the concrete, and repeating this cycle in a progressive fashion throughout. As an early critic of Modern Math observed:

> *In the early teaching of mathematics,*
> *there is no danger of making the subject too concrete.*
> *The danger is rather that the subject gets so far from the concrete*
> *that it comes to mean nothing at all.*
> Sawyer (1962)

Telling tales is an essential pedagogic tool for mathematics and statistics. Students love stories, interesting stories. These include historic and contemporary episodes told in an enticing garb. The rewards of a story-based approach are lasting. It can make students who dislike these subjects change their attitude towards it, creating a new learning atmosphere in the classroom.

Take the case of how I introduced linear equations in two unknowns during my teaching practice at Popatlal Secondary School. I could have done better by starting with talking about, say, fruits; those they like best; those they ate yesterday; the fruits in season; and how much they cost.

After some noisy banter, I tell a story:

> *Juma and Salima go to the market. Juma buys two bananas and three mangoes. From the same seller, Salima buys three bananas and two mangoes. Juma has paid one shilling and ninety cents but Salima pays one shilling and sixty cents.*

As they nod their heads, I ask:

> *If you want to buy four bananas and two mangoes, how much will you have to pay?*

A scratching of heads ensues. A smart girl gets the correct answer by guessing. But she cannot explain how she got it. Then I say let us put x cents as the price of a banana and y cents, the price of a mango. And then we formulate the two equations in the two unknowns. Now the equations have a down-to-earth meaning. This is followed by graphing the equations and finding an approximate answer. The next hour is spent on the traditional methods of solving the equations.

I take the exercise a step further by reading aloud a short story about a father who buys a bag of oranges for his children on the way home from work. They love the fruit. His funds are stretched but the image of the young ones running excitedly upon seeing the oranges in his hand drives him on. He is tired, the bag is heavy. Along the way, he has to cross a busy highway. The fast moving traffic is blind to pedestrians. It takes him half an hour to cross the road, only to realize that the bag of oranges remains on the other side. Too exhausted to turn back, he trudges home benumbed and empty handed (Salaam al-Mundhri 2008). Reading takes five minutes, an unusual activity in a mathematics class. Yet, it brings tears to their eyes, and cements the lesson of the day firmly in their minds.

For changing the attitudes towards mathematics and improving the performance of the students, we must mobilize a veritable battery of tools — stories, poems, humor, history, puzzles, sports and games, anecdotes from the lives of famous mathematicians, instances of practical use and misuse of the discipline. Field trips, practical tasks and experiments should also be utilized when opportune (see *GUWTZ* for details).

Foremost, it is the mathematics teacher who has to be versed in the diversity of the educational methods. Yet, her training is sorely deficient in that respect. A typical teacher in secondary school is not aware of the intrinsic beauty or history of mathematics. Having come to it as a routinized discipline, she teaches it accordingly, through rote learning and drill. Is it a surprise that her students end up hating the subject? I reflect further on these and related issues in the final three chapters.

3

TUTORIAL ASSISTANT

You do not really understand something
Unless you can explain it to your grandmother
Albert Einstein

+ + + + + + +

PALPABLE TENSION PERVADES THE AIR. A week ago, we had heaved a collective sigh of relief upon exiting the exam hall for the last time. Our undergraduate studies were over. But the euphoria is short lived. Now we hold our breath for the verdict.

Yesterday, our job postings were announced. I am to join the Kibaha Secondary School, a well-run boarding school twenty six miles from DSM. The prospect of teaching Form VI level mathematics at my old high school is not a displeasing one. Actually, its semi-urban setting accords with my temperament. Nevertheless, I am not too thrilled as my goals are loftier. I thus accept the job with equanimity.

The posting is conditional: No degree, no job. In late March 1971, as I pack my bags for Kibaha life, the exam results emerge. Not only do I have the BSc(Ed) degree but it has come with First Class Honors. That alters everything. The next day, I am told that I will be retained by the Department of Mathematics at UDSM. It means I can pursue advanced studies in my favorite subject. It also means that my work will be teaching degree level courses and doing research in mathematics. As a bonus, I can as well continue indulging into the myriad of progressive activities that are underway at UDSM, and that in the fine company of dedicated local and international comrades I have come to know intimately over the past three years. Needless to say, I am ecstatic.

THE UNIVERSITY

The place where I have spent my last three years, and where I have been posted is spread over on a hilly terrain some ten kilometers from the city center. Popularly, it is known as the Hill.

As you enter its gates, you enter a new world, a far cry from the messy urban environment you have left behind. You find an elegant expanse of winding tarmac roads, alongside which stand modern one and two story staff houses with wide gardens, high rise student dormitories, two large cafeterias, a complex comprising a bookstore, bar and coffee place, bank and post office, and a dense academic area with lecture theaters, seminar rooms, staff offices, libraries, science labs and administration block. A huge sports arena, a swimming pool, large open fields and hilly interludes complement the imposing concrete structures. The well maintained lawns and shrubs, trees of all shapes, shades and sizes, at times bunched but mostly blooming in isolation and a shallow spring here and there retain the semi-dominance of nature over cement and tar. Spread out over some 25 square kilometers, it is a world in itself.

For the year 1971/72, the student population of UDSM stands at 2,200. Of these, 1833 are undergraduates, 264 are non-degree students and 103 are pursuing postgraduate studies. Among the last group, there are twenty five doctoral degree students.

In addition to the main campus at the Hill, the university has two other campuses. The Faculty of Medicine, adjoined with the national hospital in the city center, has 145 undergrads, and the Faculty of Agriculture, 150 kilometers away in Morogoro, has 114 undergrads.

The UDSM student population is predominantly male; just 15% is female. But it has an internationalist flavor with nearly a fifth of the students non-Tanzanians, most of whom hail from nearby Uganda and Kenya.

The university currently employs 417 academic (teaching and research) staff, of whom 219 or 53% are expatriates. In fact, the dominance of expatriates is greater if you take away the junior 84 Tutorial Assistants, who are all Tanzanians. Of the thirty full Professors, only two are Tanzanians. It is an academy in transition. The potential for growth and development is vast (UDSM 1973).

My initial title is Tutorial Assistant (TA), a probationary post. For a permanent job, a higher degree is a necessity. So the first thing my departmental head has me do is to apply for advanced study at universities abroad, and fill out several scholarship application forms.

I apply for the doctoral programs at the Oxford University in the UK and Stanford University in California. In response, both request my transcript and the syllabuses for the courses I have done. Within a month of transmitting that material, I am accepted into their programs.

+ + + + + + +

Comment: I note this minor detail to emphasize that in those days, the degrees conferred by the UDSM were, and were recognized worldwide as, high class degrees. In comparison, today the degrees from the same institution are, in most areas, not worth the paper they are printed on. It is common to find a modern day honors level UDSM graduate talking like an ignoramus in his or her discipline. Unfortunately, conditions are similar or worse at the other Tanzanian universities.

+ + + + + + +

In addition, I apply to the London School of Economics for a master's degree in Operations Research (OR). OR is a branch of applied mathematics of relevance to industry, agriculture, transport, education and health. It is a one-year program. Acceptance is swift. With the scholarships lined up, I have to choose from one of the three places. Professor Phythian prefers I join a doctoral program. But I am hesitant. First, I have yet to figure out the area of mathematics I eventually want to specialize in. And, second, I want to explore OR. A relatively new specialty, it intrigues me. My plan is to get the master's degree in OR, lecture for a couple of years at UDSM, and then tackle the heavy duty doctorate. Upon some persuasion, he consents. So London it is going to be, with scheduled departure in late August 1971.

During this long vacation, I am in a relaxed mood. It has been a long while since I have felt as such. I do not have onerous departmental duties; just a minor task occasionally. I read a lot, mathematics and other matters. I assist the new editorial board of the student magazine, *MajiMaji*, on a new issue. I visit UDSM friends who are now teaching in Moshi, Morogoro and Iringa, and give talks on African and world affairs to their students. And importantly, Henry Mapolu and I read and give comments to Walter Rodney on the draft chapters of his magnum opus, *How Europe Underdeveloped Africa*. This terse volume embodying a trend setting method of historical analysis is to one day morph into one of the five most important works on African history written in the 20th century. At this time, we have no inkling about that future.

Two female cousins, Rumina and Shamim, have been close to me from a young age. With an only-boys family, they are my sisters. Shamim has just got her driving license. What bothers her is that keen as she is go to the drive-in cinema, her mother does not permit her, even if it is in the company of her female friends. But if I was with her, that would pose no problems. The cinema is located halfway between the Hill and Upanga, where they and my parents live. So on the weekends I am at my parents, she rarely fails to rope me into a movie show. Not that there is any reluctance on my part. Three hours of Bolywood fare inundated with song, dance and romance, and the few socialy uplifting flicks shown once in a while come with pop-corn, ice-cream, and the swell dinner her mother prepares. It is a failure proof recipe for a relaxing weekend.

GRADUATION

Yet, all good things must end. The month of July is upon us. The campus brims with hundreds of new, eager faces. And I am loaded with responsibilities. But first, a milestone in our lives is to be celebrated. July 7th, a public holiday, is also the annual UDSM graduation day. It is with joy I greet my old friends once more. The Chancellor, Mwalimu Nyerere, will confer the degrees and we will acquire the right to be called a bachelor or master of science, arts or some such thing.

Only a year ago, this institution was a part of the University of East Africa. Now it is an autonomous university, holding its inaugural graduation ceremony. Marked with due pomp, with excited parents, relatives and friends among the crowd, the event, for all that is apparent on the surface, unfolds without a glitch. For the hundreds of graduands and their families, it is a day of joy. I too am in high spirits.

Yet, something is seriously amiss. It stems from the speech given by the Vice Chancellor (VC), Mr Pius Msekwa. His words are to catalyze a turbulent phase in the life of this young institution. As we head home to party with family and friends, none of us has a clue that in just two days, life at this university is to turn upside down. This upheaval is described in Chapter 5.

On a personal angle, while I am proud and happy on this day, I do not join my compatriots in one critical act. I do not mount the podium to get the Chancellor's blessings. It is a conscious decision on my part. Little did I anticipate that it would color my academic life over the next forty years (see Chapter 9).

VECTOR ANALYSIS

Once life at the campus settles down, I get my first formal taste of conveying university level mathematical concepts to others. I am now the Teaching Assistant for the Vector Analysis class taught by Professor Phythian. It is a higher level course with a full year of calculus as its prerequisite. A vector is an entity that has a numeric value and a direction. For example, the velocity of a vehicle is a vector but the weight of a stone is not. Vector Analysis investigates the panoply of intricate patterns that emerge from combining vectors and their functions over space and time. Though it is a subject strewn with abstract ideas and beguiling formulas, it is applied in diverse areas like physics, chemistry, astronomy, economics, all areas of engineering, transportation and the analysis of data in health and social science. When geometry is cast in a vector format, the enhanced elegance and analytic power is stupefying. Not just in real life, but in mathematics too, initial appearances can be quite misleading.

I attend the lectures, conduct two tutorial sessions per week, and grade homework assignments. It dawns upon me that passing a subject, even with a high grade, does not, by itself, give you the ability to teach it. I am unable to answer off hand some questions the students pose. The bright ones raise the difficult problems in the textbook, obliging me now and then to approach the good professor. Typically, he shows me the way. Occasionally, and with his typical loud chuckle, he declares, 'Karim, you know this,' leaving me to sweat it out on my own.

Professor Phythian is not just an astute mathematician, but in my view, one of the two best teachers in our department. He is also an open-minded person. I have, since my student days, tended to discuss with him things like the content of, and approach towards, mathematics in the schools and colleges of the developing nations of Africa. With my radical stance, our views frequently collide. Nonetheless, I hold him in high esteem and continue to gain a lot from him.

One positive outcome of tutoring his class is to bring home to me the centrality of developing good blackboard skills. The material I had taught during my secondary school teaching practice was easy stuff. I had known it like the back of my hand. Vectors and their compatriots reside on a higher plane. When explaining a formula on the blackboard, I pause to consult my notes or the textbook. At these moments, I feel the attention of some students wanders off, never to return for the duration of the class. While using the board or talking, it is critical to maintain a smooth flow, and face the class directly. To be able to do that, I must master the concepts and theorems. As it is, almost all the students are intimidated by them. And if the tutor waffles in class, their confusion will double. So I slog to dissect the innards of the partial and directional derivatives, chain rule, gradient, divergence and curl, and their relatives. My aim is to explain the arcane ideas as simply as possible during each encounter.

LSE

I land in London in late August 1971. Luck is on my side. Issa Shivji, a recent graduate from LSE, has a week more in London. He shows me the ropes, around the city and school. Two things awe me: you approach a door, and it opens up; you step onto a stairway, and it takes you up! The ultra-mini skirted girls titillate me. And there are the mega-sandwiches; the amount of cheese in one sandwich exceeds my three months' consumption in DSM. That is, if it is found at an affordable price. No doubt, I am on a new planet.

My intoxication is soon dampened by the cold insularity of the Londoners. Deadly silence on buses and subways is the norm. On my way to LSE, I see a lady who has collapsed on a central island of a busy street. Likely, a homeless person. No pedestrian or car stops to assist her. Those who pass near her are as expressionless as zoned out zombies. If this is civilization, it is not for me.

And there is unmistakable racism; black people are Darkies and brown people are Pakis. On a visit to the famed British Library, I see an unoccupied reading booth. The desk light is on and a book lies open. Maybe its occupant has temporarily gone elsewhere. I ask the man in the adjacent booth. 'Is any one sitting here?' He looks at me, looks at the chair, under it, and under the booth. 'I do not see anyone!' With those terse words, he calmly returns to his book. Would a white person have elicited that insulting response?

My study program is jam packed with courses that take up much of my time. My classmates, bright minds from many nations, are scattered across the metropolis. I do not come to know them well. I also take part in external activities like supporting the people of Vietnam against American aggression and the South African people against Apartheid rule. Attending demonstrations, discussions, and reading books on political economy and world affairs takes up a chunk of my spare time. Here, in contrast, I make several good friends.

The courses at LSE are not appealing for the most part. Many are not well taught. The two I like best are (i) Characteristic Functions and (ii) The Distribution of Quadratic Forms. I do not recall who taught the first but, for the latter, we have Professor Alan Stuart of the encyclopedic *Kendall's Advanced Theory of Statistics* text fame (Stuart, Ord and Kendall 1987). As a teacher, he stands in a class of his own.

At UDSM, I had developed an aversion to statistics mainly due to the course on Multivariate Statistical Analysis. It had the worst teacher I have ever encountered. Entering the classroom, he mumbles an incomprehensible sentence, scribbles a formula on the blackboard, and places another one in a slanting way in another corner. At times, he writes over what he has written earlier. From day one to the last, we have no clue what is going on. There is no room for questions. Once the rigmarole ends, he walks out and is not available for consultation. We complain to Professor Phythian — the only time in the three years we do such a thing — but he asks us to be patient, saying that the lecturer is a top class statistician in India. Whatever the case, as a lecturer, he is the worst of the lot. I do not know how we were able to pass his exam.

That was eighteen months ago. Professor Stuart stands in sharp contrast. He first tells us in a grand-fatherly style what the topic of the day is, explains his notation, and declares his starting point. In a gentle but systematic and rigorous exposition, he then leads us to the goal. Most of the steps are not that difficult to ascend, but a few pose a real challenge. The fault lies not in his teaching but reflects the nature of the beast.

+ + + + + + +

Comment: Modern day students do not realize that in any subject, some concepts are intrinsically abstruse. Sustained effort is essential for acquiring even a modicum of comprehension. Wanting their goods on a silver platter, they reflexively cast the blame on the teacher when rapid understanding is not attained.

+ + + + + + +

Professor Stuart's exposition exposes me to the elegant foundation of statistical analysis. Invoking the language of vectors and matrices, he puts up a logical edifice that sparkles with gems of serene beauty. Remarkably, the gems are pertinent to the endeavors to unravel the truth in the natural and social sciences.

+ + + + + + +

Comment: With hindsight, I see that Professor Stuart's integration of beauty with practicality did distinctly influence my eventual decision to specialize in the field of medical statistics. Because I had to focus on OR, I did not do the more application oriented statistics courses. Therefore, it was a decade later that I came to appreciate the centrality of the statistical mode of thinking in all pure and applied branches of science including medicine and the social sciences.

+ + + + + + +

During this period, I regularly spend a part of my weekend with three cousins who are in London; Yasmin, Karim and Rumina. We go to the movies, savor spicy delights at Indo-Pakistani eateries and walk around the city. Yasmin is a nurse; Karim pursues accountancy. Rumina, my de facto sister, struggles to find her feet in an alien environment. She works by day and studies in the evening. As my UNESCO scholarship gives me a generous allowance, I pass on a quarter of it to her for six months.

It is in the company of Yasmin that I have a unique movie going experience. The academy award winning, Soviet-made film rendition of Tolstoy's War and Peace has come to town. The snag is that it is of nearly **nine** hours duration. The show starts at 8 pm on a Saturday, with a snack break at midnight, and continental breakfast at dawn. The food comes with the ticket.

We marvel at this cinematic majesty; as enriching as tackling Tolstoy himself. The scene of the injured Prince Andrei Bolkonsky first passing a lifeless looking grand oak in the depth of the winter, and later, as it begins to sparkle with life in the spring persists in my mind to this day. When the director was queried why he made such a long movie, he had a cryptic reply: 'Can you do justice to Tolstoy within a shorter time?'

Towards the end of my stay in London, I learn that the Tanzanian Vice-President

Karume has been assassinated. The details are not in the public domain, even to this day. But one consequence is that a number of Zanzibari comrades, both on the mainland and the island, are detained without trial. Word spreads that those in Zanzibar are subject to torturous ill-treatment. Some of the mainland detainees – Abdul Rahaman Babu, Colonel Ali Mafoudh, and Harko Bhagat – I know in person.

If there is evidence against them, it should be presented in a court of law, where they would have a chance to defend themselves. Indefinite detention without due process denies one of one's basic human right. Three Zanzibari exiles in London (Ali Said, Ahmed Rajab and Mohamed Ali) and I start a campaign to publicize this fact. We aim to pressurize our government to follow the norms of justice. Our work complements the work of comrades at home and in Sweden and Denmark.

We write articles for general distribution, urge Amnesty International to take up the case, and petition progressive members of the British establishment. A face-to-face session with the director of Amnesty International is fruitful. He promises to devote due resources to look into it. Former progressive lecturers at UDSM, like Lionel Cliffe, join the effort. But by the time I leave for Dar es Salaam, no achievement is discernible. The comrades in London will continue the struggle.

+ + + + + + +

Comment: All the detainees were released without any charges pressed against them some five years later.

+ + + + + + +

By the time I left for DSM, I had visited places outside London. With Rumina, I spent a weekend in Brighton visiting another relative who was working there as nurse. It gave me an exposure to the touristic attractions of the southern English seaside. I also went to Birmingham for three days to visit my maternal great uncle. Originally from Zanzibar, he had moved to the UK after the 1964 revolution on that island. I had not seen him for many years. Though quite frail now, he was distinctly pleased to see me. And I spent a pleasant but freezing weekend in a coastal Scottish town at the home of my teaching practice supervisor, Elizabeth Connelly. This was my only contact with an indigenous British family. Her mother's fine meals made it more than possible for my radically oriented mind to patiently withstand her father's arch conservative political views. To round up my visit, Elizabeth took me for a long, illuminating stroll around the town. Unlike London, I did not see black or brown faces.

4

A VISIT TO ZANZIBAR

Life is the great teacher
James Joyce

+ + + + + + +

MY PATERNAL GRANDMOTHER was born in Zanzibar in the year 1896. It was also the birth place of my parents. Later they moved to the southern region of mainland Tanzania where I was born. I first visited the island in 1959, a visit that forms one of my fondest childhood memories (See *GWTZ*). My second trip to Zanzibar was in 1969, this time as a member of the UDSM TANU Youth League. As it was a short, officious trip, I did not get to see much of the place.

The forced marriage saga of the 1960s gave the government of Zanzibar much negative publicity, especially in the Western media. Besides, its bilateral ties with the socialist governments of the Soviet Union, East Germany and China made it an automatic, Cold War driven target of the capitalist nations. In order to remedy that image, it invited the Tanzanian academic staff of the University of Dar es Salaam to visit the island for a week and see what was going on there. Three trips, with some twenty academics per trip, were organized. I was in the second trip, which occurred in May 1971.

I maintained a daily diary during the trip. Each evening, I wrote down a summary of what we saw, whom we met, and other events of the day. We were taken to both parts of the island nation, Unguja and Pemba. We visited villages, townships, farms, factories, health centers, youth camps, housing schemes and educational institutions. We talked, collectively and individually, not just with officials but also ordinary people in all walks of life. An eye-opening visit, we saw a face of Zanzibar outsiders rarely see.

Many historians and scholars have written about the 1964 revolution in Zanzibar and the subsequent developments. The revolution was a product of the injustice and inequalities established during the British colonial era and the fact that the attainment of political independence largely left these feudal, racial and economic structures intact. For an overall, integrated history of Zanzibar up to 1964, the book *Zanzibar Under Colonial Rule* (Sheriff and Ferguson 1991) has no rival. What happened after that is, however, another unclear story. The picture that emerges from the existent scholarship regarding post-1964 Zanzibar is a contradictory and confusing one. You find many claims that lack a firm foundation.

I do not aim to delve into this contentious discourse. In this chapter, my objective is to describe the picture I formed of Zanzibar from my personal observations. It is mainly based on my diary and memories. The visit taught me many things, and I am of the view that what I saw continues to have an educational value.

THE TRIP

May 9, 1971: After a short, bumpy flight, our plane lands at Zanzibar airport in the early afternoon of a sunny day. A group of officials from the Afro-Shirazi Party youth league wait for us. Warm words of welcome are followed by a bus ride to the Nkrumah College, a teacher training college. It is our place of residence for the week. The students are on vacation. The rooms are airy, beds have mosquito nets, and there is water and electricity. After a hearty meal of freshly made *pilau*, a rice and meat dish cooked with spices, we are taken to a traditional Zanzibari music performance. (This is to be our standard daily lunch.)

A large audience is present. Accompanied by a superb orchestra, the *Taarab* singers captivate us with enchanting melodies. It is a refreshing start to our trip. The only thing that disturbs me is the continued feudal custom of dishing out bank notes to individual performers. Now and then, someone from the audience throws a five or ten shillings note to a singer or musician. Such commercialization, in my view, degrades the art and dignity of the performer.

May 10, 1971: We are served an early breakfast of bread with margarine, eggs and steaming tea. At 10 a.m., we are taken to the State House to be officially welcomed to the island by the Second Vice President of Tanzania (and President of Zanzibar) Mr Abeid Karume. In a long speech, he tells us that the main problem facing the nation is insufficient food. Therefore, ensuring adequate food supplies using mechanized agriculture is the first priority of his government. Though he places a great deal of emphasis on technology, he ridicules modern experts who are good at talk but deficient in action. He openly declares that higher education is not an essential thing. The most important task is to impart technical skills through practical education. At the end, he notes the importance of equality and social justice.

It is a rambling speech littered with mystical pronouncements that leaves us in the dark about the actuality of his government's development policy. There is no room for questions.

After this two hours long session we go to the headquarters of the ASP. First we get a brief tour of the premises. Then the party's secretary goes over the history of the party. It is an interesting but selective talk. Crucially, the key role of the Umma party led by AM Babu in the Zanzibar revolution is not mentioned. He highlights the role of present day leaders but does not adequately dwell on the concrete changes in Zanzibar after the revolution.

Our tour has begun with an overdose of the official side of the story. We hope that from this point on, we will be able to see the reality on the ground with our own eyes.

Our hopes are realized after a late but hearty lunch. We are taken to a public housing scheme near Unguja town. It has four to five story structures recently built with assistance from East Germany. All weather roads to the area are under construction. The existing units plus those still under construction are expected to house 12,000 people. The well-built flats are supplied with a stove and other items. The residents will not pay rent but will pay 36 shillings every month for water and electricity. In comparison, the rent for such a flat in Dar es Salaam is about 300 shillings per month. And water and electricity are extra.

Just 10 years ago, living in such a flat for an ordinary person in Zanzibar was but a dream. These housing schemes demonstrate a concrete benefit of the Zanzibar Revolution. We are highly impressed and feel that the mainland government has a lot to learn from the construction methods. But we have concerns. Is the initial investment sustainable? Cement, an essential material, is being imported. What about building a cement factory? Assistance from East Germany is expected to end soon. What will happen after that?

We also visit an old people's home nearby. It is a well-organized place. But since we do not spend much time there, I could not draw any definite conclusions.

At night we are in for a surprise. The Minister for Education gives us a very frank and straightforward talk on the education system in Zanzibar. First he summarizes the progress made in the seven years after the revolution. The schools are now run by the state, and racial and religious discrimination has been abolished. There are 98 primary schools with 50,000 pupils and 49 secondary schools with 4,000 pupils. Twenty new secondary schools are to be opened in 1972. But only two of them reach up to Form VI level.

The official target is to provide ten years of basic education to all the children in Zanzibar. The emphasis is on science subjects, agriculture and political education. Some colleges offer technical and vocational training like teacher training, nursing, mechanical trades, typing and accountancy.

The minister does not hesitate to reveal the problems facing the education system. There is a big shortage of competent teachers. The quality of education is poor. No review of the curriculum has been done. The internal examination system does not maintain the desired standard. He is also concerned about the official policy of not sending students for university level education. He answers our questions in an open manner, and we have a good discussion. This is the only time during our trip that we encounter an open-minded high official.

Our first day has exposed us to a bellyful of experiences and voices to ponder over.

May 11, 1971: Early in the morning, we go to the tractor repair plant built with Chinese assistance. The technology is quite advanced. Machines for performing different operations have been installed. Students from an adjoining technical college do their practical work at this repair plant. After a quick tour of the place, we pay a short visit to the Lumumba College. As it is a hurried visit, we mainly see the classrooms from outside.

Next is the Zanzibar shoe factory, the highlight of the day. We spend more than two hours looking at the different sections of the place. It is a striking example of an integrated, appropriate technology industrial enterprise. The tanning section cleans, processes and cuts cowhides obtained locally or from the mainland into appropriate sizes. There is no complicated machinery. Everything is done by hand by skilled workers. After being dried and softened the pieces are sent to the main area, which is divided into several sections. There are the sole and base making area, the main body making area and the shoestring holes making area. These items go to the assembly area where expert shoemakers with anvil, hammer, nails, needle and string assemble the shoe. Then it goes to the final stages of polishing, coloring and inspection. The entire manufacturing process is labor intensive, and uses locally available skills and materials for the most part.

The final product is a sturdy, affordable shoe. Though it cannot compete with the imported brands in terms of attractiveness, it lasts longer. Several different types of shoes are made here. It is hoped that over time they will become as attractive as the imported shoes.

In an earlier visit in 1969, I had also come to this factory. I note two changes. The Chinese supervisors are not there anymore. The quality and variety of the shoes seems to have declined.

Next on the agenda of this hectic morning is the Chelechele youth camp. We are told that 300 young people reside at this camp but only a few are girls. A small number of Asian and Arab faces are also seen. The camp population is expected to increase to 800 within two years.

The residents are paid 150 shillings per month, out of which 60 shillings are deducted for maintenance and upkeep. The remaining 90 shillings are deposited in a bank account. The camp has a large farm with 600 acres under mechanized cultivation. Most of the area is devoted to rice but with 50 acres for sugarcane. The latter will be expanded in the future as there are plans to build a small sugar factory nearby. Besides working on the farm, the camp residents also help nearby villages. Last year they helped plow 400 acres of land for the villagers.

Upon leaving the camp, we tour the Mji wa Chemichemi flats. The rural buildings are not as large as their urban counterparts but each flat is well laid out and has water and electricity. These flats are rent free too.

Next we stop at the Upenja state farm. We see several large poultry sheds and are taken to the edge of a 1100-acres rice field. The three Chinese experts stationed here speak broken Swahili and are quite friendly. The workers live in tin-roofed but well built houses with water and electricity. The state farms on the mainland lack such facilities for the workers. As in many other places we visit, there are a number of water storage tanks on the premises.

In the afternoon, we first go to a historical site. It is a change from the routine. The slave market and cells at Mangapwani area. Then comes the tunnel where slaves were kept. Both are reminders of the grisly past. A tour of a natural underground water reservoir rounds up the afternoon.

After dinner we board SS Africa in Unguja harbor, our destination Pemba. It is a long trip. The sleeping arrangements are far from comfortable. We spend much of the night talking to each other and reflecting on what we have seen thus far.

12 May 1971: The 7 am. breakfast refreshes us with steaming tea with milk and sugar and plentiful *vitumbua* and *maandazi*. We land in Pemba around 9:30 am. Party officials and a large bus await.

It is the busiest day of our visit. We pass through several rice plantations. A few are state run but most, we are surprised to learn, are privately owned. The latter also get assistance from the state in terms of tractor usage and subsidized inputs.

We also spend time at a youth camp. The arrangements here are identical to the camps on Unguja. But there is a major readily apparent difference. These young residents are more disciplined. They talk to us with great respect, standing upright all the time. We wonder if the reason is greater political awareness or fear.

Just as in Unguja, there are water tanks and a water pumping station. We pass through two rural townships under construction, witness road ways being built and a multiplicity of housing schemes at various stages of competition. By the time we end the day, we are exhausted.

13 May 1971: After a heavy breakfast of porridge, bread with margarine, boiled egg and tea, we head to Fidel Castro College. It is an education college with science bias. One hundred and sixty students reside on the campus. We visit a couple of classrooms and examine the curriculum. The contents and manner of teaching resemble that in teacher training colleges on the mainland. The main difference is

that the political education here is more rigid, dealing more with the history of the ASP and glorifying its leaders.

In the afternoon, we first go to the Kiwani village dispensary. Built in 1969, it is an organized, compact place with a good stock of essential medicines. The hard working doctors and nurses ensured that overcrowding was minimized. Next we are taken to the site of a new township under construction. We find people cutting down trees and clearing the area. We also join in, though only for a short while.

Then we are transported to the Abdallah Mzee hospital, a decently equipped and staffed facility with 12 Chinese doctors. Besides the general practitioners, there is an eye doctor, a pediatrician, a dentist, two surgeons and two gynecologists/obstetricians. It treats most of the common diseases and carries out simple and complicated surgical procedures. The Chinese doctors also train local assistant doctors. The doctor-in-charge says that they are implementing Chairman Mao's call to serve the people of the world. Along the way, we hear that at the outset, the doctors were well liked by the people because they work hard and take good care of the patients. Of recent, there have been rumors of mistreatment of some cases. The truth is not known but the talk has dampened the morale of the doctors. On the way back, we pass through two rice plantations that are similar to what we had seen earlier.

In the evening, we go around Mkoani town on our own. It is a strange experience. There is not much to see apart from small rundown shops in derelict structures. Be it a grocery or clothing outlet, little merchandise is on sale. Notwithstanding the many large rice plantations in Zanzibar, rice bins are empty or almost so. Basic items like soap, cooking oil, kerosene and sugar are hard to find. The tea rooms offer little other than black tea and *mandazi*. The traders say that the distribution of basic goods by the state wholesale agency is erratic in the extreme; one item could be supplied in abundance while other essential items would be missing. This tour is an ideal opportunity to talk on a one-to-one basis with local people. I learn important aspects of the unofficial story about life on the island, especially from a man called Mr Haji.

Near the market I see a fierce bullfight in progress, my first time to witness such an event. A large crowd is cheering at what is plainly an ugly, cruel exercise. I walk back to our residence in disgust.

14 May 1971: The entire day is spent at sea, sailing to Unguja in the same vessel that brought us here. The ocean is calm, the waters, crystal clear, the gentle breeze soothing the spirit. Occasionally, I spy a large fish gliding elegantly beneath the surface. A white bird with an extended beak swiftly swoops down on an unsuspecting prey. The wonders and contradictions of nature unfold before us like a movie on a giant screen.

Our contingent has partitioned itself into three chattering groups. My compatriots and I reflect the differences between what we experienced in Pemba and Unguja. The reception accorded to us in Pemba was more formal and official. At the Fidel Castro College, we encountered an elaborate welcoming ceremony; at the Kiwani dispensary site, almost the whole village including school children had lined up to receive us, clapping and dancing as we passed by. It was astonishing that all productive and educational work had ceased just to impress us.

In Pemba, there was greater presence of security forces. It was apparent that the ASP Youth League exercised stricter control here. In a group encounter, people did not say things other than praise the ASP and its leaders. The divide between the leaders and the led was acute, and people were more afraid to speak their minds. If Mwalimu Nyerere or Sheikh Karume was mentioned in a public speech, someone in the crowd would invariably shout, *Mungu ampe maisha marefu* (may God grant him a long life). Superstitious beliefs also seemed more prevalent.

On a one-to-one basis, and especially if no one else was in the vicinity, people did speak up. One issue they raised was the beneficiaries of the housing schemes. They complained that common folk were often left out. Officials of the local and central government, party leaders, members of the security services and those related to them had the first priority. Such favoritism also applied to the distribution of basic commodities. People felt that their island was unfairly dominated by the leaders from Unguja.

In Pemba, we did not visit any industrial site. Overall, people here seemed poorer than those on the main island. Apart from getting a plot of land, and free education and health care, many do not seem to have benefited from the revolution. (I return to these matters below.)

15 May 1971: There is no organized activity on our last full day in Zanzibar. After breakfast, I walk around Zanzibar town. Before the revolution, its commerce was dominated by Indian traders. Over 90% of them have emigrated. Now the sector is under the control of state wholesale and retail establishments. A handful of influential Indian merchants remain. These state and private shops carry imported, expensive items, like canned food, perfumes, fancy clothing and shoes which are beyond the reach of the ordinary person.

In addition, there are many rundown small shops owned by Africans and Indians, and a few Arabs. They have limited supplies of stuff like sweets, salt, biscuit, soap and cooking oil but little else. Things such as rice, bread, maize flour and kerosene are hard to find. Supplies are, as in Pemba, erratic. Bread takes effort to procure. You queue from morning to evening to be lucky to get a loaf. Maize flour, mainly imported from the mainland, is costly. Meat is very expensive and rare. Popularly consumed fruits like pineapple and *shelisheli* (bread fruit) are rising in price. Surprisingly, the price of rice is also going up.

The distribution system of the state trading corporation, managed by a member of the Karume family, is inefficient. Food can rot in the depot while there is shortage in the street. Mosquito nets are in short supply, although the official story is that they are plentiful. Rumors of embezzlement in the corporation are rife but no one says it openly. In my walk, I come across shoe makers, electricians and plumbers who are barely making ends meet.

I spend the afternoon at the home of the sister of a comrade from UDSM. I get a warm welcome. Besides homemade Zanzibari food, there is plenty of revealing conversation. This is a family of dedicated activists who played a significant role during the colonial and revolutionary days. Now it has been marginalized, with some of its members getting horrible treatment from the state. I am well fed and learn a lot (I note some of it below).

Tomorrow morning we return to Dar es Salaam. I retire to bed early with my mind on the most inspiring moment of this trip. It occurred during a visit to a health center in Unguja. We were told there was a senior Chinese surgeon at this place who used acupuncture anesthesia while doing some operations. At UDSM, some of us had seen a film about acupuncture, and thus were interested in meeting this doctor.

At the gate of the health center, we found an elderly Chinese man in baggy attire sweeping the entrance area. He greeted us in broken Swahili and we explained who we were. Immediately, he smiled, dropped his broom, and said in fluent English that he had been told to expect us but had not been told at what time. To our astonishment, this sweeper was both the center director and the famed surgeon we had come to meet.

He left us for a moment, returning dressed in a doctor's uniform and a professional aura. We were first taken to different parts of the center. Later he took us to the backyard and told us about the health problems they encounter at clinic and the type of health education they were giving to the area residents. He also told us about the organization of the health system in China. One important feature of the system was the combination of modern medicine with relevant traditional Chinese medicine.

We left the center highly impressed with not just the work being done here but more with the simplicity and humility of this eminent surgeon. He was a genuine embodiment of Chairman Mao's edict to serve the people. Was this the 'New Man' Che Guevara had talked about?

REFLECTIONS

I now give my overall reflections emanating from our trip. There is no question that the Zanzibari society has been transformed fundamentally after the revolution of 1964. The colonialists are gone and so are the classes of large land owners and the local commercial bourgeoisie (mainly Asians) who were allied to them. In racial terms, the vast majority of Asians and people of Arabic background have moved to the mainland or migrated abroad. On the other hand, the highly exploited classes comprising plantations workers and dependent peasants have benefited from the ensuing allocation of three acres of land to each family.

Yet, new structures of domination have emerged. The chasm between the rulers and the ruled is wide and is widening over time. The high hopes generated by the revolution are fast dissipating and the prospects are bleak.

The Economy: Though the colonialists are gone, the economy retains the import/export structure of the colonial era. Cloves and coconuts remain the main export crops and virtually all manufactured consumer goods are imported. Despite expanded cultivation of rice and sugarcane and the few industrial projects, the economy is dependent on external forces. Unlike in the past, this dependency is now mediated through the state sector which is controlled by a tiny elite.

The export market for cloves is more diversified, with the USA, Britain, China and the USSR being the dominant destinations. Though the international price has gone up substantially, the proportion paid to the rural producer has remained around 10%.

There is a dual economy in the rural areas. Residents of youth camps and workers in state farms have an improved standard of living while the income of peasants has hardly improved. The latter, however, do have better access to education and health services than in the colonial era. But here and there, one sees a few well to do farmers. In the urban areas, jobs and opportunities for self-employment are quite limited and the majority of the people have very low income. Over the past decade, only the ruling elites, managers of state companies and their associates have reaped substantive benefits.

The major problem is the absence of comprehensive economic planning. Due to its myopic vision, the ruling elite manages the economy in a haphazard and inefficient manner. Technical education, for example, is emphasized, yet the issue of where its graduates will be employed is neglected. It is only because of the projects initiated, funded and implemented by the socialist nations that the rulers are able to make bold claims with regard to economic progress. But that cannot go on for long.

Social Services: The post-revolution years have seen a major growth of primary and secondary schools, especially in the rural areas. The number of teacher training colleges has also increased. As noted earlier, the quality of education is low, and essential items like textbooks are often missing. A few technical colleges have been established with assistance from East Germany. Surprisingly, sending students for university level education on the mainland is not only accorded a low priority but is actually looked down upon. The island is thereby being deprived of the highly skilled manpower required to formulate and implement sound long term policies in the various sectors of the economy and society. For instance, the shortage of experts in the various academic disciplines means that critical activities like curriculum reform and evaluation of academic programs cannot be undertaken.

The population of Zanzibar has benefited from the substantially enhanced basic health services. This has occurred mainly due to assistance from China. Though some auxiliary health personnel are being trained, the shortage of local doctors is acute. The USSR gave scholarships for training doctors and modernized the VI Lenin Hospital in Unguja. A small pharmaceutical compounding facility was set up within the hospital. The number of students who have sent for medical training in East Africa and the socialist nations is, however, small.

Other state run projects through which segments of the population have benefited include the housing schemes, construction of water storage tanks, tractor plowing assistance from the state farms and establishment of homes for the elderly. But their scope is limited and the question of fairness remains.

Foreign Assistance: Timely and appropriate assistance from the socialist countries has been a crucial developmental factor for Zanzibar. The initial aid came from East Germany and the Soviet Union. Later China joined the fray. The type of projects they developed are described above. The experts and doctors from China were more popular since they were hard working and worked closely with the ordinary people.

Unfortunately, such assistance has been used in an opportunistic manner by the ASP leaders. Instead of taking the projects as steppingstones to develop the economy in a planned and integrated manner, they were using them as showpiece devices to portray the benefits they have brought to the nation. Hence the long term impact of the assistance from the socialist nations is questionable. The milk and sugar factories are already rumored to be in trouble. One deleterious aspect of the East German assistance was the training provided to the security service. Its effect could not be anything other than enhancing the repressive nature of the state apparatus.

The Western nations have generally shunned the Zanzibari government, despite their full scale engagement with the mainland authorities. One exception is the malaria control program funded by the USA.

Politics and Governance: The ideology of the ASP, which governs the politics in Zanzibar, is a curious blend of nationalism, racial identity and unpredictable day-to-day pronouncements of the top leaders. It is also marked by a distinct anti-intellectual streak. Aspects of Islamic religiosity are also frequently injected into the political pronouncements.

Racial equality was a key demand of the anti-colonial struggle. Instead of sticking to that fine principle, the ASP leaders have turned the colonial era racial equation upside down. Now, the darker your skin, the more authentic a Zanzibari you are. Those with a lighter skin tone are treated with suspicion. Further the top leaders of the ASP strive to promote racial equality through intermarriage, which at one point was implemented in a coercive manner. The exercise was only halted after the ensuing international condemnation and intervention by Mwalimu Nyerere.

On the mainland, the policy of *Ujamaa*, as spelled out in *The Arusha Declaration*, is supposed to guide the national policy. No such document exists for Zanzibar. In fact, President Karume has made it clear that this declaration does not apply to the islands. In particular, the leadership of ASP is disdainful of its leadership code that restricts ownership of commercial entities by government and party leaders. Many senior officials and their family members here run private businesses and farms. These enterprises get free state assistance. Throughout our tour of the rural areas, we did not come across a single collective village of the sort commonly encountered on the mainland but saw several large individually owned farms, particularly in Pemba.

Political education is provided not only in schools but in all public institutions. In addition to covering topics like the local and union constitution, it is mostly a one-sided rehash of the colonial history, the 1964 revolution and praise for what the ASP, guided by President Karume, has achieved since then. No one finds it of interest but, out of fear, people regurgitate the contents anyways.

Mwalimu Nyerere is not popular in Zanzibar, not just with the leaders but also the general public. It is felt that he does not intervene to curtail the repressive practices that go on all the time or alleviate the shortage of essential commodities. AM Babu, who once upon a time was quite popular, has also lost his standing. It is said that he is comfortably ensconced on the mainland and no longer fights for the rights of the people of Zanzibar.

The government of Zanzibar operates in a rigid top-down style. Party and state edicts are enforced through the ubiquitous presence of political commissars in all societal institutions. They claim to have a direct line to the top leaders and tend to function like demigods. The ASP youth wing is highly organized and active. It is in charge of the youth camps and the general security. The colonial era practice of paying informants persists. A person who passes on useful information to the ASP youth wing is entitled to receive 7.50 shillings, just as in the past. Because of this system, people are afraid to speak their minds. Attendance in political rallies is compulsory. If you miss a political education session, flag raising ceremony or a rally, and the matter is reported, you may find your salary cut, or be demoted. Fear, intimidation and harsh repression are the primary mechanism through which this government functions. Arbitrary detention and even execution is a clear risk faced by any person seen to oppose those in power.

Eight years after the revolution, and despite some visible gains, the negative has come to outweigh the positive. The popular enthusiasm of the early days appears to have largely dissipated. The tension is particularly acute in Pemba.

Under the influence of the Western media, a widespread notion prevails that this nation has landed into its current quagmire because it has adopted a socialist or communist form of government. Nothing can be further from the truth. The land owners and commercial bourgeoisie are gone, the state sector plays a dominant role in the economy and the nation receives much assistance from the Eastern Bloc. But these characteristics do not suffice to make the economy and society socialistic in nature. The ASP leaders have disdain for socialism and the economy resembles a bungling form of underdeveloped state capitalism.

At outset, the Zanzibar revolution had a great promise; it could have embarked on the construction of a society based on social justice and attempted to bring the genuine development for all the people. It could have exhibited a new relationship between the masses and those in power. However this promise was derailed with assistance from Mwalimu Nyerere who was under strong pressure from the West. The progressive leaders in the Umma party and other activists were quickly isolated. Some were exiled on the mainland or abroad, and some were locked up. Consequently, the leadership was monopolized by people whose outlook enjoined petty populism and racialism with heavy handed authoritarianism.

PROSPECTS

Upon returning to UDSM, I ask myself four questions:

- Does the ASP have a vision and strategy to bring about fundamental change in the conditions of the people of Zanzibar?
- Are the leaders and cadres of the ASP primarily dedicated to promote the interests of the people?
- Has the ASP been learning needed lessons from the experiences other African and socialist nations?
- Is the ASP appropriately utilizing the assistance it has been receiving from the socialist nations?

From what I saw during the wide ranging visit, the only answer I can give to each question is a resounding 'No'. Instead of building a society based on equality and progress for all, the ASP is taking the nation in the opposite direction. It is rapidly being transformed from a 'populist autocracy' (Sheriff 1991, page 261) to 'one of the worst bungling and tyrannical petty-bourgeois despotisms in Africa' (Babu 1991, page 244). I feel sad for the people of Zanzibar. It is tragic that the hopes and dreams unleashed after 1964 are being ground to dust.

Note: The aim of the ASP leaders in inviting academics from UDSM was to showcase the development projects in the hope that we would write about them and rectify the prevalent image of Zanzibar. However what we saw had positive and negative features. My colleagues did not just want to highlight the former and be regarded as political propagandists. On the other hand, to make critical comments was a risky proposition that could jeopardize one's career. So as far as I know none of them wrote an article for a newspaper or magazine.

I wanted to write an article on the Zanzibar trip for the student magazine *MajiMaji*. But my priorities were to deal with the numerous arrangements for my postgraduate studies in London and prepare for my first university level teaching assignment for a course that was to commence in a month's time. I began to write the article just as the new academic year was about to start in early July 1971. But to everyone's astonishment, the hitherto tranquil University of Dar es Salaam was rocked to its foundation by a major convulsion. Students boycotted classes for a week and the ensuing crisis dragged on for much longer. I, like many others, was swept away by its momentum. Before departing for London, I ended up by writing about this momentous crisis. This is the topic of the next chapter.

The article on Zanzibar was put on the back burner. So what I have written above is the first time my impressions and conclusions about the revealing May 1971 visit to Zanzibar have come to light.

5

A PRO-DEMOCRACY UPRISING

*Experience is the best teacher
But the tuition is high*
Norwegian Proverb

+ + + + + + +

A SPARK CAN IGNITE A PRAIRIE FIRE. But, as Mao Zedong declared, the conditions must be ripe. The first graduation ceremony of UDSM on 7 July 1971 occasions the issuance of a potent spark. Taking the form of a rambling, vacuous oration by Vice Chancellor (VC) Pius Msekwa, it, to everyone's surprise, catalyzes a major upheaval on the campus the very next day. The discontent that led to it has been brewing for a year now.

The acute phase of this episode is of one week in duration. But it will have unprecedented features and exercise a major long term influence on how the university will be governed.

A BRIEF HISTORY

Until the 1960s, institutions of higher learning in the West and the Third World, while claiming to be citadels of independent thought and inquiry, were beholden to the dominant capitalist and imperialist system. They generated a sizable creative output in science, technology, social science, medicine, art and literature. Yet, most of their endeavors were constrained by the values and demands of the prevailing system. Research, publication and teaching were, by and large, underpinned by capitalist ideology, corporate interests and national security priorities. A minor presence of academics who queried the *status quo* was tolerated. Overall, however, views at variance with the existing social order were rare.

Moreover, these institutions had rigid hierarchical structures. The atmosphere favored a pro-*status quo* bias in thought and practice, not broad academic freedom and discourse. Behind a superficial facade, these universities were elitist institutions run by the elites for capitalist and imperial interests.

For varied socio-economic and political reasons, the decade of the 1960s brought to the fore student movements that challenged that state of affairs. The influence of dissident academics grew disproportionately in relation to their numbers. The ivory towers were rocked to the core by massive and intense protests making demands of local and universal character. These movements sought inclusion of voices promoting social justice, racial and gender parity into university affairs, and demanded basic curricular reform, especially in law, social sciences, economics and education. They struggled to end the entanglement of the academy with pro-corporate policies at home, and policies of war and neo-colonial domination abroad. A key aim of these student movements was to democratize the governance of the university (Ali 2005; Chomsky et al. 1998; Derber, Schwartz and Magrass 1990; Schalk 1991).

The academy in Africa, Asia and Latin America, often a couple of decades old, faced further obstacles arising from overt interference from local politicians and intellectual dominance by expatriate academic staff, mainly of the conservative mindset. While protesters in the West faced tear gas and batons, in Africa, they braved bullets, arbitrary incarceration and regularly, torture and death (Legum 1972).

UDSM was no stranger to student agitation. It had become a hot-bed of radical action from the year 1967, the year of the Arusha Declaration and initiation of the policy of Socialism and Self-Reliance for Tanzania. Demonstrations, in-class confrontations, faculty sit-ins, self-education classes on Sundays, public lectures and debates, leafleting and petitions had become integral to the campus environment.

Mounted by left wing students, allied with like-minded academic staff, they invoked issues like curricular reform, the hiring of lecturers, discussions of national development policies, liberation of Africa, support for the people of Cuba and Vietnam, exposé of visiting pro-imperialist groups, among other things.

The UDSM students of those days fell into three ideological groupings. Some 5% subscribed to socialist, Pan-African politics. Another 5% had pro-Western, right-wing leanings. The rest, while imbued with nationalistic feelings, kept a distance from socio-political activism. Unless it was an issue of Apartheid rule or colonialism, they stood on the sidelines. In tandem with their elitist aspirations, they focused on study, entertainment and personal affairs. (These are order of magnitude estimates based on personal experience.)

The right wing students and staff promoted agendas of their own and mounted offensives to counter the innovative leftist initiatives such as launching an interdisciplinary course in development studies. But the favorable political climate of the era made it difficult for them to roll back the progressive gains on the academic front (see *Cheche* for details).

A NEW UNIVERSITY

In July 1970, this college of the University of East Africa becomes an independent academic institution, the University of Dar es Salaam (UDSM). More than that, it now comes under the purview of a socialistically inclined government. The ball is set in motion at the founding event by inspirational words from Mwalimu Nyerere, the Chancellor. While calling for an academy that champions excellence in scholarship and operates under the umbrella of academic freedom, he also expects it to graduate dedicated experts armed with knowledge and skills of relevance to the socio-economic development of the nation. He implores the new university to promote the vision of socialism and self-reliance.

The man placed at the helm to set this grand project in motion is Pius Msekwa, the former executive secretary of TANU, the ruling party. The new VC arrives on the campus in a pompous style, on a motorcade organized by the TYL headquarters in town. The party paper boasts the next day that TANU is set to take over the university. All segments of the university community, irrespective of political inclination, are alienated by this statement. For, in the four years that have transpired since the Arusha Declaration, one thing has become apparent. There is a wide chasm between the rhetoric from the political leaders and concrete actions of the state. The ruling party is dominated by opportunists and demagogues who seek to further their own positions. They talk about socialism but have no clue or intention to implement policies that will benefit the broad majority and launch the nation onto a trajectory of genuine development. No one at the university, Tanzanian or not, progressive or conservative, looks forward to an administration with such a narrow minded and self-centered outlook. It is not that the staff and students dislike socialism as such. What they do not want is a pretentious brand of socialism undoing the strides made during the first decade of the existence of the university.

Within a week of the arrival of the new VC, our worst fears are confirmed. The substance and style of his leadership elicit grumblings from every segment of the campus community. He operates like a yes-man political appointee and shows no sign of a decent academic or social vision. He smiles all the time and at everyone, but few are taken in by his superficial geniality. It takes little time for students and academic staff, basically from all disciplines and political leanings, to query his credentials to lead the university. As the academic year rolls on, his actions not just confirm but magnify their misgivings.

He takes major decisions without prior consultation with affected parties. None are based on sound investigation. The directive to elongate the academic year to 40 weeks, thus, comes as a surprise to the university community. Even the Deans of the Faculties were not adequately involved. Seasoned academics declare it of dubious pedagogic value. Matters like teaching practice, research projects and other practical activities done during the long vacation are not factored into the vague plan. The academic staff require time away from teaching and routine work in order to do research and write. Does he regard the university environment a regular office type of situation? People wonder.

There is a serious shortage of teaching staff in many departments. Students and staff point to this problem through different avenues. Yet there is no satisfactory response from the VC or his administration. Extending the academic year will add to the teaching load of the already overstretched lecturers.

Over the past three years, the main radical student groups, the University Students African Revolutionary Front (USARF) and campus branch of TANU Youth League (TYL), and the progressive staff allied with them had confronted obstacles on two fronts. First, the ruling party leadership in town had developed strong misgivings about the stand they were taking on national and international matters. Second, these student groups had to conduct their activities in the face of practical hurdles placed by the conservative university administration. Support normally accorded to most student groups was either delayed or denied. Now, with the potent call for a socialistic reorientation of the university from Mwalimu Nyerere, they feel the situation may turn around. They harbor great progressive expectations. As a DUSO letter to the Chancellor written a year later put it:

> [With the] appointment of a party cadre to the high post of Vice Chancellor of the National University, progressive elements at the campus and throughout the nation, hoped that the spirit of the Tanzanian Revolution would be enhanced at the Hill. (ACD-14).

But it proves to be a magnificent illusion. The first blow lands on none other than the leftists. In November 1970, in a move that transmits shock waves across the campus and beyond, the VC oversees a ban on USARF and its magazine, *Cheche*. This magazine, of which I am the senior editor, has, within a year of its existence, acquired a solid national and international reputation. The order emanates from the state house, i.e. the President's office. The stated reasons, one being that the name *Cheche* (The Spark) is of Soviet origin, are clearly spurious. The ban elicits consternation among the African liberation movements that have their main office or a branch office in Tanzania. USARF has formed strong ties with these movements, both in terms of vision and activities. They find it strange that a government pledged towards socialism and Pan-Africanism has silenced an organization committed to the same goals (see the book *Cheche* for details). Pius Msekwa is now seen by the progressive groups as the front man for the implementation of a long term project to silence the genuinely socialistic voices on the campus.

Additionally, his administration enacts bylaws affecting the students in an abrupt fashion. They take particular offense to the rules restricting student movement at the residence halls. There is palpable anger: Are we primary school pupils? As adults, we have the right to determine our private lives. If an unruly student creates a disturbance during a late night visit, he or she has to be disciplined using existing regulations. It is unfair to punish all for the misdeeds of a few. When asked about it, the VC says with a straight face that he consulted the Tanzania Parents Association, a reply that incenses the students further. And, in a typical evasive style, he passes the blame onto the University Council.

Another point of friction is the opening of a university cooperative store. Though it is basically a welcome move, the associated absence of transparency irks everyone. Rumor has it that the top university officials want to use it for personal gain.

The campus workers, from cafeteria staff to clerks and messengers, have a mounting series of unaddressed grievances. These include payment of transport allowance, improved terms of service, enhancement of overtime pay, and loans for bicycles. The VC deals with them in a typical top-down style. Instead of negotiating with their campus leaders, he liaises with the officials of the national workers union in town, and over whom, as a former ruling party senior official, he can exercise greater influence.

The new VC's administration differs in one major way from the previous administration of Dr Wilbert Chagula. While progressive staff and students had numerous run-ins with him, Dr Chagula was respected as a seasoned academic who had a good grasp of how to manage a traditional university. The new VC, on the other hand, is rapidly showing lack of credibility on all fronts and, within a few months, has no constituency left on the Hill.

A NEW STUDENT LEADERSHIP

UDSM was born out of the University of East Africa, and retains its international character, in terms of student and staff composition. The narrow nationalistic rhetoric associated with the ascendance of Mr Msekwa does not sit well in this environment. Like their Tanzanian counterparts, Ugandan and Kenyan students have participated in the broad spectrum of social and political activities on the campus. The ban on USARF narrows the avenues for them to be a part of left-wing student pursuits. Thus far, the main student union and the left-wing groups have had an antagonistic relationship. In the academic year 1970/71, that is set to change. A few ex-USARF members and new students with a leftist orientation manage to win leadership posts in the Dar es Salaam University Students Organization

(DUSO). Two among them are Symonds Akivaga and Mauri Yambo. Jenerali Ulimwengu becomes a dynamic presence on the broader student political arena.

Akivaga, the DUSO president, is a popular leader. Exuding charisma, people listen when he speaks. In a departure from the student union leaders of the past, he harbors an enlightened social vision. With other progressive members of his cabinet, he successfully persuades students to view issues like the new bylaws broadly in terms of the basic right of the students to participate in decision making.

During the academic year, the administration functions like an unseen boss behind the curtain projecting a multitude of unnerving directives at the least expected time. In theory, students (and academic staff) are represented at the various levels of decision making, including the University Council. The Chairman of the Council claims at the first graduation ceremony a year on that it is the only university in Africa with such a representation (ACD-00) (The specific references for this chapter are coded and listed separately). But he does not note that in practice, it is a token presence. Their views do not count. Whatever they say, the higher ups do what they want to do anyways. Reflecting that spirit, the Chairman's speech, though rich in flowery analogies, does not have specific references to the multitude of issues that had concerned the university community in the previous academic year.

One concern mounts on top of another. The DUSO leadership requests, time and again, an audience with the VC and other senior officials. Mostly, they are rebuffed. When a meeting is held, the VC appears sympathetic. But once the students exit his office, he proceeds with business as usual.

By the end his first year in office, he has alienated all on the campus apart from those within his narrow inner circle. For the first time at this university, students, radical, reactionary or moderate; academics, progressive, liberal or rightist; and the ordinary workers have come to develop strong feelings of disaffection towards an unmistakably inept, uncaring VC. The Hill is at a boiling point.

THE OPEN LETTER

Wednesday, 7 July 1971: And now comes that pompous speech from the VC at the first graduation ceremony. Both he and the Chairman of the University Council give a topsy-turvy portrait of the first year in the life of this university. The VC concedes that there were a few problems. But he ascribes them to 'misunderstanding.' The other pressing issues are pushed under the rug. For the student body, it is the final straw. Water is about to turn into steam.

Akivaga summons his cabinet for an emergency session the same evening. The consensus is that all the matters have to be brought out into the open. This is to be done in the form of an open letter to the VC. Somehow, the VC gets a wind of this effort, and tries to mollify them. But the DUSO cabinet sticks to its plan.

Thursday, 8 July 1971: The letter is brought out in the morning. Though signed by Akivaga, it expresses the view of the cabinet as a whole. The grievances outlined are genuine. Though, reflecting the accumulated frustrations, its tone breaches the norms of polite diplomacy. The VC is accused of making 'major policy announcements in public places without prior discussion, consultation or even information.' The cases cited relate to the 40-week academic year, the cooperative shop, and issuance of misleading declarations on the nature of the cleavage between administration, lecturers and students. The letter boldly calls a spade a spade:

> [T]he university is like a floating ship without competent leadership to direct it. ... Mwongozo, para 15 declares that leaders should desist of telling lies but you [VC Msekwa] publicly do and you know this. (ACD-01).

It concludes that the students will hold a general meeting to discuss these issues in a *baraza* the next day, and invites the VC to attend and explain his stand on the relevant issues to the students.

The *Mwongozo* invoked in Akivaga's open letter is the shortened Swahili name for the TANU Guidelines (TANU 1971), a ruling party document issued three months earlier in March 1971. After the Arusha Declaration (TANU 1967) and Education for Self-Reliance (Nyerere 1967), this is the third key policy document on the implementation of the policy of *Ujamaa* in Tanzania. Its outstanding feature is the excoriation of the prevalent leadership and management style in the nation. In its place, the new policy calls for honest, humble leaders who respect people and their views. Participation of ordinary people in the making of the decisions affecting their lives and work is made into a firm requirement. The qualities it specifies for a leader exemplify its radical spirit:

> *There must be a deliberate effort to build equality between the leaders and those they lead. For a Tanzanian leader, it must be forbidden to be arrogant, extravagant, contemptuous and oppressive. The Tanzanian leader has to be a person who respects people, scorns ostentation and who is not a tyrant. He should epitomize heroism, bravery and be a champion of justice and equality.* (TANU 1971).

Leadership styles proscribed above are rife in governmental and para-statal bodies as well as in schools and colleges. This pro-people document is the work a few leftists in the ruling party who seized an opening in the brick wall of tradition to push it through. Though it is an official ruling party document, high party functionaries and senior management personnel in state bodies dislike it. Walter Rodney explained the contradiction in a speech given five years later:

> *In many ways [the Mwongozo] is an even harder hitting document than the Arusha Declaration..... [T]he majority of Tanzanian people stood in [its] framework and that anyone who wanted to oppose it had to do so surreptitiously.* (Rodney 1975).

No wonder, it gains wide and fast popularity among workers, peasants and students. The people treat it almost as a sacred text, citing key paragraphs in a bid to hold leaders with authoritarian practices to account. Soon a nationwide series of protests, some leading to occupations of offices, factories, schools and the university, are to erupt. When workers and students stand up against these autocratic, wasteful, elitist management bodies, they speak the truth. The consequences, as we shall see, are, however, far from what they expect.

Symonds Akivaga is a pioneering personality in this historic movement against heavy handed bureaucracy. His open letter is a key record of that eventful era when ordinary people across the nation decided to rise up in efforts to control their own destiny.

The DUSO open letter is duly delivered to the VC's office. The copies posted on noticeboards attract crowds. Sentiments of agreement from students and staff dominate the scene. The officialdom responds instantly, in a pungent manner. A blunt note from the Chief Administrative Officer, AC Mwingira, charges Akivaga with three counts of indiscipline: libeling the VC, promoting disharmony at the university, and inciting disobedience among the students. He is ordered to appear for a disciplinary hearing early morning of the next day (ACD-02).

RUSTICATION

Friday, 9 July 1971: He reports on time. As the open letter was approved by his cabinet, they too are present. Yet, no one is called in. He is told to return after two hours. Shortly after 10 am, he climbs up to Mr Mwingira's office. Immediately, he is handed a letter declaring that he is guilty as charged, and has consequently been rusticated from the university (ACD-03). He is told to pack his bags.

This procedure violates basic tenets of decency and justice. He has not been given even a modicum of a chance to defend himself. Furthermore, the University Disciplinary Committee is a one-man body, consisting solely of the Chief Administrative Officer. It cannot be expected to be fair and impartial, especially in a case that affects his boss and the administration as a whole.

As the stunned student leader and his cabinet appear at the exit of the administration block, a couple of hundred students are gathered outside. The exit is adjacent to the Senior Common Room, and it being the morning tea hour, quite a number of lecturers also look on. I am one of them. Among the crowd, I see some student comrades: Henry Mapolu, George Hadjivayanis, Munene Njagi, Joe Shengena (the campus TYL chair), Ramesh Chauhan, Naijuka Kashivaki and Wilbald Kavishe.

Everyone is eager to know the outcome of the disciplinary hearing. Standing atop the small stairway leading out of the building, Akivaga reads out the letter he has been given (ACD-03). 'What does 'rustication' mean?' It is a new word even to this educated crowd. 'An indefinite suspension.'

There are loud cries of dismay and anger. Some students want to storm the administration block right away and confront the university bosses. But Akivaga has the good sense to calm the crowd. The Speaker of the Student *Baraza*, Mr Swai, brings order by formally declaring the gathering to be a baraza, an open meeting that constitutes the highest decision making body of DUSO. With the students seated on the ground, a spirited exchange is soon underway. 'What is the next step?' That is the main question.

The proceedings, however, are short lived. As if out of nowhere, a contingent of about fifty Field Force Unit (FFU, the riot police) officers swoops down from the main gateway of the administration block. Armed to the teeth, and with a reputation for ferocity, it is the most feared entity in the nation. Apparently, the VC has had it on standby. Interestingly, and astoundingly to the students, the officer in charge is Said El-Maamry, who graduated from UDSM with a law degree just two days earlier. Following his order, two policemen go four steps up the stairway and one seizes Akivaga by his arm. As he is pulled down, one student shouts loudly. He is hit with a rifle butt and arrested as well. Two students try to hold on to their leader but eventually submit to the strong pull of the policeman. Akivaga is placed under arrest and marched to the waiting police vans.

As the initial shock wears off, intense shouts of dismay are heard. A large group trails behind the retreating contingent, chanting for the release of their leader. In front of the main building underpass, the FFU forms a no-go barrier. Those who come close are roughly pushed away or struck with the butt of the rifle.

George Hadjivayanis is the boldest. He approaches the officer in the middle and calmly tells him that Akivaga and the students have violated no law. He goes on to say that what the FFU is doing is contrary to the national policy of *Ujamaa* that promotes participation of the people in decision making. At first, the officer is expressionless. As George goes on with his tirade, he says they just follow orders. Whether someone has committed an offense or not will be decided by the courts.

A whistle is heard. The FFU retreats in a reverse formation. Akivaga is huddled in one van, but we do not see him. The students follow. About fifty emerge from another direction onto the grassy lawn not too far from the police armada. As the

FFU prepares to depart, a few hurl small stones at their vehicles. None strikes the target. In minutes, the contingent is out of sight, leaving us aghast in disbelief. We are to learn later that Akivaga was taken straight to the airport and put on a plane to Nairobi.

The gathered students simmer with anger. Calls to storm the administration building are heard once again but the DUSO Vice President and the Speaker manage to restore calm. As the *baraza* resumes its deliberations, loud calls for the VC to come down from his high perch are heard. After a while, it is not the VC but the Chief Administrative Officer who comes to talk with the students. But the students want the big boss in person. Mr Mwingira's words are met with such angry verbiage from his audience that he has no choice but to retreat. About an hour on, George, Jenerali and two other hot-headed students lose their patience. They climb up the flights of stairs to the VC's office, barge in, grab the stunned boss by his arms, and roughly escort him down. The moment he arrives, he is asked by the gathering to explain why Akivaga has been arrested. The seemingly shocked VC is initially unable to utter a single word. He is visibly shaking, perhaps afraid that the angry lot will beat him up. Finally, he says: 'Comrades ...'

That deceptive start ratchets up the temperature. Loud boos ensue. He stutters and cannot go on. Just then, fearing the worst, the Speaker urges students to continue their meeting. For the pathetic VC, it is a chance to bolt away from the scene. But he does with a promise that he will attend the next student *baraza* and explain his actions.

The resumed debate shimmers with harsh verbiage, but remains orderly. In a short while, four resolutions are passed with unanimity: (i) Students will boycott lectures and seminars until Akivaga is returned; (ii) They will not cooperate with the Administration in any way until then; (iii) The VC must resign; and (iv) They remain loyal to the Chancellor, Mwalimu Nyerere.

By this time, all academic activities have come to a halt. A group of students had gone from lecture theater to lecture theater, passing on the information about what was happening near the administration building. But, contrary to what university officials were to claim the next day, no act of violence or vandalism was committed. Many academic staff also stand in the vicinity.

Around four in the afternoon, a group of academic staff, exactly sixty four in number, gather to discuss the unfolding crisis. They are directly affected in that no student is expected in class tomorrow. Reflecting the overall staff composition at the time, one fifth are Tanzanian and the rest, expatriate. Critically, most in attendance identify with the progressive faction of the staff. All back the students. The academic staff too have misgivings, minor and serious, against this inept bureaucracy, and yearn for a change. A three-person ad-hoc committee (Joe Kanywanyi (law), Marjorie Mbilinyi (education) and Kighoma Malima (economics)) is empowered to convene a meeting of all academic staff the next day. The VC, his two senior deputies and the DUSO Cabinet are invited to attend (ACD-04).

Another vibrant *baraza*, this time in the main assembly hall, transpires after dinner. It starts by naming, amid applause, the academic staff who signed the petition supporting the students. Despite his earlier promise, the VC is not present. There is an extended discussion on how to implement the resolutions passed earlier. It is agreed that the *Mwongozo*, the document that emphasizes the importance of democratic decision making in the principal institutions of society, should be central to promoting their cause. There is little doubt that the university administration has transgressed it in spirit and substance. It is resolved that the next morning, students at each hall of residence should hold a mini *baraza* to discuss these guidelines, and come up with suggestions on how to promote their struggle.

With a few other academic staff, I stand at the back. Towards the end of the meeting, I raise my hand. The Speaker beckons me to the stage. The few words I say convey the message that their cause is just, that the authorities have acted in a disgraceful, illegal way and that members of the academic staff stand solidly behind them. There is loud applause. Two other staff follow suit.

+ + + + + + +

Comment: I remain proud that I was the first staff member to speak up openly in support of the students. As a lowly Tutorial Assistant with a tenuous position, I took a risk. Dismissal was a possibility. But some historic junctures generate a momentum of their own. What has to be done, must be done. I did not, though, realize that my act hammered the first thick nail into the coffin that would unceremoniously extricate me from the university in two years' time.

+ + + + + + +

REACTION

Saturday, 10 July 1971: The campus is abuzz with a host of gatherings as each student hall of residence convenes its own *baraza*. The one in Hall III, the female residence hall, stands out. Its activist chair-person Fausta M Materu steers it to pass a creative resolution urging students to do practical work like kitchen duties and cleaning the residential areas (ACD-07). Accepted by the general student body, its implementation begins right away.

After the mini *barazas* are over, the campus TYL Branch holds an open air meeting in the Revolutionary Square. Over four hundred members take part. TYL Chairman Joe Shengena and leaders of the Kenya and Uganda students' associations jointly condemn the administration actions. A long TYL statement issued subsequently expresses 'complete solidarity' with DUSO, and full agreement with the resolutions adopted by the student body. It as well condemns the 'fascist' measures taken by the administration, calling the VC's speech on the graduation day an 'example of chicanery and loud-mouthed lies.' Declaring the UDSM students' demands to be in line with the national policies, it calls upon the youth and workers nationwide to support them. (ACD-06; ACNR-03).

The TYL statement, translated into Swahili, is distributed broadly not just within the campus but also in the city, particularly the adjacent working class neighborhoods. At the same time, DUSO releases a letter in Swahili, and addressed to the workers on the campus. Explaining the position of the students, criticizing the actions of the administration and the police, it says the workers and students have a common cause. Both support the national policies while the higher ups actively work against it. It also warns that the action taken against Akivaga may one day befall the workers. It concludes with the adage that unity is strength while separatism is self-defeating (ACD-08).

In those days, university TYL remained a radical organization, having inherited that mantle from USARF. For it, the issuance of militant statements was a part of its normal operation. But it is the first time in the history of the university for the main student organization to release a statement espousing unity with workers and peasants and declaring support for socialism.

The TYL and DUSO statements immediately get highly favorable reception from the workers at the Hill. They also welcome the participation of the students in work at the cafeteria and the halls of residence. In that respect, the students' struggle gains a major boost.

The news of the class boycott at the main campus has reached the medical campus in the city and the Faculty of Agriculture in Morogoro. Students at both the places have now joined in.

The newspaper headlines are dominated by the class boycott at UDSM. The coverage is fairly balanced. The *Daily News* has a revealing photo taken at the moment of Akivaga's arrest. (ACNR-01).

The academic staff hold their second meeting. Nearly two-thirds of the staff are present. Joe Kanywanyi chairs the session. At the outset, the VC is in attendance. It is obvious that his explanation and responses do not satisfy the audience. EA Moshi presents the students' case. He, on the other hand, gets a favorable hearing. Ultimately, the meeting resolves to back the students and sets the return of Akivaga as a precondition for a peaceful and just resolution of the current standoff. The three-person staff ad-hoc committee is empowered to continue its work and draft a consensus statement expressing the views of the academic staff (ACNR-03).

The Dean of Students issues a curious public relations statement declaring that

Akivaga has not been deported, only rusticated. It is a deceptive play of words. There is no doubt that the student leader was put on a plane and, as confirmed by the local media, now sits in Nairobi.

Sunday, 11 July 1971: No meetings are held today. But a good number of students engage in cleaning work and kitchen duties. In the process, they discuss socio-political issues with the workers. It heralds a new dawn. A spirit of camaraderie between the segments of the campus community hitherto alienated along class lines begins to sprout, mildly but surely. A couple of literacy classes for the workers are conducted by the students.

The *Sunday News* has four separate pieces on the crisis at UDSM (ACNR-02, ACNR-03, ACNR-04, ACNR-05). One reports that the University Council is to hold a special meeting to discuss the university crisis the following day. Another gives detailed and accurate accounts of the staff and TYL meetings held on Saturday. A third reports an interview with VC Msekwa in which it is revealed that the decision to rusticate Akivaga was made after consultation with the Chancellor, Mwalimu Nyerere. Other than that, the VC gives evasive and misleading answers to questions on the main aspects of the crisis. The editorial opinion in the paper gives a fair overview of the ongoing situation at the Hill and raises key concerns about the actions taken by the administration and the police.

The DUSO cabinet meets in the evening to draft an explanatory letter to the Chancellor of the University. Another highlight of the day is the issuance, by Andrew Chenge (law student) and Andrew Lyall (lecturer in law), of a pointed assessment of the legality of the recent actions taken by the administration. They conclude that basic tenets of natural justice as well as national laws have been breached. The deportation of Akivaga to Kenya, in particular, violated current rules and occurred without prior approval from the Minister for Home Affairs (ACD-11).

Monday, 12 July 1971: The day begins with a mammoth student *baraza* at the Revolutionary Square. The open letter to the Chancellor prepared earlier is read out and approved. It explains, in a systematic and diplomatic manner, the stand taken by the students. The large crowd, with creatively designed placards, sings and chants as it marches to the location where the University Council is to meet. In parallel, a small group of students proceed to hand deliver the letter to the State House.

During the day, quite a number of students work in the university farm and the cafeteria, and conduct adult education classes. Informal discussions of a political nature with the workers occur in several locations.

Unknown to people outside, the Council deliberations at the outset are fairly even handed. A series of voices critical of the administration are heard. The student representatives also get a fair degree of attention. Three hours on, Council Chair Nsekela is called to an important phone call. It is from Mwalimu Nyerere. He is told in a forthright manner that the language used in Akivaga's open letter is unacceptable and the rustication of the student leader must stand. When the Council meeting resumes, the tone is changed. The august body spends as many hours to dissect the language of Akivaga's letter. The contents are ignored.

The Council deliberations end at 10 pm. All this while, the tranquil student vigil has continued on the grass lawn outside. Yet, that night, there is no official word on the outcome for them. Though it is quite late and everyone is exhausted, a *baraza* is convened. It is addressed by the student representatives on the Council. Not authorized to release the Council resolutions, they can only give a general description about the deliberations. Their tone, however, indicates that what is going to come will not be favorable to the students.

Council Chair Nsekela raises the bogey of foreigners manipulating the students behind the scenes. He warns foreign staff not to indulge in local politics. The leadership of DUSO rejects this obviously false accusation outright but it features prominently in the national media.

Tuesday, 13 July 1971: Mr Nsekela conveys the Council's verdict to the entire university community at 10 in the morning. It is a morale-shattering verdict: nothing but unqualified support for the VC and his officials. He further directs the students and staff to resume normal academic activities, and ends with two promises: that Akivaga will get a chance to appeal, and the Council will launch a probe into the roots of the crisis. To the staff and students, they sound like empty promises that most likely will produce in a bureaucratic whitewash.

After this meeting, the DUSO convenes a *baraza* to discuss the implications of the resolutions of the Council. The adverse verdict from the Council presents a stark choice for the students: continue the class boycott and most likely face retribution like mass expulsion, or compromise and continue the struggle by other means. The ensuing debate was summarized in a paper written two weeks later by a student activist:

> *The main theme of the deliberations that ensued was this: The Council had let us down and the only thing that remained for us was to choose whether to clash with the highest authority, the Chancellor and therefore the President of country, or to appeal to him to intervene on our behalf. To choose the latter we would have to make a gesture of goodwill because we did not intend to give the Chancellor an ultimatum but an appeal. The best gesture would be to go back to classes. The other side of the argument went as follows: If we gave up [at this stage] we would likely lose all we were fighting for and that would mean the whole battle had achieved nothing. Suppose again that the delegation we were*

to send to the Chancellor was told that we had to go back to classes without being given any guarantees as to our requests, should we still go on to obey?

It appeared as if there was a balance in the opinions. Some other bit of argument turned a majority of the students towards weighing the consequences of coming into direct confrontation with state power. If we refused to go back to lectures the Chancellor would probably order that the University be closed down, and those students who would ever come back would be completely cowed down into yes-men of the Administration. Further, scattered as we all would be, we would never be able to do anything as a student body and even the struggle for getting Akivaga back would die in the wilderness. On the other hand, if we went back to class, the Administration would have no pretext for trying to stop student leaders from carrying on the struggle now and in future. The student leaders could therefore rally all other sympathies, could lobby all those in power and build up enough pressure that could perhaps help in remedying the situation at the Hill. This is what was aptly described as a "tactical retreat". Njagi (1971).

The students are aware of the dual nature of the *Ujamaa* policy which combines flowery words with pungent acts. Invoking a hallowed ruling party document and having the facts on your side do not guarantee a positive outcome. The sharp divide among the students is not a divide of spirit, but of fear of the consequences. The fact is the FFU has not left the campus; its vehicles still linger at the main gates of the university campus. Upon hours of wrangling, the conciliatory wing prevails. The *baraza* resolves to end the class boycott. And a two person delegation is chosen to visit to the Chancellor. At present, he is in Dodoma. This will give the students a chance to make their case to him directly.

But the situation is not all bleak. After the vote, a firm letter of support written by the Workers Committee of UDSM, entitled Grievances of the workers on the Hill, is read out. It both expresses unrestricted solidarity with the students and lists the numerous grievances the workers have in dealing with the university administration. It is met with 'deafening cheers of appreciation from the students.' (Njagi 1971; ACNR-12).

Furthermore, the majority of the academic staff continue to support the students (ACD-11). They have issued a statement urging far reaching changes in the governance structures of the university. Only a few reactionary academics, evidently promotion seeking lackeys of the administration, have expressed dissenting, anti-student views.

On a broader front, another thing that boosts the morale of the students is that the two main English language newspapers in the country, the government owned *The Standard* and the party run *The Nationalist*, have covered the crisis at the Hill in a fair manner. Their editorial opinions have taken issue with the actions of the university administration and have queried the legality of expelling Akivaga from the country. From what can be discerned, public opinion leans on the side of the students.

But the DUSO leaders are aware of something others are not. Earlier they were summoned to a secret rendezvous with the personal assistant of Mwalimu Nyerere. Held at the home of Lionel Cliffe, Head of the Department of Development Studies, the message from the Head of State was no different from that conveyed by the University Council: First end your class boycott. Then your demands will be considered.

That afternoon a five-person delegation composed of the VC, the Chairman of the Council, the Minister for Education and two students (EA Moshi and IM Dewji) flies to Dodoma. On arrival, they are immediately taken to meet with the Chancellor who is in a village some miles from the town. At first Mwalimu confers with the three officials. An hour later, the students are called in. While commending the UDSM students for going back to class, the Chancellor forthrightly declares that the rustication of Akivaga was in order. The language of the open letter was unacceptable. In an indirect gesture of recognition of the legitimacy of their demands, he however promises that the act of parliament that established the University of Dar es Salaam would be rectified to institute more participatory governance structures.

But this is far from satisfactory to the student delegates. They need something concrete to take back to their constituents. In particular, they need a word on the fate of their leader, Symonds Akivaga. But Mwalimu is in no mood to dwell on that point. When the delegates repeat their request, he expresses his annoyance by abruptly standing up and leaving the room. As if on cue, the army officers present in the background approach the students, place them under arrest, and march them to a detention room nearby. They remain under lock and key for about two hours before being escorted back to their hotel in Dodoma town. Profoundly unnerved and shaken by this unexpected experience, the duo are barely able to sleep that night.

Wednesday, 14 July 1971: EA Moshi and IM Dewji are up early to have breakfast and catch the flight back to Dar es Salaam. In the dining area they see Amir Jamal, the Minister for Finance, at one table. Much to their surprise, he calls them over. He tells them Mwalimu is profoundly sorry about what had happened to them the previous evening and wants to assure the students that Akivaga would be allowed to appeal his rustication. It is an attempt to mollify them. They also get a hint that for their future cooperation in bringing back normalcy to the campus, there would be tangible rewards for them in terms of their career prospects (This account derives from a personal communication with IM Dewji).

When the two return to UDSM in the afternoon, they find that classes have resumed. A final *baraza* is convened that evening. But it is a low key affair. Less than half the usual number turn up. As their representatives present their report from the visit to the Chancellor, a spirit of resignation prevails. Despite all their efforts, their leader remains in Kenya, his ultimate fate uncertain. And the VC whom they despise can, with impunity, continue his reign of error and intimidation. Having been brazenly let down by those whom they had trusted to be fair and just, the university from now on functions under an atmosphere of despondency that affects not only the students but also the workers and the academic staff. There is fear that a witch hunt may be in the offing.

Thus ends the acute phase of one of the most significant, and in crucial ways, an historically unique student uprising at the UDSM.

SUBSEQUENT DEVELOPMENTS

I resume tutoring the Vector Analysis course and plan my departure for study at LSE. Shortly, Munene Njagi and I write articles on the history, features and significance of the Akivaga crisis. Published a month later in *MajiMaji*, they get a decent reception at the Hill (Hirji 1971; Njagi 1971). Students and staff express their appreciation to us in person. To this day, these articles remain the only detailed firsthand accounts and analyses of this momentous episode.

Apart from a few committed leaders, the student body recedes into a state of political apathy. The lecturers perceive them as docile and demoralized. The mood of the hour is synthesized by a radical student:

> The Revolution has been betrayed, hijacked and lost. Let me go to the Library and be consoled by the whisper of books, books – m m m – It was a beginning but how soon it subsided like ripples in the wide ocean. DUSO (1971), page 12.

Yet the Crisis-related contradictions rumble on. The 23 July 1971 letter from DUSO Vice President EA Moshi to all the students (ACD-20) describes the pressing issues:

- Though the students are back in class, the FFU maintains a presence on the campus, and the administration has put undue obstacles on the conduct of normal DUSO activities.
- The administration goes on spreading the claim that the whole crisis was instigated by foreigners. The students reject it outright: they are 'capable of thinking independently.'
- While eleven 'opportunist' academic staff took a pro-administration stand during the crisis, more than seventy signed the petition supporting the students.

- DUSO is making preparations to launch the appeal on behalf of their rusticated President.
- The administration is sowing seeds of discord among the students. They are urged to resist and remain united.
- The Council is about to launch an inquiry into the roots of the crisis. The inquiry team will include two students.
- The students are to be commended for the oneness, patience and restraint they have displayed throughout these critical times.

From this point on, I give a summary of the ensuing events. For details, consult the documents, media reports and articles noted in the References.

On 25 July 1971, the University Council appoints a Special Committee to probe the university crisis. Chaired by Joseph Mungai, MP, it is dominated by pro-establishment figures. The key shortfall is that the university community is not adequately represented. At the outset, DUSO rejects composition of the committee. Later it agrees, albeit reluctantly, to cooperate with it. The Mungai Committee begins work in early August. Within a day, DUSO once again declares its strong dissatisfaction, this time with the Committee's mode of operation.

On 26 July 1971, DUSO submits a formal appeal against Akivaga's rustication. The DUSO President is allowed to return to DSM in the middle of August for his appeal to be heard. In a clear indication of bureaucratic obduracy, he is not allowed to enter the university campus. He remains outside in the city, presumably under the watchful eyes of security officers. And, in an obvious contravention of conflict of interest rules, the Appeals Tribunal is chaired by the Chief Academic Officer. The one-sided appeals process arrives at a swift, harsh, vindictive verdict. Akivaga's rustication is changed into expulsion. As of 19 August 1971, he is no longer a student of UDSM, and thus must return to Kenya. Not only is the verdict unjustified, but also the Appeals Tribunal has ignored a key fact: that Akivaga did not sign the open letter to the VC as an individual but on behalf of the DUSO cabinet. If he is guilty, then so are all the members of his cabinet. Expressing their rejection of this gross miscarriage of justice, the DUSO cabinet resigns four days later, and the student representatives to all the university bodies withdraw as well. It signifies their complete disenchantment with the Msekwa administration.

After suffering one demoralizing blow upon another, the students return their attention to the traditional mundane bread and butter matters. Their interest in utilizing existing avenues to make their voices heard in the corridors of power is at an all time low. The level of participation in the election of student representatives to faculty boards, for example, is plainly abysmal. A generalized sense of disinterestedness towards everything but purely educational issues seems to prevail (ACD-21; ACD-24).

The University TANU branch calls an open meeting on 8 September 1971. The sole item on the agenda is the ongoing standoff at the Hill. It is the first time the main campus-based organ of the ruling party has tackled the matter. The meeting, chaired by economics lecturer Kassim Guruli, is well attended by the staff and workers who are TANU members. An extended but contentious discussion ensues. While most members voice their disapproval of the actions taken by the VC, senior administration officials staunchly defend them. The outcome is the opposite of what had been earlier anticipated by the students. The meeting votes by an overwhelming margin to pass a resolution criticizing the actions of the administration, asking for the removal of incompetent leaders and calling for the unconditional return of Akivaga. This clear vote gives a clear lie to the contention oft voiced by the VC that those who oppose his administration are doing so because they basically oppose TANU and its policies. The fact is that not just the youth wing but also the main wing of TANU on the campus is dissatisfied with his performance as the person in charge of running the national university.

The report of the Mungai Committee is released in November 1971. The presentation of why and how the Akivaga Crisis occurred in the report is biased and incomplete because it has chosen to ignore the views of the students who were members of the Committee. Both former DUSO cabinet members and the TYL University Branch reject it outright. The latter holds a public forum to explain its rejectionist stand. In late December, *The Standard* carries two detailed analyses of the flaws of the report. The one by Naijuka Kasihwaki is particularly noteworthy for its thoroughness (ACNR-31). Kasihwaki, who was the Chairman of USARF at the time it was banned, has played a central role in ensuring that the newspaper reports of the Akivaga Crisis, especially in *The Standard*, were as comprehensive and balanced as they were.

The sole redeeming feature of the Mungai Committee Report is the recommendation to enhance the level of participation of students and staff in the major decision making organs of the University. The details and nature of the recommendation though fall far short of the thorough changes proposed by the academic staff. The two exemplary proposals from the staff were inclusion of the non-academic staff and institution of the right to recall of university officials (ACD-12).

The academic year flies by. The authorities seek to end the impasse with a delayed gesture of goodwill. In July 1972, Akivaga is readmitted to UDSM to complete his final year of studies. As no election was held in his absence, the students continue to recognize him as the legitimate President of DUSO. But that is not what the administration and the external powers desire. As he subsequently boasted in his memoir, the VC conspires with a group of ultra-nationalistic students to carry out an unconstitutional overthrow of the Akivaga-led student government. As expected, the new leaders adopt a far less confrontational stand towards the administration. By that time, the student body is too alienated to care. The counterrevolution is complete. (see Appendix B for details).

In the history of struggles against injustice, such an outcome is not unusual. For example, the first genuinely socialist local government, the Paris Commune of 1879, was, after murderous suppression by the state, followed by prevalence of divisive, myopic tendencies among the masses. The inspiring civil rights and Native American movements of the 60s in the USA were followed in the 1980s by gang violence, drug usage and a youth without a sense of direction in these communities. Other examples abound across continents.

LONG TERM EFFECTS

The solid unity across the social spectrum, the astute manner in which the students and staff comported themselves, and the statements issued by them fueled a number of eminently laudatory long term effects. The three major positive long term effects of the Akivaga Crisis were:

- It galvanized a movement to counter an incipient trend to bureaucratize the university and bring it under TANU control.
- A few reactionary staff had, in writing, declared that the gatherings of the academic staff during the crisis were 'unconstitutional.' This raised the awareness among the staff of the need to have their own organization, and set in motion a long but fruitful effort in that respect.
- The official report on the crisis led to legislation that further democratized of the governance of the university.

The state and university authorities were, however, shaken by the solid grassroots unity displayed during the crisis. A potentially wayward bunch of students, staff and workers had to be placed under greater control. The spread of radical leftist ideas had to be curtailed. With the manner in which he dealt with leftist students at the campus right from his first day, and leading up to the ban on *Cheche* and USARF, it is evident that VC Msekwa had come to the Hill with a mission to stifle leftist activism. After the Akivaga crisis, the dilution of the influence of the genuinely socialistic voices, expatriate and local, gained renewed intensity. Non-renewal of the contracts of expatriate left-wing academics; reduced hiring of progressive academics from abroad; removal, in one way or another, of local leftists and strategies to de-radicalize student politics gained speed. Due to the entrenched left-wing momentum of the early *Ujamaa* era, this process took time and was met by resistance from below. It was in large measure completed under Pius Msekwa's successors, who also were of identical retrogressive mindset.

The radicals, old and new, continued to promote their cause in varied ways for about two decades after the Akivaga Crisis. They held ideological classes on

Sundays, published issues of *MajiMaji* with well researched, critical analyses on key topics, organized public lectures on contemporary matters, visited schools and colleges to give talks and organize events, and took up activities designed to promote the cause of African liberation, socialism and pan-Africanism. For at least four years after July 1971, the issues of *MajiMaji* contained numerous astute papers of critical relevance to these topics. A number of them were in Swahili, making them more broadly accessible outside the university arena. The ex-student activists like Issa Shivji and Henry Mapolu who taught at their alma mater played a significant role in these future struggles.

But the process entered a new, less-rooted phase. The neo-liberalism of the 1990s finally placed progressive struggles by students and staff in an extended state of hibernation that continues to this day. The UDSM experienced major expansion in terms of student intake, departments and types of courses offered. But the quality of education and scholarly output plummeted drastically. This decline of a once most stellar of the academic institutions in Africa can be attributed to a multiplicity of factors related to national and global economic and socio-political trends. Yet, its roots lie in the systematic assault of the left-wing scholars begun under Pius Msekwa. The succession of inept VCs appointed by Mwalimu Nyerere entrenched that trend. Hence, we now have an academia that does not shine either on the socialist or the traditional dimension. We have the worst of both worlds.

In an atmosphere of continued demise of progressive developments and politics, both in the nation and the university, the mechanisms for democratic governance at UDSM instituted after the Akivaga Crisis thereby increasingly became a formal shell devoid of substance. What is the meaning of democracy when the matters at hand are far from the lives and interests of the common folk. A significant portion of the blame for this outcome has, in my opinion, to be placed on the ultimate authority, Mwalimu Nyerere. Whether it was a question of dealing with workers', peasants' or student struggles, he was the person who made the final decision. This is a key point that present day analysts of left-wing persuasion have avoided. Thereby, they have left the rightist scholars an unchallenged venue to give simplistic, ideologically driven answers.

A SUMMARY

The Akivaga Crisis remains a one-of-a-kind, salutary event in the history of UDSM. Its signal features were:

- The students had two immediate demands, return of their leader and resignation of the VC, and a long term one, effective participation in the university decision making bodies.
- Throughout the crisis, the students acted in a peaceful manner.
- It was a mass movement. Residence hall and general *baraza*s, where all

the major decisions were taken, were held on an almost daily basis. A lively grassroots democracy matured into action.
- The students raised their own demands and brought up issues affecting the university community as a whole.
- The majority of the academic staff and workers firmly backed the students. This level of unity among the campus constituencies has not rematerialized to this day.
- The statements issued by the student and TYL leaders during the crisis were translated into Swahili. This improved communication with the workers and further enhanced their bonds.
- Students, male and female, held political and campus related discussions with the workers. They worked side-by-side with them in various campus facilities. Once more, this was a first-time occurrence at this place.
- Female students played an exemplary, progressive role during the class boycott. Prior to the crisis, their participation in left or right wing student politics had been abysmally low.

Most of the academic staff were non-Tanzanian. And Akivaga was Kenyan. Known stooges of the administration as well as the Council Chairman used these facts to raise the bogey of foreign instigators. But it failed to gain traction. The students knew that citizenship had nothing to do with why things were as they were. In any case, the staff who played the leading role in the crisis were all Tanzanians.

These exemplary features of the Akivaga crisis are recorded in the original documents and statements of the period, and are summarized in three first person commentaries published in *MajiMaji* and the Workers Committee statement issued at that time. I quote these to give a flavor of the spirit of those days.

> *While we commend all students for the staunch stand, we feel we have to note the special role played by the female students. During the boycott of lectures, they were the first to come out with the brilliant idea that students take on workers' duties and hold political discussions with workers in their hall. This is a very good example of revolutionary political agitation, and the fact that it was set by female students who have in the past been notorious for their apathy makes it doubly important.* Chauhan, Kavishe and Minja (1971).

> *Students, a large number of the academic staff, and the workers at the University stood together to express their absolute dissatisfaction with the University administration. All had tolerated maladministration and arrogance for long enough.* Njagi (1971).

> *On the whole, the effect of the [Akivaga] Crisis has been educational..... The*

limitations of petty-bourgeois politics prevented the neo-colonial setup itself from being questioned. But it is the first time in the history of this University that the student body as a whole has taken a progressive stand. Hirji (1971).

In a statement of solidarity entitled: *Grievances of the workers on the Hill*, it was reported:

Never before had a [?] people on this University felt a sense of Unity to put right what was felt wrong, as this period of crisis, said one workman. (ACD-17).

The human struggle for material, social and cultural improvement is a long term, ongoing, worldwide struggle. It has ups and downs, gains and setbacks, but it never ceases altogether. The important landmarks in the struggle sometimes exercise a salutary, cumulative effect. The lessons they convey are used by people to elevate future struggles to higher levels. But sometimes, those landmarks are lost sight off, and people are then destined to reinvent the wheel.

Earlier struggles can positively affect later struggles through two mechanisms. One, they may institute lasting changes at personal, institutional and societal levels. And two, their memories may persist in a reasonably accurate manner through various cultural venues like popular and scholarly literature, songs, poems, plays, movies and art.

The long term effects of the July 1971 Pro-Democracy Movement at UDSM have been noted by several writers. But sound and comprehensive accounts of what actually transpired during this inspiring struggle do not exist. In fact everything that has been written about it after 1972 has been flawed, misleading and distorted in the extreme. One cannot expect otherwise from those who were close to the Msekwa administration. Even centrist, bourgeois scholars are prone not to reveal the singularly progressive features past historical events. But what is unexpected is that all the left wing scholars who have written about it have given us accounts that are selective and biased. Often what they have presented is either purely fictional or the exact opposite of what actually happened. I discuss this critical issue in depth in Appendix B.

6

ASSISTANT LECTURER

Teachers touch the future.
Author Unknown

+ + + + + + +

UPON MY RETURN TO UDSM in July 1972, I was bestowed the grand title of Assistant Lecturer, and was handed a full load of courses. Now I was a confirmed teacher at a university.

ON LECTURING

In each of the next two academic years, 1972/73 and 1973/74, I taught four regular courses and one advanced course. It was a big load, making me slog from morning to late evening, weekends rarely exempted.

In the regular courses, each lasting three months, there were students with subject combinations like mathematics and physics; mathematics, chemistry and education; and mathematics and economics. The regular courses were: (i) Linear Programming; (ii) Finite Mathematics I; (iii) Finite Mathematics II; and (iv) Basic Statistics. The last course had first year students from the Statistics Department as well. Class size ranged from 80 to 125. Each course comprised three hours of lectures, and two hours of tutorial sessions. All these courses were related to what I had studied at LSE.

The advanced course, Non-linear Programming, was attended by final year double mathematics students. The class size the first time was six, and the next, it was ten. It too had three one-hour lectures and an hour for the tutorial session.

In the first and second quarter, I had ten contact hours and in the last quarter, five contact hours per week. Compared to a secondary school teacher, who typically is in the classroom thirty or more hours a week for ten months of the year, this seems a lighter work load.

In actuality it is not. First, preparation is more exacting; you need to read and reflect at length. A single lecture normally covers a wide ground. Grading takes up time. Second, you as well need to conduct research and publish papers. On both fronts, you confront complex issues that tax your mental energy. It is a daunting situation at first. But you get acclimatized to the world of ideas. Ingesting and imparting knowledge, and attempting to innovate ideas, abstract or concrete, comes to define your life. It is not a nine-to-five job. Your brain cannot be switched off and on like a radio. To flourish well in the academia, you have to indulge in reflection without regard for time or place. Only that habit enables you to reach the frontiers of knowledge and probe uncharted territories. There is no short cut.

They say lecturing differs in a major way from teaching. In a school, you dish out standard material in an established style and gently guide your students through it. At the university, you present varied ideas in a dense fashion, and let your students struggle to disentangle them.

In my view, that is only partly true, and depends on whether you deal with general courses or special courses. The former have large class sizes and are attended by students of various backgrounds and major fields of study. This was the case in the four regular courses I taught. Even though such students have a higher aptitude for mathematics than a typical undergrad, they still find the university level mathematics a big leap from high school mathematics. They must be led through the subject matter with patience. If you cannot communicate the basic concepts well, they will remain stuck in one place. I only appreciated later that relevant mathematical or statistical activity, and real life examples from diverse areas form a crucial part of the learning process in this arena as well. I was not taught these subjects that way, and in my teaching during these two years, I modified the traditional approach in only a marginal fashion.

The special courses, taken by advanced students, are another matter. Here you plunge into the abstract from the start and drive them to the limit. You give hints but let them figure out the rest. Yet, it certainly does not entail rambling at random as our Multivariate Analysis instructor had done. You must devote sufficient time to prepare the lectures and systematically build up a coherent edifice. Effectively teaching each type of course is a challenging task but in its own distinct way.

In addition, there were departmental meetings and academic seminars to attend. I took part in the activities of the Mathematical Association of Tanzania, wrote papers for its journal, went to secondary schools across the nation during the long vacation to supervise teaching practice, and presented one academic seminar each year. I was appointed as the Faculty of Science representative on the Board of Examiners of the Department of Development Studies. It was a full plate, but I had room for more.

ACTIVISM

The UDSM of that era led the African universities, at least on the intellectual front, in left-wing and Pan-Africanist activism. Curricular reform was a center piece of that effort. Concerned staff, local and expatriate, in alliance with progressive East African students, endeavored to confront the conservative bias in the traditional syllabuses and textbooks, and produce relevant, forward looking, intellectually rigorous content. All areas of learning, from the natural sciences to law and the social sciences were affected to one degree or another. A key innovation, emulated subsequently by universities globally, was a structurally integrated course on human development. Initially the proposal to introduce this course faced strong opposition from the Westernized, micro-discipline oriented academics who were in the majority. But through tactics like faculty occupation, production of well formulated scholarly alternatives, public debate, academic exposé and in-class confrontations, the progressive block gained the upper hand. Two new courses, Development Studies (DS) and East African Society and Environment, entered the university curriculum. The first course was required for all non-social science students and the second, for all students in the social sciences.

Progressive students set up their own radical journal dealing with socio-economic matters. Its first incarnation, *Cheche* was banned within a year, but soon it was replaced by an equivalent, *MajiMaji*. Both magazines gained global fame. All departments within the university seethed with outstanding research work more relevant to the African condition, and many important books born at this university gained international recognition (see *Cheche* for details).

Throughout my undergrad years, I was fully engaged in varied aspects of such left-wing activism. After joining the academic staff, I continued in that spirit. I helped the editorial board of *MajiMaji* to produce the new issues and wrote articles for the initial issues. Together with comrades like Henry Mapolu and Nizar Visram, I wrote book reviews and articles for newspapers, took part in public lectures and demonstrations, and worked on the cashew nut *shamba* operated by UDSM TANU Youth League branch.

In my third year of studies, I had led tutorial sessions for DS classes. I continued doing that and also gave two lectures on the history and current status of science for the course on East African Society and Environment. Dr (later Professor) Mahmood Mamdani was the course director at that time.

Progressive activism was, however, not confined to the university campus. One major initiative we took was to coordinate the activities of the genuinely socialist minded former students of UDSM but who now taught in schools and colleges across the nation. Charles Kileo was in Tabora, Ramadhan Meghji, Zakia Meghji and Ramesh Chauhan were in Moshi, Shiraz Ramji was in Iringa, George Hadjivayanis and Salha Hamdani were in Morogoro, and so on.

Political Education (*Siasa*) had by then become a compulsory subject. As it was being taught in the dogmatic style favored by the TANU bosses, it had the effect of making students and teachers despise progressive ideas and ideals. To counter that retrogressive tendency, our group convened meetings in Morogoro, Moshi and Dar es Salaam to work on an alternative educational strategy. We produced socialistic material both in Swahili and English, distributed latest issues of *MajiMaji*, helped set up student run magazines, sent university people to schools to talk about contemporary socio-political issues, and assisted school libraries to obtain progressive and Pan-Africanist books. On these latter three fronts, Shiraz Ramji, teaching physics at the Mkwawa High School in Iringa, produced outstanding results. In the context of the national school system, what we did was but a drop in the bucket. Yet, it set the ball rolling, giving a locally crafted, practical example of what could and should be done.

Our inspiration came from Mwalimu Nyerere's philosophy of *kujitegemea* (self-reliance). Thus our efforts did not in any way rely on the local political bosses and business entities, or external funds. But we did not form a separate political movement or party. We worked within the system to push it, using educational activities, in a socialistic direction. We saw that while Mwalimu's call to build a socialist society was sound, his party and state bureaucracy were dominated by hypocrites who wanted to undermine it and use it to their own advantage. Something had to be done to counter that unhealthy state of affairs.

On my part, upon invitation from resident comrades, I visited schools and colleges in Moshi, Morogoro, Iringa and Dodoma. I took general knowledge and socialism related books, papers, copies of *MajiMaji* and gave talks on world affairs and African liberation to the students. It was a far cry from Vector Analysis. Yet, it was an integral part of my life. An academic is foremost a human being, and especially in a poor nation like ours, endowed with a responsibility to devote his/her energy to further the wellbeing of his fellow human beings. I did not view these two sides of my persona as contradictory. Rather, for me, they were eminently complementary.

MATRIMONY

Yet, life went beyond mathematics and politics; there was laughter, love, union and children. After I started visiting Issa Shivji at his home in 1968, I became acquainted with his lovely sister Farida. Our relationship progressed gradually. Her tradition bound parents, typical of the parents of that era, would not allow their youngest daughter to freely associate with boys of her age. But by the time I went to LSE, she would often be in our group when we went to the beach or movies. Her parents had no issue with it provided her elder brother was present as well.

Upon my return from London, something clicked. I began to see her in a different light and looked for chances to talk to her on her own. The opportunity materialized in a novel way. She was a secretary at the headquarters of the National Development Corporation. So as to enhance her proficiency at work, she had enrolled in an intermediate Swahili course at the Adult Education Center in Lumumba Street. It would be held twice-a-week in the evening. She mentioned it to me, and the next day, I enrolled in the same course!

Actually, her father was relieved when he came to know that I too was in the same class. He was worried that she would have to drive back alone after dusk. Farida drove the family Volkswagen Beetle, a compact, durable small car of the type you do not see these days. Now that a reliable friend of her brother would accompany her, he felt better. No one inquired into the coincidence!

On class days, I took a bus from the UDSM campus to the Adult Education Center, and returned with her to Upanga, spending the night at my parents' place close to her flat. In no time, we started parking at the Upanga beach for half-an-hour before going home. On the last day of the course, as we parked at the seafront, I posed a query to her, speaking in a somber mood:

> *Farida, I want to ask you a question. Your reply will determine whether I will jump into the ocean or not.*

It was a full tide day with the strong waves striking the concrete barrier and raising whitish foam high into the sky. Conversant with my habit of talking in odd ways, she started to laugh.

> *What is it this time, Karim?*

> *Will you marry me?*

Without a moment of hesitation, she sweetly replied:

> *Of course I will.*

So did a new phase in my life emerge. Our parents were overjoyed upon hearing our decision. A formal proposal from my family to her family ensued, a small engagement ceremony was held, and the auspicious date was set to be the Fourth of August, Nineteen Hundred Seventy Three.

In line with my radical orientation, I had sought a simple civil ceremony. But our parents would have none of it. Farida was neutral on the subject. There were the dresses and jewels to be purchased for the bride, some pre-wedding rituals, and finally a traditional prayer house ceremony to be followed by a large banquet at the Diamond Jubilee Hall. There being no point in starting a new life in acrimony, I acquiesced and left them to handle all the preparations.

There was but one point on which I refused to compromise. I would not, under any circumstances, bow down before the photo of any spiritual deity. My stand made all in the family distinctly unhappy. The maid of honor threatened to pull out of the whole thing. But in the end, concluding that nothing could be done to sway this 'crazy character' and, in consideration of Farida's future, they acceded to my demand.

Everything went well on this most joyous occasion. With her poise, gorgeous eyes, elegant hair style and endearing smile, Farida was a stunning bride. The banquet was the high point. Relatives, colleagues, friends and comrades from the campus and upcountry joined in the celebration. In May of the year following, we got the best gift of our life. Rosa, a sweet baby, came into our lives.

It takes persistence to adjust to a new mode of living. From a close knit family, Farida found it hard to be away from her parents. I had had an irregular, independent schedule. There were ups and downs. Both of us had to compromise. Now, as we traverse the fifth decade of our coexistence, I know that I could not have had it better. I am blessed with a generous, gentle, loving partner. All who come to know her recognize her as a selfless, caring person. And we have been further blessed with a dear daughter, Rosa, and Samir and Emma, two endearing grandchildren.

TEACHING PRACTICE

In April 1973, I reentered the teaching practice circuit, but now as a supervisor. It was an odd feeling: I, a trainee just a couple of years back, a novice teacher with little exposure to secondary school teaching, and whose training had not been of the optimal variety, dishing out advice to others on how to teach. I am sure those whom I supervised had concerns of a similar kind as I had had of my supervisors. Though in terms of stressing the need for relevant examples in the teaching of mathematics, I gather I did a better job.

For me, it was an educational trip, visiting schools in Arusha, Dar es Salaam, Dodoma, Moshi and Morogoro. I interacted with the trainees from UDSM, talked to local teachers and students. It complemented my earlier visits to schools at the invitations of fellow comrades. Later I also held discussions with the trainees I had not visited. All that provided me a fair picture of the conditions of our secondary schools and the teaching of mathematics.

As a socialist, one thing I keenly sought to know was how Education for Self-Reliance (ESR) projects had fared, and if the staff and students had come to terms with the policy. Had the situation changed since my days at the Popatlal school four years earlier? I was distressed to find that if anything, it had worsened. My visits and discussions painted a rather bleak picture. A school with a well-run ESR project and contented stake holders was a rare entity. Instead, complaints, from teachers, pupils and parents, abounded. I did not come across a single teacher or trainee with positive words about ESR. They followed it because it was a compulsory requirement set by the political authorities.

As a sign of the level of underlying discontent, even the controlled state and party newspapers had now started to carry letters to the editor and articles from people who were unhappy with the policy. Their contention was that frequent, unplanned manual work was lowering educational standards, and did not have an educational or practical value. These views were countered by a vocal group of politically connected supporters who, after noting a few cases of successful ESR projects, declared that the current problems were transitional obstacles and would be resolved with the accumulation of experience.

I found the quality of the debate unsatisfactory. Both the critical faction (the realists) and the supportive faction (the idealists) used selective evidence and dogmatic arguments. None presented a grounded socio-historic analysis of the role of education in society. The academics at the Department of Education of UDSM should have led the nation by presenting a factually sound case and alerting the nation on the actual state of affairs in our schools. But being a generally timid lot, their papers dealing with ESR raised marginal issues. Some wrote critical academic papers, but went on to declare the contrary in their newspaper pieces.

Through my readings, I came to know of socialist and non-socialist nations where academic and practical education had been integrated quite successfully. This had, to a degree, taken place in Tanzania as well. Viable secondary technical schools had been established in the early independence days and I had attended one of them. But now, under ESR, instead of being utilized as a sturdy foundation for building the new system, it was being side-lined.

Delving into the history of education in Tanzania, and based on my observations and interviews, I wrote a long article on the issue for *MajiMaji*, a UDSM student magazine. Its title was: *School Education and Underdevelopment in Tanzania* (Hirji 1973). I first laid out the historic background:

- Agricultural and vocational training in schools had been introduced in the colonial era. It had been a standard aspect of missionary run schools. It was not a new idea.
- Such training was enforced only in schools attended by the African students.
- Students in Asian and settler schools received quality education of the type given in schools in the UK.
- Asian and European school leavers were more qualified for higher pay

- white collar jobs while Africans were relegated to low wage, manual jobs or unemployment.
- Abolishing of discriminatory system and provision of the high grade education to all had been a major demand of the movement for national independence.
- Immediately after Independence, a national, merit (not race) based education system was set up, many new schools were built and teacher training expanded considerably.
- The policy of ESR, with its emphasis on practical work, coming just seven years after *Uhuru*, was viewed with deep suspicion, especially by the African majority.

Mwalimu Nyerere had, however, presented ESR as an integral part of an overall policy for building a new society based on social equality and economic progress for all. As a popular leader who spoke to the nation in a unique fatherly, persuasive manner, he was trusted by the people. Apart from the mainly Asian, disgruntled business community, elements of the Church hierarchy, and the newly minted political elite, Tanzanians stood ready to march with him to the promised land.

Yet, his *Ujamaa* policy began to unravel within three years. On the educational front, numerous obstacles were seen.

- ESR was a policy document, without a detailed plan on how it was to be out into practice. The Ministry of Education, for its part, made practical work a formal requirement but did not produce sound guidelines on how it was to be done.
- ESR activities were not integrated into the curriculum in a formal, systematic manner. They became an appendage stuck onto the existing white collar oriented system.
- Since evaluation of school performance remained as it was, that is, through traditional exams, teachers, students and parents had little motivation to devote time and energy for ESR work.

These negative incentives were compounded by the general trends in the economy.

- The rewards structure in the jobs pyramid remained as before. Despite the idealistic rhetoric, white collar jobs paid much more than manual work.
- Despite the talk about self-reliance, the stress was on dependency generating, export-import oriented economic activities.
- Despite nationalization, expansion of the state sector and opening of new industries and firms, job growth was slower than the output of the education system, especially at the lower levels.
- Hence, rural urban migration and urban unemployment expanded.

As the competition for good jobs intensified, parents and teachers did not want their students to waste their time in unrewarding practical work. At the same time, a widespread feeling of discontent became manifest among the students. A variety of reasons fueled that discontent.

- In contrast to the rhetoric of democratic participation enunciated in ESR, the education system became more top-down and authoritarian in nature.
- The Ministry issued unsystematic orders to the headmasters, who in turn made unreasonable demands on the teaching staff, who for their part, began to discharge their duties with less diligence and dedication. The teachers were also unhappy about their remuneration and terms of service.
- And the brunt of the ensuing dislocations in the schools was borne by the students who now faced an environment of harsh discipline and poor learning conditions.
- On top of it, *siasa* (political education), now a compulsory subject, was taught in an insipid, sloganeering style. Students heard lectures on grassroots participation but encountered a singularly authoritarian reality which paid no heed to their voices. Abundant hypocrisy only bred cynicism and fueled discontent.

Despite the fine political rhetoric in ESR, Tanzania had a chaos ridden educational system lacking a sense of direction. Nations like Cuba and China had successfully combined basic subjects with practical work at various levels of the education system. Some non-socialist nations too had gone a long way in that direction. Instead of learning from these models, we were stumbling along from error to error.

Consequently, not only was the traditional educational system breaking down but it was not being replaced by a sound socialistic alternative as well. People in all walks of life, including those who had initially backed it, thereby started to hate the very word socialism. My summary of ESR was:

> *The major contribution of ESR is neither any profundity of analysis nor any spectacular success in implementation but the fact that it has pioneered the injection of progressive ideas into the education system. It is these ideas that are inspiring the youth to assert themselves.* Hirji (1973)

My words came in the context of a well-grounded school of radical analysis that had emerged at the UDSM. Local and external scholars like Walter Rodney, Issa Shivji, Henry Mapolu, Adhu Awiti, Andrew Coulson, John Saul, Tomas Szentes,

Justinian Rweyemamu, and Clive Thomas wrote pioneering papers on key issues affecting Tanzania and Africa.

The contents of my paper on ESR posed a direct challenge to Mwalimu Nyerere and TANU. It stated bluntly that what was being devised for the education system now was not much better than what was done under colonial rule. For the ruling party, I had crossed an unacceptable line. The senior administrators at UDSM were, for many reasons, also thoroughly displeased with me.

This article was the final solid nail in the coffin that was to bear me out of this place within the next twelve months. It came out in September 1973. And the order for me to be ejected from UDSM was issued in March 1974. I was one of the first victims of the post-Akivaga crisis purges at the university.

7

PLANNING OFFICER

Life is like riding a bicycle
To keep your balance
You must keep moving
Albert Einstein

+ + + + + + +

A SIMPLE, TERSE LETTER, NOTHING MORE. Yet, it packs the power of a swift lightening strike that turns my life upside down. These are the end days of March 1974. A hectic period of marking final exams has ended. Farida is seven months pregnant. It is high time we prepare to welcome a new being into our home. I have plans for the long vacation: two research projects and a pile of readings. Also, the applications for my doctoral study program have to be sent off.

The letter comes from the Chief Administrative Officer. I look at it in disbelief: It proclaims I have been, as is commonly said, 'decentralized.'

In the past two years, the government has unrolled a new regional administration system. In theory, it is the implementation of the *Mwongozo* for the rural population, a novel mechanism to give power to the people. Paradoxically, it has been constructed for Tanzania with the expertise of the Mckinsey Corporation, a global American consultancy firm that facilitates the smooth operations of the international capitalist order.

Under this system, development of hitherto stagnant rural areas will be stimulated by regional and district development directors, each with a sizable technical staff. It will be coordinated by the Prime Minister's Office (PMO) in Dar es Salaam. Many civil servants, technical personnel and officers of para-statal organization have been recruited into this burgeoning system.

The letter in my hand says that the PMO has posted me to be a Planning Officer in the office of the Regional Planning Office (RPO) of Rukwa Region. My job location is Sumbawanga, the regional capital. And I have one week to report at my post. With a word of congratulations, it requests me to contact the appropriate university offices to process the terminal benefits, if any, that are due to me.

Minutes later, Dr David Cappitt, the Head of Mathematics, walks into my office. He also has a copy of the ominous letter.

What is the meaning of this, Karim?

I have no idea, I am as surprised as you are.

He feels for me, and does not want to lose an upcoming member of his academic team. We wonder how a mathematician steeped in arcane theory, having zero experience of relevance, can fill the shoes of a planner of the transport, agriculture, health and education sectors for rural communities.

And, of all places, why Sumbawanga? It is one of the most remote and superficially developed places in the nation, in the chilly South. Other than a major supplier of *ulezi* (red millet), an indispensable ingredient for producing mbege, the traditional brew in the North, and dried sardines, it is known for one other thing: During the colonial times, it was a location for exiling political dissidents. Physically and politically, it is the veritable Siberia of Tanzania. The implications are clear, to him and me.

Do not worry, Karim. I will launch a strong appeal to the Dean of Faculty of Science and the VC. Maybe we can reverse this.

Thank you, David.

But knowing what I know, I say to myself: 'Fat chance.' At home, Farida is flabbergasted. Her first words are: 'What will happen to our baby?' I give her a big hug and tell her we are young and strong. We can give the best of care to our baby wherever we go. The news spreads like wildfire across the campus. Many friends and comrades come to inquire in person. A meeting of my close comrades is held at the home of Joe Kanywanyi. Their comments are:

It is a nasty form of political retribution, no doubt.

It is payback for your activism, Karim.

We should protest. But how?

There is no room for questioning the legality of the move. According to the contract I signed at the start of my undergraduate studies, I am pledged upon graduation to go, for the next five years, wherever I am posted by the government. Politically, it will sound particularly odd. The rightists will mock:

> *You radicals, you shout in the name of workers and peasants. Now that you are being sent to help the peasants, you wish to remain in a comfortable environment.*

The university authorities could have appealed my transfer on the grounds of misallocation of qualified manpower. But obviously, they are also behind it. So I give my friends my decision:

> *It is not the end of the world. If the mathematics department cannot do anything, then I am going to Sumbawanga. There is no need to do anything else. It won't work.*

The next day, as I pack my books and files in my office, Dr. Cappitt enters in a clearly dejected spirit:

> *I am sorry about this. Karim, I am told there is no way to reverse the decision. It comes from the highest office. What a shame!*

That evening, we meet Farida's mother and my parents. They too are shocked. My father has an instant solution:

> *All your friends have left for Canada. You are smart. Go study at a university there. You will get a scholarship, and I can pitch in financially. Call Farida over a few months later, and start a new life, away from this godforsaken place. You have been a stooge of Nyerere. Where has it taken you? Into the jungle. Forget him and think of your family.*

He refers to the ongoing exodus of the Ismailia community to Canada. Most of my relatives and childhood friends are now in Toronto, Calgary, Edmonton and Vancouver. But all in my immediate family remain here. So he wants me to initiate our move to the new land.

But I am in no mood to be disloyal to my land of birth. It has nurtured and educated me. I distinguish between the people and the government. Fundamentally, my contract is with the former, not the latter. The government that is treating me unfairly is at the same time oppressing my people. I will stand with them, be it in Sumbawanga or elsewhere.

Farida's mother is not happy at this turn of events but does not object. The most heartwarming thing is the unconditional support from Farida. While a bit apprehensive, she categorically says that she goes wherever I go. She too has the nationalistic spirit, imbibed from her staunchly leftist brother, Issa Shivji.

So Sumbawanga it is. As Farida's pregnancy has been a complicated one, we decide that I will go first, and come to collect her after the baby is born. She quits her job as the secretary of the Dean of the Faculty of Science, and puts up with her mother in the city.

TO SUMBAWANGA

I board the bus to Mbeya, a major town in the south, around noon time in the first week of April 1974. By the dawn of the next day, I am there. It has been raining. The trip along the recently paved Tanzania Zambia highway was not tiring. A tad short on sleep, nothing more.

The second phase of my journey, from here to Sumbawanga, is about a third of the distance covered thus far. The bus is full, and it is raining. After the initial 20 kilometers, the rest of the 200 kilometers traverse a muddy and hilly terrain. The noon time bus is scheduled to arrive at my final destination at 6 pm in the evening.

It continues to rain; the road is slippery. To avoid skidding, the driver reduces speed. Now and then, we feel a jolt from a tire dipping into a watery pothole. The real trouble begins when we reach the first steep hill. Barely twenty meters up the incline, the bus begins to skid back. It cannot ascend any further. The driver has no choice but to bring it to a full stop. He explains the situation:

> *The road is too steep and slippery. The bus is too heavy to go up.*
>
> *Do we have to go back?*
>
> *No. All the passengers have to disembark. Then I can take the bus up.*
>
> *What about us?*
>
> *I am sorry but you have to walk to the top.*

Fortunately for us, it has ceased to rain. So that is what we do. And that is what we do again and again, six times in all, during this trip. If it is raining, we wait until there is a pause before disembarking and trudging up the hill.

As the roosters croack, we enter the awakening town, exhausted to the bone. It is chilly, windy but dry. A six hour journey has taken eighteen hours. Dragging my bag, I make my way to the home of Mehdi Mitha, a distant cousin who runs a clothing and household goods store. He is a veteran of this town.

I am received warmly. A hot bath, a load of fresh *chapatis* with honey and a boiled egg later, I hit the sack. The next morning I report to the office of the Regional Development Director (RDD). It is in a newly built one story complex, a twenty minute walk from where my cousin lives. I am expected. My first task is to fill out work and salary forms in the personnel office. My job title is Planning Officer.

I am shown the office of the Regional Planning Officer (RPO), my immediate boss. He is not around. I am to sit in a room adjacent to his office. I find a friendly young fellow, an Assistant Planning Officer. A large table with three chairs is in the middle. It bears a few files and office papers, and a large pile of newspapers. Four filing cabinets stand near the walls.

He tells me his name is John. He has his own chair. I can choose any from the other two. With the RPO, we constitute the entire regional planning team.

> *What am I supposed to do?*

> *The mzee (old man) will tell you. Just relax and get used to this place for now.*

Then he gives some crucial advice. Punctuality is essential. I must report at work by 7:30 am, and leave the office at 2:30 pm. A few minutes late will get me a warning letter from the RDD. If I am persistently tardy, I will be in bad trouble. He says it gravely, but he does not spell out what it means.

After showing me the washroom and water taps, he points to a place where vendors sit. They sell bananas and roasted groundnuts. I am pleased to find a friendly, helpful office mate. I like him. It is a good start in a new place. Back in the office, he tells me:

> *There are newspapers here. You can read them if you like. But the latest one is two weeks old. The office of the prime minister in Dar sends them by bus every two weeks. If we are lucky, your bus has carried a new batch. Once the senior staff have looked at them, they are placed in our office.*

That is how the rest of the day goes. The next day I do the same. It is in the middle of the third day that a short, stocky jovial man walks in.

> *Ah, you must be Hirji. Welcome, welcome. I have been waiting for you. We need a person who knows about data collection and statistics. You are from the university, so I am sure you will be of great help to us.*

He is my boss, the RPO. An informal, friendly boss, I tell myself. Maybe I can make a worthy contribution to this region.

> *Thank you, I will try my best. Where should I start?*

> *Ah, Hirji, there is no hurry. You need to settle down. John will show you our previous reports to the PMO. Read them and look at our files.*

This I do for the next three weeks. During this time, the RPO is away on safari. John tells me he is inspecting projects in the villages. Towards the end of my first month, the boss calls me.

> *Karim, the financial year is soon to end. I need information from the Regional Agriculture, Education and Health Officers for our report. I want you to remind them to give it to us on time. I especially want to know if their budget allocation has been appropriately spent and what their needs for the next financial year are. This is very important.*
>
> *I will do that promptly. I have read our reports as you told me to do, and have made a plan for a region wide survey to get more accurate and relevant information on education and health.*

He eyes me sharply, but then smiles.

> *Oh, Hirji, that is good, very good. I am going to a meeting in Mbeya tomorrow. We can talk about it when I come back.*

Tracking down those officers and reminding them to send in their reports is accomplished in no time. But the talk about a regional statistical survey never transpires. He is rarely around. And when he is, he is always rushing to a meeting, talking with the RDD, or signing important papers. Yet, every day I am at work before 7:30 and leave exactly at 2:30. My office mate does the same. We munch roasted ground nuts, read and reread newspapers. We make sure a work file is open in front of us all the time, and a pen and a notebook are handy. It is essential that a passerby sees office staff engaged in work. As far as planning for regional development is concerned, that basically is going to be the norm during my time in Sumbawanga.

FAMILY LIFE

I talk to my boss about family issues. I desire to go Dar es Salaam. He is most helpful.

> *Look Karim, some important papers have to be sent to the PMO. You take them. I will authorize your trip.*

On the third day of May 1974, I am reunited with Farida at her mother's place. And I am just in time. Two days later, she gets the contractions. I speedily take her to the nearby Agakhan Hospital. Her mother comes along. She is admitted immediately into the maternity ward. Anxiously, we wait outside. But it is a short wait. In less than an hour, an all smiles nurse emerges:

Congratulations. It is a baby girl. Baby and mother are both fine.

Farida had a breech delivery; our baby is underweight. A long bus trip is not advisable at the moment. We agree that I will come back after two months. Before I return to Rukwa, a queer name changing episode transpires.

Farida and I like the name Rosa, the first name of the heroic German socialist, Rosa Luxemburg. But my mother does not approve. She says it is a European name. She wants a name that reflects our traditions. At the baptismal event in the Ismaili prayer house that evening, she puts an Ismaili name, 'Rozemin,' on the birth form.

Farida is not aware. When I see it, I am livid. The first thing I do in the morning is go to the Registrar of Births, have the form nullified, and a new form filled with the name changed. The clerk says it is the most rapid name change he has ever witnessed. I say that there was a misunderstanding, and as the father, I have the final word. Yet, to my mother, our baby is 'Rozemin' for about a year. Eventually, she relents and fondly begins to call her Rosa. It is a sign of the culture wars of that era, a clash between provincialism and humanistic cosmopolitanism.

In late June, I am permitted to go to Dar es Salaam to collect my family. Fortunately, a husband-wife team of expatriate researchers from UDSM are heading to Sumbawanga at that time. They kindly agree to give us a ride. With a night in Mbeya, we are at our new home in Sumbawanga in thirty six hours. Only one problem arises during the trip. An hour from Mbeya, Rosa develops an excruciating earache. She cries uncontrollably. It only subsides when a doctor in Mbeya gives her ear drops. To our relief, she falls asleep instantly. For the rest of the trip, she is as playful as ever.

Three days after my first arrival in Sumbawanga, I had found a place to stay in the backyard of a building owned by a local businessman. It consists of a 6 by 6 meter room and a tiny outhouse, with a hole-in-the-ground toilet. The walls and roof are tin sheets. Cooking is done on charcoal and kerosene stoves outside the room. The rent is low but it is not what I prefer for my family. I fill a housing application at the regional office. But my rank in the hierarchy is not high enough, and I am on my own. So my application is put on the back burner.

This is the new home for my family. Yet, we are happy. We are together; we play with our child, and enjoy the fine dishes Farida cooks. The room is pretty cold at night. We keep warm with two blankets, and by huddling together. Two weeks later, my father comes to visit. He has supplies like powdered milk and a bundle of snacks cooked by mother. He is appalled at what he sees:

Is this the place for a London educated university lecturer?

Fortunately, just a week later, seeing that my wife and child are now with me, the housing office allocates me a governmental house at the outskirts of the business area, a mile from my work place. It is a large single story structure built for colonial officers in the 1930s. The walls are of mud plastered onto wood beams. The roof is tin sheets. But there is a ceiling board, though an ancient one, under the roof.

It has a living room in the center, an 8 by 8 meters bedroom on the right, and on the left, a bedroom half that size plus a small store room. The living room opens on the other side on to a large low walled backyard, at the end of which there lies four small sheds, next to each other. From extreme right, you see a hole-in-the-ground toilet, a water heating shed with a Samovar and piles of logs and charcoal, the kitchen and last, a storage shed. The backyard is jagged stones from one end to another. You have to walk with care.

The place has not been maintained. Small holes and cracks pepper the walls. Paint is peeling wherever you cast your eyes. Nonetheless, for us, it is a heavenly delight. At last our baby can sleep in a warm place, better protected from wind and rain.

So begins a comfortable ritual that will last fourteen months. Waking up at six, I light the ancient charcoal samovar in the shed. After freshening up with the hot water, Farida prepares breakfast in the kitchen as I dress. My belly full, I depart for work while she wakes up Rosa, cleans and feeds her.

At 3 pm, I am back at home. Rosa is crawling around the living room. She grins and scratches my face as I pick her up. Hot, aroma laden lunch awaits. After a short siesta, on most days, the three of us take a long walk around town.

Our favorite route goes up hill to the Catholic Church. Built in the colonial times, it is the most elegant structure in town. What especially draws us is the expansive, well maintained, colorful garden that lies around it. We traverse the multiple mini-paths that run across it. Rosa is set down in places to allow her to quench her unlimited curiosity. Though, we have to be watchful. She can pluck a leaf or take a stone and put it in her mouth with astonishing speed.

Twice a week, we visit my cousin Mehdi. Rahim, their baby boy, is of Rosa's age. It is enchanting to see them engrossed with each other. Invariably, we are given dinner. Razia, his wife, is an expert cook. There is a mountain of *chapatis* and delightful vegetable or meat curry. After the edifying dinner, we walk home with a sleepy Rosa around 7 pm, a flash light in hand. It is a five minute walk.

Evening time has its own ritual. As darkness descends, Rosa is placed in her cot. I light a regular kerosene lamp, and *Petromax*, a pressurized kerosene lamp. The latter brightens up the living room like a large electrical tube light. Soon Farida has dinner laid out. We eat our meals on a mat placed on the floor. As she feeds Rosa, I set ten mouse traps, each with a piece of bread as bait. I place them under the cot, under our bed and near the walls. After Farida securely places Rosa in her cot, and she is under the mosquito net, I put out the two lamps and crawl into the bed as well.

The moment it is dark and quiet, the top of ceiling board seethes with life. The resident mice scurry around: they smell food. We hear them descending the walls. Suddenly, there is a snapping sound, then another, then another, until the entire colony of pests takes flight in fright. I emerge from the bed with my flashlight to find three to five mice writhing in the traps. Picking them up with due care, I toss them into the backyard, and return to bed in relief. For this night, our baby will be safe from the nasty creatures. As an added measure of protection, each long leg of Rosa's cot stands in a bucket of water.

Our young house worker, Hamisi, comes in around eight. The first thing he does is to collect the dead mice and bury them in our small garden outside. He has planted maize, tomato and green pepper. The mice fertilize it well. A jolly fellow, he helps Farida with washing, cleaning, sweeping and buying fruits and vegetables from the market. He looks after Rosa when her mother cooks. By and large, that is the normal manner of our life in Sumbawanga.

MATHEMATICS CLUB

The Kantalamba Secondary School lies two hundred meters from our office. Enrolling about 350 students in Forms I to IV, it is the only secondary school around. There are twelve teachers on the staff. One of them is Mehdi's younger brother, Firoze. Having been there for more than five years, he has a ton of tales to tell me about the place.

One day I find a 'data collection' type of excuse to visit it during work hours. My actual aim is to meet the mathematics teachers and discuss issues about teaching. To my pleasant surprise, I find that the only mathematics teacher was my student at UDSM.

We talk. I propose that we start a mathematics club at the school. One afternoon per week, I will give hour long talks on different topics and assign a variety of exercises. He likes the idea, and so does the headmaster.

For the next six months, each Wednesday from 2:30 to 3:30 in the afternoon, I conduct the club activities. About fifteen students attend on a voluntary basis. I talk about mathematical paradoxes, logical conundrums, and enigmas, a field now known as recreational mathematics. After demonstrating the solution to a puzzle, I at times set a similar problem they can tackle on their own. Now and then, I mention practical applications of mathematics in agriculture, industry, health and transportation.

I aim to give them an introduction into the early history of maths. I have a book on the subject, and I had borrowed another one from the UDSM library using the card of a fellow university lecturer. The students are fascinated by the diversity of ways in which mathematics developed in ancient Babylon, India, China, Egypt and Greece. I venture into the general history of these societies as well, and relate mathematics to the level of economic development.

It is a fun and rewarding activity. Instead of rereading old newspapers, I read relevant books and prepare the club lecture in the office. So long as I am seen doing something, no one gives a hoot what it is.

To my surprise, the self-reliance farming project at the school is well organized and fairly productive. Upon five years of operation, the revenue from the project was used to start a small shop. Located in the school compound, it is run by the students. But this is not the norm. Other school self-reliance projects in the primary schools of this area have failed due to mismanagement and misappropriation by the head teachers.

Yet, there is a high level of discontent among the students. It is manifested in frequent incidents of rebellion like fights and class boycotts. The headmaster is too strict. Some teachers punish students in very painful ways. One day a student is hit on the head with a stick, has a deep gash and is sent to hospital. The case is hushed up.

As this type of instability continues, I am not comfortable with showing up at this school on a regular basis. The higher ups can say or do anything. They may say that it is this radical fellow from UDSM who is inciting the students.

The club runs on a regular basis for six months. A foundation is laid. The mathematics teacher can build upon it. I donate my book to the club and bid them farewell. I also write a short article on aspects of the history of mathematics., based on my talks at the club. It is published in the journal of the Mathematics Association of Tanzania a few months later.

A FORAY INTO HISTORY

I open the three old, rusty filing cabinets that have not been touched in ages. Perusing systematically, I see that files date back to the 1940s. I am transported to the colonial and early Uhuru days. A wealth of material on the developmental initiatives undertaken by the government officials lies buried herein. I learn about what transpired and the eventual outcomes.

Once upon a time, this region was a major food producer. It exported dried fish, beef, millet, fruits and vegetables, much of it to the copper mining areas of Zambia. There were a few large settler farms, but most of the produce came from small scale peasant farmers and fishermen. Apart from a couple of exceptions, that productive configuration lies by the wayside now. I see no current plans to revive that highly promising potential.

One thing strikes me. Time and again, colonial and later day officials come up with the idea of making the peasants grow some new commercial crop. No peasant is consulted; no serious feasibility study is undertaken; the initial planning is poor and hurried. It usually meets resistance from below; direct and indirect coercion persuades some farmers to grow the crop; the success attained is minimal. The soil is unsuitable, or the market not adequate. Eventually, it is abandoned. The region awaits another day a bureaucrat has another brilliant idea.

Other than this informal foray into local history, I undertake a formal one. I meet Abdul Sheriff, a rising star in history at UDSM, during a visit. He has read my paper on education for self-reliance.

> *Karim, would you like to write a paper on the history of the education system in Tanzania during the German colonial era? I have access to archival material in Germany. We are in the process of translating those records into English. I can give what we have to you, and you can work on it.*

My interest is piqued. With much time to spare, what do I have to lose? Sure, I say. Armed with three typed rolls of archival material and several history texts, I begin the work in Sumbawanga. By the time my family and I depart from this place, I am half way done. I present the paper at a conference on the history of colonial mainland Tanzania held at UDSM in 1978. It comes out later as a chapter in a book edited by HY Kaniki, *Tanganyika Under Colonial Rule* (Kaniki 1980, Hirji 1980).

My paper reinforces the Marxist thesis that the structure and function of the education system in society accords with the interests of the dominant class. In normal times, it plays a role in the formation and consolidation of the existing social structures. But at critical moments in history, elements of the education system pose a challenge to that structure. In the period I cover, the later aspect does not manifest itself in a marked way.

Education can block fundamental change, or it can enhance such change. That is a crucial message of history. For us, the educators, the choice is: serve the *status quo* or educate in ways that will promote equality and social justice.

BOOKSHOP

My elder brother, Mohamed, suffers from a mental condition, schizophrenia. For about eight years, he has regularly gone through an unpleasant cycle: uncontrolled behavior, hospitalization for a couple of months, release and a few months of respite. Then it starts over again.

A year into our stay in Sumbawanga, I suggest to my father that he could come and stay with us. I would find a gainful activity for him. My father happily agrees, though mother is understandably reluctant.

One person I now know well is Pyrali Meghji, elder brother of my UDSM comrade, Ramzan Meghji. Currently unwell and unemployed, he can maintain a minimum level of subsistence for himself and his family. Financial assistance from his brothers keeps him afloat. But it is irregular and small. His backyard has a small shed that opens outwards. It can be converted into a small shop with minimal repair.

I suggest to him that it become a books and stationery shop that would be run by Mohamed. His task is to do the repairs. I will do the rest: get a couple of wood shelves, a glass cabinet, a chair, a sturdy lock and the merchandise for the shop. The profits from the venture would be split on a fifty-fifty basis between him and my brother. Pyarali agrees and embarks on the repairs. I find second hand shelves and the cabinet from town merchants. Then I write a letter to my brother.

September 1974

Dear Mohamed:

How are you and how is everyone at home. Fine I hope.

I am writing to you about the possibility of you coming to Sumbawanga and starting a bookshop. There is not a single bookshop in this town, so I think the prospects are good. I have already acquired a room for the shop. Some minor repairs have to be done, the place has to be painted, and the furniture has to be bought before the shop can be started. All this should be ready in about two months.

In the meantime, you should do the following. First register yourself as a member of TANU and get a TANU card. This will be necessary in order to get a trading license. You should post the card to me as soon as you get it. Then you should go to Elimu Supplies and inquire about the prices of things like stationery, pens, minor office equipment, etc. But don't buy anything at the moment. The bookshop can initially stock the following types of items: stationery, pens, newspapers, magazines, novels, story books, educational books, toys. And miscellaneous items.

Let me know your views as soon as possible. Regards to all at home.

Yours, Karim

Happily, Mohamed is all for it. Our father accompanies him on his bus trip. He is now relieved to see us in a better house. Mohamed sleeps in the extra bedroom. Rosa gets along with him splendidly, always crawling up to him to be carried and taken out, which he invariably does.

Mohamed has brought the merchandise which I had ordered. It is a modest start: Thirty books, four dozen notebooks of varied sizes, two packs of ball point pens and pencils, six writing pads, paper clips, stapler and staples, rulers, coloring pencils, pencil sharpeners, erasers, elastic bands and items like small balls and balloons. Apart from books, two town merchants carry such items. But the Sumbawanga Bookstore is the first dedicated book and stationary shop in this area.

I put the equivalent of two months of my gross salary into the project. Father also makes a contribution. If all goes well, Mohamed and Pyarali can make a decent living from it as it takes root and expands.

Trading begins as desired. Opening the shop door at 10 each weekday morning, Mohamed runs it until 2:30 pm, returning home in time for the family lunch. Farida helps him maintain the accounts and control the cash. The net profit in the first month is 100 shillings, less than a tenth of my salary, and for the second month, it is 150 shillings. Both those amounts are evenly split between the partners.

In the third month, it gets unhinged. Mohamed is erratic at home. It is difficult for him to sleep. He paces up and down in his room well after midnight. After opening the shop, he walks around town, leaving it susceptible to theft. Medicines from the local doctor do not affect his mood. He clearly needs specialized psychiatric care in Dar es Salaam. To our dismay, he has to return to Dar es Salaam. Rafik, my young brother, comes to take him back.

+ + + + + + +

Comment: Only much later do I come to discern the root of the problem. He had come here with a three month supply of his medication. It has unpleasant side effects: dryness of mouth, tremors, tongue protrusion, etc. When he feels better, he skips on his dose. The dosage needs to be gradually reduced so as to maintain a balance between stability and undesired effects. This crucial matter has not been communicated to our father or me by his psychiatrist. We are not told that he will need his medicine for a life time, but the dose has to be modified according to his status.

Doctors are good at writing prescriptions but weak at conveying crucial information in an understandable manner to the patients. It has a negative effect on the long term outcome of mental conditions. Patients and their supporters must be informed that the withdrawal effects of psychiatric drugs can often be more unpleasant than the symptoms of the disease.

Yet, doctors begin with doses that are too high. They do not well attend to the choice of the drug. Of the many available, careful trials are needed to select the most suitable for each patient, as well as the dose needed. They also do not stress the centrality of gradually tapering the dosage. Thereby too many patients suffer needlessly and manageable cases turn into chronically unstable cases, as was the case with my brother (Whitaker 2010, 2011).

+ + + + + + +

The short lived Sumbawanga Bookstore carried three types of books: a third were books for schools, another third were popular Swahili and English novels, and the rest, books on current affairs, history and politics. In the last category were progressive works like Walter Rodney's *How Europe Underdeveloped Africa*, Frantz Fanon's *The Wretched of the Earth*, Kwame Nkrumah's *Neo-Colonialism: The Last Stage of Imperialism*, *The Autobiography of Malcolm X*, and William Hinton's *Fanshen: Fanshen: A Documentary of Revolution in a Chinese Village*. (Fanon 1965; Hinton and Magdoff 2008; Nkrumah 1966; Rodney 1972).

Books in the first two categories have a good turnover. Those in the last one mostly remain on the shelves. At the end, I donate some to colleagues at work and Pyarali. The only person who buys a couple of books of this type is from the regional security service. I once see two of them talking. One has a copy of *The Wretched of the Earth* in his hand. Are they investigating what this radical exile from the university is now up to? Anyways, I hope they did learn something in the process.

All in all, I report with sadness that my effort to assist my brother and, in the process, introduce progressive ideas in this intellectual hinterland were both majestic failures. It is a financial setback too. I console myself by saying that at least I gave it a reasonable try.

NATIONAL EXAMINATIONS

I am fortunate to be able to maintain, even in this isolated place, a connection with the profession I want to pursue. In 1972, while at the UDSM, I was appointed as a marker for the national Form VI exam in Statistics. The following year, my role was upgraded. I set the two exam papers for the subject, prepare the marking scheme, oversee the marking and am made a member of the national subject committee. I continuously serve in this capacity until 1977.

The National Examination Council of Tanzania is in charge of the entire exercise. My particular assignment comes under the able chairmanship of Dr GRV Mmari, the coordinator for all the mathematics related examinations.

By the time I am dispatched to Sumbawanga, I have set the examination papers for the year 1974. Later I receive the summons to participate in marking, scheduled for December. My boss raises no objections.

On the set date, I report at the Kibaha Secondary School, one of the national marking centers. Located twenty six miles from Dar es Salaam, it is my former high school. I see hundreds of teachers and some lecturers from UDSM congregated here. It is endearing to meet friends and past students. My buddy Shiraz Ramji, who sets the A-Level Modern Mathematics papers, is invariably present at these gatherings. While in Sumbawanga, I set the papers for the 1975 Statistics exam.

Form VI Statistics is a specialized subject taught at only four schools. Usually, about half the exam candidates are private candidates. During the years I was involved, the total number of registered candidates varied between twenty to fifty. And not all turned up for the examination.

For Statistics, there are but two markers. My partner marks Paper I, I mark Paper II. When done, we audit each other's work to ensure that all papers are graded fairly and as required. Then I compile the marks for each candidate and write out the subject report.

As the setter, I am required to ensure that the exam questions reflect the syllabus and are at the appropriate standard. A moderator reviews my draft before it is finalized. Our aim is to maintain the standard set in the Cambridge High School Certificate Examination. Yet, over the years, it declines as topics like analysis of variance, bivariate distributions, study design and survey methods are deleted from the Tanzanian syllabus. Further, like exam paper setters for other subjects, I have to follow a strict procedural guideline to ensure complete confidentiality and secrecy.

I maintain a balance between theory and applications related questions, with the latter based on local data of relevance to social and economic development. Some reflect the socialistic orientation of the era. For example, one question talks of rate of surplus value instead of rate of profit, and another, about measures of income inequality.

In any year, the pass rate does not exceed 50%. Often it is less. The marks can range from 2 points to 85 points out of a total of 100. Several reasons contribute to this lackluster outcome. The few qualified teachers for this subject need retraining. Textbooks with relevant, realistic examples do not exist. I raise these issues in the committee meetings. Other apparently more urgent matters take a priority. For, the bigger problem is that the pass rate in all mathematics related papers, in O-Level and A-Level examinations, are abysmally low. It is a perennial malady that has not been remedied as I write these words in the year 2018.

My recollection has it that Statistics was removed as a high school course in 1980. During the time it was offered, I played my part to nurture and sustain it. In the years 1974 and 1975, that work provided a needed respite from the monotony of inane bureaucratic life in Sumbawanga. During marking it is refreshing to see hundreds of hardworking teachers busy from dawn to dusk grading the hundreds of scripts piled in front of them. It is heartening to see the supervisors applying due diligence to ensure that grading uniformity is maintained with random spot and script checks. It is an atmosphere enjoining banter with seriousness. My specific task takes three to four days. The rest of the time, I help the overall coordinator in other duties. During the entire week I feel unusually cheerful. For this is the only activity that helps me retain a formal link with the subject to which I seek to devote my professional life.

PLANNING AND DATA COLLECTION

My boss is rarely in his office. At times he attends a meeting in Mbeya or Dar es Salaam. This is what I learn from John, though he does not know their purpose. At other times, the RPO goes, in an office Landrover, to townships and villages in Rukwa Region. Once in a while, John is asked to accompany him. These are called 'project inspection and data collection' trips. I am puzzled about the numeric information emanating from these trips, for I never see so much as a sliver of such data. My perplexity ends after six months on the job. On a bright day, my boss tells me:

> *Tomorrow you will join me to inspect an education project in the Lake Rukwa basin. We may return late.*

We leave at 9 am, with him sitting in front with the driver. I am at the back in this four-wheel drive with comfy seats. It is an uneventful ride in a sparsely populated, lush green area until we reach the edge of the canyon overlooking the lake. The descent is steep. I hold my breath. Luckily, our driver is familiar with the twists and turns of this roadway. His skilled maneuvering of the all-terrain vehicle lands us at the lake basin in no time.

And what a grand sight it is: like you are on another planet. A light blue, calm water expanse stretches to the horizon. It is a shallow but wide lake. The surface area varies according to rainfall. I am told it is populated with crocodiles and hippos. On that day, we do not sight any. It as well abounds with fish. Traversing the sandy basin, we spot a fishing vessel at irregular intervals. I also sight one salt pan.

Just after noon, we reach our destination, a primary school where two additional classrooms are being constructed. The man in-charge shows us around the place. He speaks with deference. The RPO asks some questions, and occasionally jots down something in his mini-notepad.

And then we are off. Now we search for farmers who grow papaya, pineapple and water melon. I am astonished at what I see. Tons of such fruits and vegetables can be had at dirt cheap prices. A papaya or pineapple costs a fifth of what it does in town, which itself is a half or a third of the cost in Dar es Salaam.

I buy one large papaya and one giant pineapple for home. My colleagues fill up the vehicle with their purchases. I wonder, but maintain a diplomatic silence. Back in town a little after 4 pm, I am grateful that the boss tells the driver to drop me at my doorstep. I do not have to carry the heavy load from office to home.

Rosa enjoys the pineapple juice and mashed papaya. Farida, Mohamed, our house worker and I gulp down the rest over the next day. On discrete inquiry with my officemate, I learn that the fruit load is generally 'passed on' to market vendors for a good sum. Data collection has its own rewards.

Over the course of my stay in this area, I recall being taken on four such 'data collection trips.' Once it was to the shore of Lake Tanganyika. We had gone to inspect a fishery project but returned with a load of premium fresh and dried fish. On two other occasions we visited interior villages. Here the 'data' took the form of fresh corn and finger millet.

That, in essence, is the grand total of the contributions of an expert with a master's degree in Operations Research from the world renowned London School of Economics to the data collection and development planning efforts for Rukwa Region. On several occasions, I draft proposals for formal data collection surveys to scientifically assess the production and marketing of fruits, vegetables, grain and fish in the region. My boss peruses each proposal with interest. In all seriousness, he says:

> *This is very good, Karim, very good. I will take a thorough look, talk to the RDD, and get back to you.*

Of course, he never does it. Rarely, out of the blue, he tells me:

> *You know, your data project, I like it. But it is not in the budget. We have to wait till we get the funds.*

At that moment, I do not know which project he is talking about. I doubt if he does either. Whatever it is, it is never placed in our annual or supplementary requests for funds from the PMO.

One day, the boss calls me.

> *Karim, a seminar for chairpersons from fifteen villages is going on in Sumbawanga town. I was supposed to address it tomorrow, but I have been called to an important meeting in Mbeya. Can you take my place?*

It is not a request but an order.

> *What shall I talk about?*

> *Oh, you have been here long enough. You know this region well. Talk about the challenges of planning for development, and anything you think is important and relevant.*

The next day, I stand in front of respectful group of elderly villagers. I do not think they have seen a *Muhindi* (Asian) governmental official before. On my part, I am a bit nervous, as I come without much preparation.

I focus on history, specifically, what I found from my perusal of the rusty cabinets. I talk of the official initiatives of the past and note how often the energies and resources of area villagers have been wasted as a result of poor planning by an uncaring bureaucracy. I stress the need to involve farmers in the formulation and execution of projects that involve them. I emphasize the need for accountability and transparency in governmental actions.

Their expressions reveal to me that, coming from an official, these are novel words. Instantly, they open up and talk in a candid manner about their recent experiences. They tell me that when the policy of *Ujamaa* was announced, they liked it and marched to demonstrate their support. They were promised water, education, health services, as well as good accessibility at the new collective villages. But when they got there, it often was empty land. Construction of a school or dispensary was just in the offing. They were told that money from the central government would arrive soon. But it took too long, and generally fell short of what they had been led to expect. Organization of the collective projects was in disarray. When a project got off the ground, the farmers were shortchanged by higher ups in the division of the proceeds. At their previous locations they had a water stream or a shallow well. The new villages had to wait a year or longer to get the deep wells dug. In the meantime, getting water became a laborious exercise. And on, and on. After a while, many were so frustrated that they decided to return to the isolated places they had come from.

By the end of the two hour session, I learn more from these humble villagers than they do from me. I end the session by saying that I will convey their misgivings to the authorities. But they as well as I know what it really means. I do write a small memo to my boss in which I summarize the complaints around the *Ujamaa* policy. He is not pleased. It is immediately returned, with the admonition that I should not listen to trouble makers, or write such unwise things.

During the 'data collection trips,' as my colleagues engage in the significant task of fruitful data gathering, I converse with the farmers, teachers, fishermen and elders nearby. I gain more insight into the realities of this region from these interactions than from any official report I read.

Talking of official reports I would be remiss if I failed to note a most crucial regional planning exercise. It occurs every six months in the office of the RPO. He summons his aides. The six monthly or annual report to the PMO is due soon, he tells us, in a grave tone. He has a draft in front of him. We get a copy. I see it notes classrooms built in Village A, the main room of a dispensary constructed in Village B, fishnets given to X fishermen, two miles of district roads upgraded, etc.

He briskly runs through it in a point by point fashion, pausing once in a while to ask:

> *Karim, is that not the case? When we visited Village A, the two classrooms were almost completed. Don't you recall?*

I could have queried his flexible interpretation of the term 'almost.' Yet, I agree with him.

> *Good. Even the Regional Education Officer (REO) visited the place. He found what we found. The latest district report also says the same thing.*

Not raised is the fact that the REO had gone there before we did. And he has another question for the Assistant Planning Officer. In three hours at most, this team of regional planning experts has complied a comprehensive development report for the PMO.

> *Very good. Both of you are doing a good job. I will make a note of it in your files.*

With that, we head back to our newspaper pile. In all likelihood, we will not see his final report until the next one is due.

+ + + + + + +

Comment: Development planners at the PMO aggregate the effusive data stream generated from our region with similarly formulated data streams from other regions to form a scientifically sounding overall picture of the development underway in the nation as a whole. It forms the basis of official claims of significant gains in the provision of water, educational and health services to the villages and towns, progress in adult education, etc., during the *Ujamaa* years.

Throughout this era, Mwalimu Nyerere continues to espouse, in flowery, inspiring terminology, the need for Africa to stand on its own feet. Self-reliance is, he declares, indispensable. Yet, it is under him that, in per capita terms, Tanzania sits at the top among the recipients of external loans and grants in sub-Saharan Africa.

Consequently, the overall data snapshot is transmitted to the international agencies like the WHO, UNDP, UNICEF and the World Bank, as well to the multitude of bilateral agencies of the Scandinavian, Canadian, British, US, Japanese and other governments. Knowing well the pitfalls of these data, they still publish them as they are in their own official reports.

As the government beats its own hollow drum, the agencies respond in harmony. They have a stake in showing to their funders and taxpayers all the money being sent to this poor African nation is being spent wisely.

In that manner arises the mythology of the spectacular gains in the provision of social and health services in Tanzania during the *Ujamaa* era. Dubious data turn into hard core truths.

+ + + + + + +

Not that the reality is totally unknown. Independent minded experts from UDSM conduct on the ground scientific surveys. Their reports generally puncture a gaping hole in that rosy picture (see Coulson 1982, Mapolu 1980, von Freyhold 1979).

Unfortunately, modern day debates about life under *Ujamaa* continue to be informed by those mythologies. Intellectuals cite what the Leader said here and what he said there, and employ mythologies to buttress their arguments. Ideological verbosity, of the left and right variety, supplants reality. In this era of instantaneous social media exchange, due examination of relevant facts is surpassed by the art of creative juggling of words.

My statistical career has spanned nearly forty five years. As I look back, I regard my own role, though tiny, inadvertent and imposed from above, in the generation of that misleading mythology to be the very low point of my professional life. It is one of the few things I regret.

POLITICS AND ECONOMICS

In the course of my stay here, I learn about fellow exiles. All have been around for at least a decade. It seems that I am the only recent arrival.

In the Mau Mau era, Kenyan freedom fighters were brought here under guard. Citizens of Tanzania by now, they are into small scale crafts and trading. Interestingly, they man most of the barber shops in the area. A number of soldiers who took part in the army mutiny of 1964 ended up in this area too. Some have small shops but a few are famed as this town's leading drunkards. Around that time, a militant leader of the Mine Workers' Union at the Mwadui Diamond Mines who was also a senior official of the Tanzania Federation of Labor was exiled here. Subsequently, he betrayed his roots and became a corrupt official in a local branch of a major state enterprise. After amassing sizable wealth through dubious deals, he at present runs his own lucrative business. However, I do not come to know any of these exiles in person.

Apart from us, I divide the population of this area into several socio-economic strata. The top stratum is composed of two segments. On the one side is the bevy of politicians in high office, senior bureaucrats in the machinery of the state, and top executives of the local branches of the parastatal enterprises. On the other side are the leading businessmen, owners of transport companies, and the like. The latter are mostly of Asian and Arab descent.

A relationship of unease prevails between the two groups. In the past seven years, the power of the private sector has waned considerably as most of their activities, from wholesale trading to large scale farming and export, were taken over by state firms. Since the state enterprises are run in an inefficient and corrupt manner, private business survives and thrives in the many interstices of the economy.

The two sectors are loggerheads in the political arena. Yet, behind the scenes, they collude, grease each other's palms and expropriate a major chunk of the economic benefits due to the people for themselves. You can spot them as they are driven around in Peugot 504s and fancy station wagons.

Below them are the mid-level farmers, teachers, office staff, small business people, clergy and the like. I count myself among them. We live a modest life, and harbor some apprehension as to the future of our families.

At the bottom are the multitude: peasant farmers, fishermen, manual laborers, office cleaners and messengers, drivers, domestic servants, itinerant traders, and the like. Living in abject poverty, they face numerous hardships at every twist and turn of life. For them, the flowery rhetoric of the political elite has thus far been devoid of meaning.

Conflict between the elements of these economic strata are an integral part of the landscape. Take the strike by the drivers at the regional headquarters in July 1974. It comes with a letter written anonymously to the RDD. The key issue is the conduct of the senior transport officer. Said to be arrogant and abusive, the letter charges him with making the drivers do extra private night time duties. Anyone who objects is dismissed.

A meeting of all drivers is called. It is chaired by the RPO, my boss. The transport officer is present as well. Instead of mediating in a fair manner, the RPO says that the strike has been instigated by a few trouble makers. Each driver is asked if he agrees with the contents of the letter. Each one, intimidated as he is, says no. The matter ends with an official letter sent to the PMO stating that the alleged complaints have been investigated and found to be baseless.

But the paramount class conflict in this region is between the peasantry and the domineering state bureaucracy.

POWER TO THE PEOPLE

Decentralizing rural administration was aimed to bring state officials closer to the people and give the latter a greater voice in the decisions and acts affecting their lives. In the adroit hands of Mckinsey Corporation, the new system just adds an additional technocratic bureaucracy on top of the already heavy machinery of governance bearing down upon people. In addition to the ruling party structure, the political machine under the regional commissioner, you have a third strand, the development directorate. With the power centered in Dar es Salaam, it remains a rigid, hierarchical system in which the people at the bottom must submit to orders from above without questions. One villager tells me that if they want to start a football club, they first have to get a permit from the district party chairman!

Other than bringing people into villages, this bureaucracy has no creative solutions to resolve existing problems. It has no ethical commitment to serve the people. With a few exceptions, it follows the economic recipes handed down by experts from the World Bank and Western organizations. It places parochial short term gain above the welfare of the people. While it excels in spouting volumes of fine socialist rhetoric, the socialism it implements seems like that of an extraterrestrial brand. In truth, it is but a chaotic form of state capitalism.

Nowhere is this more evident in how the villagization scheme is implemented in Rukwa region, and I may add, elsewhere in the nation too. As was conveyed to me by local villagers in the seminar I addressed, the widespread initial enthusiasm for *Ujamaa* has dissipated by 1974. Inefficient implementation is the key reason. Promises are not followed by action, the misappropriation of resources does not abate, and the farmers and fishermen face excessive hardships during the process.

Now it is going nowhere. Loud calls by pot-bellied politicians fall on deaf ears. Predictably, the authorities resort to force. It is a part of a nationwide undertaking named *Operation Vijijini*. Predictably, dreadful incidents occur. In the northern part of Rukwa Region people are told to move into tobacco growing complexes. They dislike the idea. When state officials come to enforce the order, confrontations occur. The FFU are called. There is indiscriminate gunfire against the gathered crowds. In Uyonga area, three peasant farmers are shot dead. It enrages the population. Calm is restored after the Regional Commissioner goes to the area and promises that no more forcible relocation to the tobacco complexes will occur.

It is but a temporary respite. The central authorities have villagization as their priority number one. A stern directive from the center is issued to all regions: People must move into the *Ujamaa* villages, one way or another, whether they like it or not. The man at the top reneges on his solemn undertaking given at the onset of the *Ujamaa* era to make the move to villages completely voluntary. The day after the edict is issued, the new bureaucracy moves into action.

At my location, it proceeds as follows: For three months in early 1975, almost each morning, there is a general meeting of all the employees. The RDD calls for twenty to thirty volunteers for the day. There is no shortage of takers, who leap on to the four trucks at hand. Some have batons and sticks in their hands. Some have bags and buckets. One day they head north, the other day, east, and so on.

Their task is to locate and catch isolated rural dwellers, and herd them to a collective village. They implement the job with gusto. The rural residents try to escape when they hear a vehicle approaching. But the trucks come from several directions. Many, especially children, elderly and women, are caught. They are taken, with just a few belongings, to the designated village, and simply dumped there. How they will feed themselves or where they will sleep is nobody's business. They are supposed to be in a village, and that is where they must be.

Items like livestock, farm harvest, domestic belongings are left behind. The militia guys have no qualms about helping themselves to the goodies. This is their reward. Volunteering for the exercise is popular among the office staff. Each fellow returns with a couple of fat chickens, or a goat, or a bagful of maize cobs, or a bucket of shiny red finger millet. They get an allowance as well.

At times, they boast that they apprehended a witch or witch doctor who has been discouraging the people from joining the *Ujamaa* villages. Amid laughter, we hear that the witch was adequately punished. It means being beaten senseless or worse. Common talk has it that some had their ears sliced off. It is a despicable undertaking, inflicting wanton suffering onto destitute rural folk. Only two other workers, Sichilima and Zaharan, both of low grade, share my opinion. I never volunteer. They do not either. Had I been asked to participate by my superiors, I would have refused, no matter the consequences. In life, one has to draw a line somewhere.

Adverse national publicity brings the exercise to a halt after a while. By then up to four million people have been forced to relocate. In our region, it lasts for three months. The RDD writes a report to the PMO saying the bulk of the rural population is now in *Ujamaa* villages. Only a tiny proportion lives on the outside. At the final meeting, he congratulates the staff for their splendid accomplishment.

+ + + + + + +

Comment: Today, different groups have their own favored stories as to what transpired in the Nyerere era. Asian bigots declare he was fervently anti-Asian. Muslims of a fundamentalist bent claim he was anti-Muslim to the core.

In that regard, I defend Mwalimu. He was not a racist or a religiously biased politician. I tell them: learn about what happened during villagization. It was not the brown skinned Asians but black Africans who suffered miserably. In Rukwa, no discrimination on the basis of religion occurred. It did not matter whether you were Catholic, Protestant, Muslim or Pagan. If you did not join an *Ujamaa* village, you were dealt with in an equally harsh manner.

+ + + + + + +

Comment: Another mythology prevalent today is that Tanzania of that era was a stooge of the communist nations, especially China. The construction of the Uhuru Railway between Zambia and Tanzania, the building of the giant Urafiki Textile Mill with Chinese help combined with Tanzania's firm support for the entry of China to the UN and the struggle of the people of Vietnam against US aggression are adduced as evidence in support of that proposition.

Let us look at the reality. In 1974, with the help of the World Bank and Western agencies, the government devises a new scheme for rural development. Under the title of Regional Integrated Development Program (RIDEP), it is to address the low levels of efficacy and accountability of foreign funded projects. These problems are to be remedied through assigning specific regions to specific funders. This process will clarify lines of responsibility and joint evaluation of the projects.

The region-wise allocation of foreign agencies include: (i) Kigoma: World Bank; (ii) Tanga: West Germany; (iii) Mara and West Lake: Denmark; (iv) Arusha and Mwanza: Sweden; (v) Shinyanga and Morogoro: the Netherlands; and (vi) Rukwa: Austria.

The list does not feature any communist nation: not Russia, Hungary, East Germany, Cuba or China. The fate of all the regions of socialist Tanzania will not be decided by some communist philosophy but by World Bank oriented capitalist planning.

+++++++

In early 1975, a team of five experts from Austria, accompanied by two high officials from the PMO, arrive in Sumbawanga. They hold talks with the RDD and his senior staff, and are given a tour of the office complex. Our room is orderly. The newspapers and extraneous stuff are gone. We have two files, a note pad and pen in front of us. It looks as we had been instructed to make it look. The RPO informs them in an officious tone:

This is my planning team. Karim is an expert in statistics.

Looking briefly at us, they nod, turn around, and leave. We learn that their mandate is to make a comprehensive assessment of the economy of our region, identify the principal bottlenecks, and devise a viable development plan. And that has to be done before April 1975.

The fate of this blessed region is now in the august hands of five Austrians who perhaps know but two words of Swahili, whose prior experience in Africa seems minimal, and who, a few months back, may have been hard put to locate us on a map. Yet, they hold the purse strings. So what they say will go.

Until I leave this place for good at the end of 1975, I do not see much progress on that front. The experts come and go. They meet the bosses. I am never given a chance to talk to them. Perhaps they explore the region, but we are not privy to their plans or movements.

+ + + + + + +

Comment: *Ujamaa* Villages in Tanzania did not represent the traditional African mode of living. For the most part, they signified a coerced existence under the control of an insensitive bunch of bureaucrats. One could perhaps justify that if it led to policies and actions that markedly improved people's living conditions. But that did not happen. The poverty entrenching export-import basis of the economy remained as it was during the colonial era.

The RIDEP episode makes a mockery of the hallowed verbiage about self-reliance. It reminded me of the partition of Africa of the 1880s. Five years later, it was, for all practical purposes, abandoned. Nowhere did it generate significant, sustainable results. Go to Rukwa region today and try to find a major positive sign of the Austrian neo-colonization of that area four decades ago. It will be like trying to locate water on the moon. It is also noteworthy that these economic occupations occur around the time that the forced moves to villages are in progress. Yet, the hallowed Western promoters of democracy and good governance do not seem to mind. They do not raise a political storm on the basis of human rights or any such platitudes. But, they do not spare any invective on castigating the violations of human rights of the people or Cuba and China, places where there are real and major improvements in the living conditions of the masses are taking place.

This World Bank approved *Ujamaa* policy at the end proves to be a majestic failure on all fronts. It is not socialism of any shape or form. A more apt name for it is: A chaotic brand of neo-colonial state capitalism.

EXIT

Well within a year of our arrival, Farida and I are in harmony with life in this land. It has its own idyllic features. Of cardinal importance to us is that our small infant is now a healthy, chubby, playful baby. Each month, her mother takes her to the local child health clinic. The friendly staff give her sound advice on the nutritional value of locally available food items and how to cook them. Rosa gets along splendidly with her playmate at my cousin's place. During the evening walks, she runs hither and thither, grabs this and that, her face beaming with intense pleasure.

Though there are no chocolates or fine restaurant delicacies to be had here, we are content with the cheap, varied and bountiful fruits, vegetables, fish, grains, and meat that Farida, moreover, prepares in a delicious style. We make up for the lack of theaters by listening to movie songs on a cassette player. I read a lot of books, at home and at work. (If you are seen reading or writing in the office, it is taken as work, no matter what it is.)

The air in town is fresh. It is quite windy and cold at times. But we take it in stride. Once, there is an ice hailstorm. One morning, I see a brighter than usual stream of light emerging from my brother's room. He is fast asleep. As I enter, I see, through a hole in the ceiling board, that two tin roof plates have been blown away. Mohamed has slept undisturbed throughout the stormy episode. I make a report to the regional works office the minute I am at work. It is repaired the same afternoon. Just a minor thorn in this otherwise almost ideal existence.

People we encounter are courteous and friendly. Besides our relatives, we visit Sichilima and Zaharan, my office mates, at home for a chat. Sometimes they come over. Personal security is not an issue. My salary is modest. But as we live in a modest style, I manage to save a fourth of the amount for a rainy day.

Yet, the paucity of intellectual stimulation bothers me. I find continued immersion in a remorseless bureaucracy that violates the basic rights of people with impunity deeply disturbing. I yearn to teach and explore the wide world of mathematics. Farida, for her part, wants to resume her work as a secretary. The prospects for her in this area are essentially nil.

But I cannot just resign and look for another job. I am still under the five year work contract with the government. If I am to get a new job, it has to be with official permission. There is a vacancy for a statistician in the Department of Epidemiology and Biostatistics at the Faculty of Medicine of UDSM. I apply. The lack of response to my letter indicates that I remain an unwelcome at that academic institution.

In September 1975, I see a newspaper advertisement for an Instructor of Transport Statistics at the National Institute of Transport in Dar es Salaam. Must be a new place, I tell myself. In haste, I submit an application through official channels. Providence is on my side. In two weeks, I am called for an interview. A month later I get a letter of acceptance which bears the stamp of approval from the central manpower allocation office.

In the middle of November 1975, Farida and Rosa depart for Dar es Salaam. Again fortune is on our side: by some coincidence, the researchers from UDSM who had driven us to Sumbawanga are here. They kindly agree to give them a ride back to Dar es Salaam in their vehicle. Farida takes her and Rosa's clothes and stuff. I have to take care of the rest: the cot, three mattresses, assorted pots, pans and plates, a bagful of my books and papers, and my personal items. The two beds and other items are distributed among my co-workers and our house worker. He is not happy to see us go, but I give him a good terminal benefits deal. Pyarali, Sichilima and Zaharan get three books each as a parting gift. They are the left over stock from the ill-fated bookstore.

I have ten thousand shillings, the equivalent of six months of my salary, in my bank account. It will be handy at our new location. In the last week of November, I make my final journey from Rukwa Region. And what a trip it is. I ride in a twelve ton lorry that is transporting finger millet and dried fish to Dar es Salaam. It has space for our belongings but the seat next to driver already has a passenger. So the loading assistant and I are at the back, sitting on top of sacks of dried fish.

It is a bumpy ride. The driver seems hell bent on making it to Dar es Salaam in record time. It does not matter whether we are on a straight or winding stretch, he maintains the same speed. I am wearing three shirts to protect myself from the wind. But it does not help. A stopover of a couple of hours in Mbeya, and then we set sail once more. We are lucky that it does not rain. By the time I am in Upanga at my parents' house eighteen hours later, I am as exhausted as a marathon runner. But when I see Rosa, that tiredness vanishes.

My first and final trips to and from Sumbawanga are the most arduous journeys I ever undertake. It is behind me now. Another adventure, of a different character altogether, and of five years' duration, awaits. But first, I need to sleep.

8

SENIOR INSTRUCTOR

Teaching creates
All other professions
Author Unknown

+ + + + + + +

TODAY IS THE DAY. Externally, I am calm. Inside, I bubble with excitement and elation. I can once again say: 'I am a teacher.' It is almost the end of October 1975. I am to report at the National Institute of Transport (NIT). My appointment letter designates me an Instructor in Transport Statistics. But first, I need to go to the head office of the National Transport Corporation (NTC) on what is now Samora Avenue. The NIT is the training wing of the NTC. I am warmly received by Chief Patrick Kunambi, the Director of Administration of NTC, and the person in charge of NIT.

We have been waiting for you, Mr. Hirji.

After I have filled out the employee forms, he tells me:

Come. I will introduce you to your colleagues.

I am taken to a room where two men sit at a round table. I guess both are in their fifties. The short, plump man is Mr Sanga, the Principal of NIT. The tall, muscular man is Mr Billa, Head, Department of Motor Vehicle Mechanics. Both shake my hand vigorously. After exchanging pleasantries, my first question to my new boss is:

Where is NIT located?

This is the NIT.

You mean this room!

Yes, for now, this room is the NIT.

I am flabbergasted. He informs me that NIT is about to open its doors. We three are its first employees. As such, it is our mandate to make sure that this educational institution takes off, and in a successful way.

According to the plan given by Chief Kunambi, NIT will have three academic units: the Department of Transport Management, the Department of Motor Vehicle Mechanics, and the Department of Transport Operations. The first one, to which I am posted, will offer a three year course leading to a Diploma in Transport Management; the second, a three year course leading to a Certificate in Motor Vehicle Mechanics; and the third will conduct short courses for drivers, conductors, loading clerks and other junior workers in transport firms.

He also tells me, with an encouraging smile, that as I am the first teacher recruited for the Department of Transport Management, I am, until further notice, also the acting head of that department.

Where is the study program for the diploma course? Does it contain detailed outlines and list of books needed for each course?

It is your responsibility to develop a detailed plan for the three year study program, formulate the syllabus for each course, including making a list of the required and subsidiary books.

What about the other teachers?

No other person who had responded to our advertisement was found suitable. We may get more applicants. But in the meantime, I need to look in different places and recruit fellow instructors.

When are we supposed to start?

In January 1976. The announcement for application to study at NIT will appear in the papers next week.

And where will the teaching take place?

Temporary wooden structures for classrooms and offices are being built behind the Urafiki Textile Mill. I went there yesterday. I am sure they will be ready for use in a month's time.

I do not sleep well that night. What a drastic transformation! From a do-nothing job that entailed reading old newspapers to pass time to a job where I have to conjure up, from scratch and in a couple of months, an entire advanced academic study program in an area I hardly know much about. Do I have what it takes to undertake that stupendous challenge?

My consolation is that two other people also have a similar responsibility. Though I am to find out that my particular task is a much more onerous one. While courses of the type they have to devise exist within the nation, no college in sub-Saharan Africa offers diplomas in transport management. I feel like a lone blind man dumped in an alien terrain without even a walking stick for guidance.

THE STUDY PROGRAM

The basic questions are: What is to be the underlying theme of the diploma program? What types of courses are relevant? How should they be structured? In addition, I need to construct at least the outlines of their syllabuses and locate required course material.

The only thing I get from the Principal is a brochure from the Chartered Institute of Transport in the UK. It lists the study topics for membership examinations of that Institute. But a major portion of their contents does not seem suitable for the African context.

I first go to the Ministry of Transport and talk to senior staff. Some of them had got advanced training abroad. I get an idea of the type of courses they had studied. I pay a similar visit to the transport unit of the Prime Minister's Office. Then I visit the UDSM, my old hangout. I go to the Economics Department, the Geography Department, the Economic Research Bureau, and the Bureau of Resource Assessment and Land Use Planning. There are several reports dealing with transport issues in Tanzania and East Africa. Some can be used for our courses but most are too advanced.

Critically, through these visits I come to know that over the years, a number of short courses dealing with transport matters (covering road, marine, rail and air transport modes) have been held in the country. For some I get the outlines and for some, I am lucky to find detailed course material. Though this material is for courses of two to four weeks in duration, for me, they are a gold mine. From other places, I find the syllabuses for diploma and degree level courses in general management and administration.

In two weeks, a broad outline forms in my mind. In the first year, our students will take courses on management at a general level, and in the second and third, we will build on that foundation to offer them specialized transport related courses. Each academic year will have three study quarters and a long vacation. During the latter, students will get practical training in the form of attachment to transport organizations and firms for a period of two months.

My priority is to pin down the first year courses, and sequence them by academic quarters. I initially decide on Introduction to Management, Economics, Accounts, Transport Statistics, Basic Commercial Law and Development Studies. The last course gives an integrated, historical perspective on social, political and economic conditions in Africa and Tanzania. It is offered at most higher education institutions in the nation, though we have to teach it with an emphasis on the development of transport systems.

The remaining years will have courses like Transport Policy and Planning, Transport Logistics, Personnel Management, Financial Management, Law of Carriage and Goods, Traffic Safety, Quantitative Methods, as well as courses covering different transport modalities like road, rail, marine and air transport.

It is, as yet, a hazy plan. To solidify it, I need instructors for the first year courses. Then we can finalize course sequencing and detailed syllabuses, and procure the relevant material for teaching.

I can do that by myself for two courses: Transport Statistics and Quantitative Methods, the courses I will teach. The latter course will contain varied mathematical methods that are applicable to transport planning and logistics. Some of these methods were included in the courses I took at LSE. Though now I have to teach them in a simplified and practical style.

THE TEACHERS

At this juncture, I need to mention a unique characteristic of NIT. Unlike many higher educational institutions in Tanzania, this one has zero foreign funding. No bilateral agency, from Norway, Denmark or Canada, or multilateral agency like the UNDP or the World Bank is slated to provide funding, experts or any other form of support. We are on our own. The NTC and the Ministry of Transport have agreed that the Institute will be funded mainly from the transport licensing fees paid by transport entities. In addition, private and public transport entities that sponsor students for study at NIT cover a part of their tuition and other costs.

I cannot count on any group of external expatriates who will overnight descend on our campus to help us get going. For now, it is like a sky high obstacle to surmount. In the long run, however, it will be a blessing in disguise.

Where to get the instructors? A couple of new applicants are to be interviewed. But their application forms leave me doubtful about their suitability for the job.

While doing my investigations about course material, I had been sounding out local experts in the ministries and educational institutions about teaching at NIT. Some are willing to do it on a part time basis and help write a preliminary syllabus. This takes care of first year courses like Accounts, Management, and Basic

Commercial Law. I pitch in too. In addition to my regular course, Transport Statistics, I teach Development Studies, and assist the Department of Motor Vehicle Mechanics by teaching Basic Mathematics to its first batch of students. This is on top of discharging the myriad of duties of a head of department.

It is thus that the Department of Transport Management of NIT starts to function on January 1, 1976. A few months on, graduates with a first degree in management and administration, economics, and political science are taken on board as teachers. Initially, they teach the basic courses. Later, they go abroad for master's level studies in Transport Economics and Planning, Transport Policy and Development, etc.

Two years on, there is an effective academic team in the department. The Tanzanian instructors include Anthony Kondella, S Kaombwe, AK Selemani, TE Mrema, Mr Swai and Mr Mwangu. Interestingly, S Kaombwe had been my student at UDSM. At that time, he had also been an active member of the transportation club I had initiated.

But there is more. Without well qualified instructors specialized in diverse areas of transportation, we cannot offer the second and third year courses in a satisfactory manner. But we do not find any suitable person locally. Overseas recruitment is essential. Chief Kunambi, our boss at the NTC makes a critical decision. We should advertise for instructors in India and Pakistan. Cost is the key reason. It is far cheaper to employ a person from those areas than from say, the UK or Sweden. I endorse it for a second reason. Experts from those nations are more likely to be aware of the type of transport problems we face and the approaches to resolving them than experts from industrialized nations.

We get several applications. Looking over their qualifications and experience, I recommend a couple. The Principal and the Chief fly over to interview them. Our first external instructor, Mr Khalifa Afzal Hussain, arrives in August 1976. He hails from Pakistan.

We could not have asked for better. Mr Hussain is to turn out to be a valuable gem for NIT and our department. In the six years he is destined to stay at NIT, he will function like a solid academic and practical backbone for the training given to our students.

In ways more than one, he is a remarkable person. After getting a BA in commerce from Punjab University in 1933, he worked in large rail and road transport corporations and public bodies. He rose through the ranks to posts like Chief Traffic Superintendent and General Manager. Along the way, he got higher training in the UK, edited the magazine, *Punjab Transport*, and lectured in Transport Studies at the Punjab University. By the time he joined NIT, he had written three books, and was regarded as one of the top experts in transport in Pakistan.

Now he is almost seventy years old. Yet, he assumes his duties at NIT with the vigor and stamina of the youth. Soon, he and I are able to formulate detailed syllabuses for second and third year subjects like transport economics, planning, development and logistics. He shows me a copy of his most recent book, *The Development of Roads and Road Transport in Pakistan* (Hussain 1973). Though it focuses on Pakistan, the technical concepts it employs for describing, financing, regulating, planning and operating road transport systems apply well to our context. It can certainly be of use in such courses. He tells me that ten extra copies are on the way. He will donate them to NIT. Most critically, with his clear and patient teaching style, and an-ever jovial personality, he is an instant hit with our students.

A year later, we recruit Mr. Choudhri, a transport economist from India. In addition to good academic qualifications, he has years of teaching and practical experience. His teaching style is systematic and rigorous. His examinations are quite challenging. His students are on their feet all the time. He sets a fine model of academic quality for other instructors to emulate. Until I leave NIT in August 1980, these are the only expatriates we have in our department. Yet, they are of greater value to us than ten experts from Europe, UK or USA.

At times, a critical shortfall occurs when an instructor is on study leave or away some other reason. Then it falls on me to teach his subject: Transport Policy and Development, Transport Logistics and Planning, or Development Studies. I have to read the relevant books. Preparing for and teaching such a class takes a heavy toll on me.

In early 1978, I come to a decision. I have been a confirmed Head of the Department of Transport Management for two years. But administration is not my forte. I prefer to teach, do research, interact with students, and write papers. I tell that to the Principal. He is surprised. It is rare for anyone to voluntarily vacate a position that comes with perks, official and unofficial. While other senior staff utilize the Institute's resources like motor vehicles for personal purposes, I never do. Such perks are not on my menu.

I suggest to him:

> *Anthony Kondella is an efficient, dedicated person who gets along well with his colleagues and students. He has assisted me often. So I know he has good administrative skills. I think he would make a good head of department.*

Earlier, I had talked with Anthony. He did not have any objections. Fortunately, my suggestion is taken up. At the outset, I assist him. Soon, he earns the respect of the staff and students. Until I leave NIT, be it in calm or rough waters, he steers the departmental ship as a competent and popular captain.

One reason why the Principal accepted my decision to step down was that now

I would not be there to tenaciously dispute most of his pet proposals in the NIT Management Committee meetings.

THE STUDENTS

The Diploma in Transport Management program admits two types of students. First, we accept persons with adequate Form VI level passes in subjects like economics, geography and mathematics. And we also consider those who only have Form IV level passes provided they have at least three years of relevant experience in a transport organization. They as well must demonstrate their suitability through an interview and an entrance test.

There is a sizable response to our newspaper advertisement. The diploma program begins in earnest in January 1976 with twenty learners on board. The wooden classroom structures pose no barrier to effective instruction. In three years, a total of some eighty students study at one time in the diploma program. The attrition is minimal. Apart from a few stragglers, most are capable and diligent learners. Though, they find my specific subjects, Transport Statistics and Quantitative Methods, to be the two most difficult ones.

Our mature age students are from diverse organizations. In the main, they come under sponsorship from public and private road transport firms. Our horizons expand as the Tanzania Railways Corporation, several manufacturers and distributors with large vehicular fleets, and the companies in other transport modalities begin to send us students. I make a special note of Major JB Gama, an officer in the Tanzania Peoples Defense Force. He has managed a large fleet of the army's vehicular armada. He joins our diploma program in 1978. Upon graduation, he returns to the military forces. Our reputation spreads beyond the nation's borders. In the 1978 intake, one of our students hails from Zambia.

The Department of Motor Vehicle Mechanics enrolls a similar number of students in the certificate program. Initially, I assist them by teaching Basic Mathematics. Later, upon my recommendation, Shiraz Ramji is hired to do it on a part time basis.

The Department of Transport Operations has two experienced and capable instructors for training bus and heavy duty truck drivers, and bus conductors. They run courses lasting three weeks five to six times a year. The courses are popular and always well subscribed.

PROGRESS

By the end of 1977, the permanent buildings for the Institute are up and in use, a hundred meters from the wooden rooms. Our department has most of the second floor of the two story academic block. The other departments occupy the first floor. Our floor has two classrooms, the office of the Head of Department and a couple of staff offices. The administrative offices of the Institute, the library, and a lecture hall are connected to it by cement corridors. The student dorms and a well-equipped motor vehicle repair workshop are at the rear. The wood structures continue to be used as staff offices, store rooms, and student recreation venues.

On the academic front, there is substantial progress along several fronts. I delve into six: short courses, international recognition, research and publication, student journal, the library, and occupational safety.

Short Courses: In its third year of existence, our department begins to offer courses of two weeks duration on varied transport related topics. One or two courses are held per year. Usually twenty to thirty employees, from transport firms and companies like the breweries and cooperative unions that maintain a large fleet of vehicles, attend. Initially, I organize the courses. Mr Hussain and Mr Choudhri are invariably the main academic pillars. Anthony Kondella and I contribute to the lectures as well. Once in a while, I invite a part-time instructor from the Ministry of Transport, UDSM, or elsewhere to give talks on specific topics.

A short course photo in Appendix D shows the instructors, students, and NIT and NTC officials. Mr Hussain is at the extreme left in the rear line. Next to him is Anthony Kondella. In front of the left pillar is Shiraz Ramji, an invited instructor. The man in the middle sporting a beard, glasses and white shirt is myself. On my right in white shirt is Chief Kunambi and next to him, stand Mr Sanga, the NIT Principal. Mr Choudhri is at the extreme right in front of the right pillar. Almost everyone else is a course participant.

Such courses are popular, and well attended. We get critical feedback at the end of each one. I am surprised at the level of positive responses we get. Most attendees recommend a follow up course building on material taught in the current one.

International Recognition: As a long time Fellow of the Chartered Institute of Transport in the UK, Mr Hussain keeps the UK institute informed about our activities and progress. He shows me the letters he gets from there. I can see that they are visibly impressed. He also sends them our syllabus and copies of the final exams we set for our students. Now, to become a member of the Chartered Institute of Transport (MCIT), you need to pass its two phase examinations. By 1980, the UK institute accepts that the NIT diploma program is of a sufficiently high academic caliber to be accorded a rare exemption. According to this, a Diploma in Transport Management from the NIT of Tanzania allows a candidate for MCIT to proceed to the phase II examination. In other words, the person does not have to sit for the phase I examination papers. It is a worthy tribute to the innovative efforts of the pioneering academic team of the Department of Transport Management at NIT.

Research and Publication: During my tenure as head of department, I encourage the instructors to conduct independent research on relevant issues of the day, and publish reports and research papers. In due course, I am appointed as the Head of the Research and Consultancy Committee of NIT. It is my responsibility to review and approve the research and consultancy projects proposed by academic staff, and for the approved projects, set the level of funding. It is a laborious, contentious task. I have to be encouraging and fair. Yet sub-standard proposals have to be returned to the proposers, on occasion, for two or three rounds of improvement. This is one of the few times when the stringent requirements I set made a couple of the academic staff grumble about me. I was told of this by other instructors.

As a new institution, we have no tradition in research or consultancy. Yet, slowly but surely, these activities take off. To give one example: AK Selemani and I compile *Directory of Transport Firms in Tanzania, 1978*. It is a comprehensive directory covering the road, rail, air and water transport firms in Tanzania. For each firm, we give the name and address. For the Tanzania Railways Corporation, the location and management contact information for each station and substation are given.

Books on the varied modalities and aspects of transportation are not hard to locate. But almost all are published in the West, are of minimal relevance to Africa, must be imported and are mostly beyond the budget of our students. Of value is the book written by Mr Hussain. In addition, we compile readers for our courses. These are cyclostyled, soft bound volumes of teaching material and papers gathered from varied sources by the instructors. Besides relevance, a key requirement is that the material be at a level accessible by the diploma students. It is a time consuming endeavor. The instructors usually attend to it over the long vacation. In the long run, it pays off.

Thus, in 1977, KA Hussein and I compile *Transport in Africa: A Reader*. A year later, TE Mrema follows up with two volumes of *Transport in East Africa: A Reader* and Mr Choudhuri comes up with a well selected *Financial Management for the Transport Sector: A Reader*. The second volume of *Transport in East Africa* has a long theoretical piece I had written earlier, *The Political Economy of Transport*. It ponders on the question whether transport is a productive value-adding endeavor, or it is a service providing activity. The answer is that it is both, depending on what is being carried and to what end. Over the course of time, other instructors contribute to this pedagogic endeavor.

Student Journal: In early 1978, I float with the idea of launching a journal run by NIT students to the President of the student organization, NITSO. He discusses it with his cabinet. The students are unanimously enthusiastic about the idea, he subsequently tells. And they already have a name for the magazine: *The Transporter*.

I place the proposal at a meeting of the departmental heads and the Principal. Their first concern is cost. I have roughly calculated figures at hand. It is agreed that for one or two issues per year, the funding can be included in the budget of NIT. While there is consent around the table about the idea as such, it comes with a proviso: The students should not undertake this project on their own, but should be supervised by members of the academic staff.

Who will do this donkey work? Instructors rarely undertake extra work that does not come with extra remuneration. Aha, but Hirji is here. After all he came up with the idea. I guess that is the way our Principal reasons.

I am hence the Chief Adviser to *The Transporter*. Two advisers are to assist me: H Bantu, Head of Department of Transport Operations and A Shebuge, Instructor in Motor Vehicle Mechanics. The Principal will be the Patron of the magazine. Needless to say, my two colleagues feature only as named entities in each issue. I do all the work with the students.

Not that I am averse to doing it. NITSO elects the first set of members of the editorial board. Elias P Matteso is the Editor in Chief. The board is willing to put in the needed effort but is unsure about how to get going. My experience as the senior editor of the student magazine *Cheche* at UDSM comes in handy. After a couple of meetings with them, they take off in earnest. Over the ensuing four years, the editors of the magazine talk to me regularly, sometimes at my home during weekends.

By March 1980, four issues of *The Transporter* are in print. Their articles mainly address the policy, practice and personnel matters connected to the transport sector in the nation. Many are well researched and articulated. Articles on student affairs and socio-political issues augmented by short narratives, poetry and humor enrich and enliven the issues. It is striking that almost all of these contributions are by the students and instructors from within. Material from external sources appears only once in a while. I contribute an article to each of the first four issues. The second issue of *The Transporter*, whose table of contents are shown below, is a case in point.

The Travails of a Tanzanian Teacher

The Transporter, NIT

Volume 2, March 1979

Elias P Matteso, Editor-in-Chief

Author	Title	Page
Editor	Editorial	0
KF Hirji	Interpretation of Road Accident Statistics	1
H Abdallah	Problems Affecting Drivers When on Safari	11
JL Mmari	Forecast of KAMATA's Required Capital Investments in Vehicles to 1982	14
AJ Kabero	The Working Conditions of Drivers and Conductors Employed in Urban Transport	42
SJ Mlaki	Working Conditions and Industrial Relations in Road Transport	52
? ?	Return Load Generation – BITCO	61

Apart from my article, the other five are written by our students. They are the product of research done by the students during the field attachment. The best five reports, reflecting sound data collection, systematic analysis and a professional writing style, were selected for publication in this issue.

Under Khalid Kachenje, the next Editor-in-Chief, issues with more varied content come out. Some articles are in Swahili, making it accessible to the drivers and conductors attending NIT short courses. Issue No. 4 has a photo of the first batch of graduates of NIT. For this issue, I write an article, under the pseudonym, A Correspondent, entitled *Democracy and Education* which overviews the relationship between students, teachers and administrators in the education sector and proposes actions needed for improvement. (As it paints a picture of a key aspect of the education system in Tanzania in that era, an edited version has been placed in Appendix C of this book.)

The Library: A couple of months after NIT takes off, it is apparent that a set of reference books to be utilized by our staff for teaching and self-education is needed. I obtain the funds and scour the bookstores at UDSM and the city center. Soon a mini library, really a single shelf of books and reports, materializes in my office. Six months later, the shelf overflows. Also, the comings and goings create too much disturbance. A small room is found. With three shelves fitted, it is our nascent library. And, who else to take care of the collection? I am designated as the librarian. The other departments, whose collection is smaller, move their books and bound volumes to the new so-called library. It is kept open for a few hours a week by our departmental secretary, the able Stella Maji. She deals with loans and returns, and I ensure that the books are well organized on the shelves and an up to date inventory is maintained. Though it serves its purpose, it as an amateurish undertaking.

In anticipation of the completion of the new library building, a professional librarian is hired. The knowledgeable, efficient, hard-working Mr JG Mkingilma is the right man for the job. I hand over the collection to his care. Having secured two assistants and a typist, he wastes no time getting down to business. Furniture is ordered and installed; import license is obtained; books, encyclopedias, and dictionaries arrive; a modern cataloging and borrowing procedure is set up; a reading area comes into operation, and orders for technical journals are placed.

Along the way, he has to tackle several bureaucratic hitches. Initially it starts operating in a small way as completion takes time. By early 1980, however, NIT boasts a state of the art library with a fine selection of material on transportation and other fields. It is the one place at NIT about which hardly any student or staff complains.

Occupational Safety: I have just read Daniel Berman's revealing book *Death on the Job* (Berman 1979). It tells me that even in the economically advanced nations, workers face major occupational and safety hazards which take a heavy toll on life and limb. The officialdom and corporations tend to play down the problem. Under reporting is commonplace.

What is the situation in Tanzania? In particular, what kind of workplace accidents occur in the motor vehicle repair shops in the country, and at what rate? I am aware of the poor state of statistics in Tanzania in general. I thereby do not expect the data in the official reports on this matter to be accurate or complete. Looking into this issue should of the task of the Department of Motor Vehicle Mechanics at NIT. But they are asleep at the wheel.

By this time, as explained later, I am in good terms with the students in that department. Summoning several of them to my office, I propose that in their next field attachment, they can be posted to various motor vehicle workshops in Dar es Salaam to conduct research on this vital topic. I can assist them with designing the research plan, data collection forms and doing final analysis of the data. They are enthusiastic as it is the first time their field attachment will have a concrete plan. I talk to their head of department and tell him that I will make the arrangements with the companies, the student assignments and supervise them. Since it takes a burden off his shoulders, he takes no time in giving his approval.

Some fifteen students participate in this project, and a detailed report describing the work conditions, safety problems and recommendations is written (Hirji and NIT Students 1980). It is the outcome of the first fully fledged and systematic field research done at the NIT. It has been done at minimal cost with the students doing the data collection in the course of their regular practical training. The students who took part tell me that it has been a highly instructive experience. The data from the research are analyzed in a statistically appropriate manner. As the Chairman of the NIT Research and Consultancy Committee, I set a precedent. It is my hope that it will stimulate the instructors to conduct well planned scientific research of relevance to the nation. Our report, printed as Research Report No. 1 of NIT, is placed in the library. This happens just before I depart from NIT.

Hiccups: In the first five years of its life, other than confronting the developmental hurdles of the sort I have described, the staff and students at NIT also encounter internal impediments on a regular basis. They largely stem the fact that the Principal has priorities other than academic excellence and efficient use of the scarce resources at our disposal.

For example, there is a chronic shortage of paper instructors can use for class handouts. Yet, Mr Sanga issues printed notices and pronouncements almost on a daily basis, often dealing with non-consequential matters. Where three copies placed on the noticeboards are sufficient, he sends a copy to each instructor as well. Ensconced in his secluded corner, he wants to issue a daily reminder as to who is the boss around the place. I suggest that only one copy be sent to each department, and the paper be used on both sides. My words, however, just irritate him.

Mr Sanga previously headed educational institutions but has little transport related experience or knowledge. Yet, he comports himself as an expert in the field, tending to second guess the academic staff. I have to fight for funds for books yet money for superfluous office equipment and out of town trips by senior personnel is always at hand. Educational visits to local transport sites are delayed because trip scheduling for our two buses is done in an erratic manner. And this at a place that teaches transport logistics! And so on.

One issue over which places us at loggerheads on an annual basis is the criteria for admission into the diploma program. Though they are clearly set down in our brochure, he wants me to relax them so as to admit more mature age entrants. It will generate more revenue as their sponsoring organizations will pay the fees. I resist him on the ground that merit must be the primary eligibility criterion for admission. Else, dubious practices may sneak into the process. What is the point of having a student who cannot adequately grasp the material in our courses? Will we change our pass/fail level for him or her? Yet, Mr Sanga persists: 'Hirji, you are too rigid.' But as long as I have a say, financial considerations do not supplant the academic ones.

Complaints about cafeteria services and the upkeep of student residence halls abound. Favoritism affects the hiring of support staff. A dark tale is afoot about the Principal's secretary. A new one comes aboard from time to time, a dainty, young girl who usually is not that competent. A few days on the job, and she is as big headed as if she is the boss. Even heads of departments find their work unduly delayed. Rumor has it that she accompanies the Principal to entertainment venues after work hours. But I cannot verify it one way or the other.

And something is seriously amiss in the Department of Motor Vehicle Mechanics. In practical terms, Mr Billa, the Head, is an undisputed expert. He can take the engine of a heavy duty truck apart and rebuild it seamlessly to make it run like new. He is an able, friendly instructor. But as far as administration goes, he is on shaky grounds. Things like teaching schedules, arrangements for field attachment and student evaluation are not done as needed and on time. And strange anomalies occur. Capable students at times get low grades and poorly performing ones get high grades. The students complain but to no avail. I hear about this and more through my students.

Inevitably, the matter reaches a point of no return. One day in 1978, I hear a loud commotion down below. As I descend the stairway, I see all the students from that department in the corridor. They are visibly angry. Many are shouting. Mr Sanga and Mr Billa are trying to persuade them to return to class but they are adamant and refuse to heed his call.

Finally, he asks them to be patient. He will convene a meeting of the NIT Management committee right away to look into the matter. So the three heads and the Principal gather, in a gloomy atmosphere.

> *What is going on, Mr Billa?*

> *I am not sure, Mzee. I think they are being incited by a few trouble makers.*

I cannot let that usual excuse pass.

> *We should appoint a Committee of Inquiry to determine the full story. Otherwise, we are risking a full scale strike.*

All eyes are on me, none too kind. That sounds distinctly disconcerting. Aware of my good rapport with the students, Mr Sanga sees how he can turn the situation to his advantage.

> *Let us assign Mr Hirji to lead the inquiry. It will calm down the students.*

He is prescient. When the decision is announced, students return to class. I feel Mr Sanga wants to buy time. The process may take a while. Eventually, my report can be implemented in part and shelved. And life will go on. Sensing his possible shenanigans, I also have a plan up my sleeve.

I am the only person in the commission of inquiry. Not discouraged, I begin the work that afternoon. For a week, I set aside all else except teaching. I slog late into the evenings, interviewing students, instructors and Mr Billa. I examine departmental and instructor records. In five days, I have sufficient evidence to make a case. Two days later, I submit my report.

I find several problems with adherence to the curriculum: some topics are taught repeatedly while some important ones are barely covered. Instructors lack clear guidance on setting assignments, exam questions and practical work evaluation. Paperwork for field attachment is oftentimes delayed. The major problem is maintenance of student records. What is in the instructor's book can be at variance with what is noted by the Head and that too may differ from what the secretary types. No checking is done. Hence the anomalies observed by the students.

Problems are numerous: The conclusion is evident. The department is not being run as it ought to be run. Mr Billa bears the responsibility for the mess. Though I do not say it explicitly, a new head has to be found. The management does not welcome my findings. Mr Billa defends himself by saying that no one is perfect and that the errors I show are few. Mr Sanga agrees and declares that my conclusions are hasty. There is a need for additional investigation, they all conclude.

The committee wants to bury my report. But I have guarded against it in advance. I had leaked a copy to the President of NITSO. Further, I send a copy to Fatma Alloo, a reporter with the *Daily News*. She comes to the NIT campus to interview the students. Much to the embarrassment of the Principal, the crisis at NIT becomes front page news.

There is no other alternative now. It has to be seen by the public that remedial measures are being taken. He issues a statement saying that a few serious but unintentional problems have been detected through an inquiry he had authorized. Steps are being taken to remedy them.

And steps are taken. Records are rectified. Instructors are assigned administrative responsibilities normally discharged by the Head. Things run more smoothly. But Mr Billa stays on as the Head. In part, the students are mollified; in part, they grumble on, but among themselves.

Within our department, I recall one dismaying incident. It is 1977. I am supervising the exam in transport statistics. The Principal's secretary enters the room: 'The Mzee wants you in his office. It is urgent.' I rush down. The boss has to send off the annual budgetary request to the NTC. He asks me to verify some items. Back in the exam room in ten minutes, I find the class silent. Each person is immersed in his/her own script.

As I mark the scripts at home over the weekend, what I find dismays me. I had set one difficult question in order to demarcate the diligent, smart students from the average ones. Yet, all have done it well. It does not smell right. All have employed an identical approach. All have the same six digit answer, stated up to four decimal digits. But there is an error in the final computation. The answers in all the scripts are erroneous in an exactly identical manner.

To have the same correct answer in twenty five scripts, while unusual, is within the realm of possibility. But to get a wrong answer within that number of scripts in the way described is not. The probability of such an outcome arising by chance alone is somewhere in the region of 10^{-150}, a tiny number less than one in which 149 zeros after the decimal point are followed by the digit 1. Something fishy has transpired. The next day I summon the class. I am visibly angry.

> *I know that when I was out of the room, all of you copied the answer to Question 5. You copied it from Mr X.*

They look down in shame. No one denies my charge.

> *I trusted you, and you have let me down.*

At this point, Mr X and another student have tears rolling down their faces. A student stands up.

> *We are extremely sorry, Mr Hirji. We made a big mistake. It will not happen again.*

I feel that they are genuinely remorseful.

> *Well, I will set a new exam. You have to take it tomorrow.*

Other than this, I do not recall any serious issue involving the students in our department. A class without stragglers who want to get by with minimal effort is a rarity. NIT is not an exception to this universal rule. Yet, in the five batches of students I teach at this institute, I have mostly diligent students putting in due and satisfactory effort in theory and practical work. Their relations with the instructors are on the amicable side. In each batch, I become particularly cordial with two or three socially aware students, who, once in a while, visit me at home for general socio-political discussions. The current editor of *The Transporter* is one of them. A cooperative, harmonious relationship prevails among the instructors as well. In the presence of the venerable Mr Hussain, the atmosphere is always jovial. His usual refrain to me is: 'Cheer up, Karim, you're too serious.'

TRANSPORT IN TANZANIA

During the long vacation, each first and second year student at NIT is attached to a transport company or organization in Tanzania. Most of these entities are public firms spread across the expanse of the nation. Besides undertaking the duties assigned by the company, the student has to write a report on how that firm is functioning and the work he or she did. An instructor from NIT pays a visit, at least once, to make an on-the-spot assessment of his or her work.

I go on supervisory visits for four years. Twice I am in the Northern Zone, supervising students in Moshi, Arusha and Tanga regions; once I traverse the Tanzania Zambia Highway, visiting students in Iringa and Mbeya regions and then all the way to Lusaka to supervise a student from Zambia. Once I elect to remain in Dar es Salaam, visiting students not in my department, but in the Department of Motor Vehicle Mechanics (The reasons for this are described elsewhere).

My teaching practice supervisory visits at UDSM taught me about how secondary schools in Tanzania were functioning. Correspondingly, the NIT supervisory visits give me lessons on the state of the transport sector in Tanzania that I could not have garnered from any book or report.

In each area I visit, an NIT student is attached with the local Regional Transport Company (RETCO). A typical RETCO has a fleet of twenty or more buses and trucks operating within the region and adjacent regions. During these three to four days of the visit, I initially meet the managerial personnel. They tell me what the student has been assigned to do and how well or not he or she has been doing.

My student shows me around. We visit the offices, depots and garages. I am informed about the company, his/her work and the challenges he or she has encountered. It gives me a chance to converse with office staff, drivers, bus conductors and mechanics. On two visits, I am at the local branch of the Tanzania Railways Corporation, where an NIT student is on field attachment.

My students know that I stand on the side of the underdog, that is, with students and workers. In addition to getting the official story, I thereby get frank opinions about that company from the other side of the workplace equation.

In general, it is a disappointing tale. Despite being publicly owned, the company runs like a typical capitalist entity. The national policy enshrined in the *Mwongozo* gives the workers a say in decision making and operating the company. In truth, it is a policy devoid of substance. What the boss says goes. Whoever takes issue with that is shown the door.

Lower tier workers are dissatisfied with pay and benefits. The long work hours on road trips are inadequately compensated. Comparing their poverty laden lives with the perks of the senior management, they ask, 'What kind of *Ujamaa* is this?' No wonder, industrial actions like work stoppages surface now and then. At times, when a manager is clearly exposed to have acted recklessly, causing major losses to the company, he is transferred to another post. Appropriate disciplinary, financial or criminal sanction is imposed but once in a blue moon.

Under such circumstances, the company is generally run in an inefficient way. Maintenance schedules for vehicles are not followed. Theft of spare parts and other items is common; a lot of funds are misspent; corruption at the top abounds. The workers talk of the collusion between private businessmen and company officials to defraud the public. Spare parts are not ordered on time, leading to cannibalization. The vehicle inventory is smaller. Records for operations like cargo and passenger loads on the trips, fuel consumption, tire and battery replacement, and trip revenues are riddled with gaps and errors. The data on company operations often are kept using faulty units and aggregating methods.

Another crucial shortcoming that makes a strong impression upon me from the field attachment visits is the lack of intra- and inter-sectoral integration. There is no centralized policy for ordering trucks, buses and smaller vehicles for the companies operating under the NTC. One RETCO has Italian vehicles, another Swedish, another British and so on. Where to get them is decided by the external financier. A policy of say two vehicle manufacturers for the whole system could drive down costs through economies of scale and enable the system to utilize a well stocked spare parts, tire and battery depot. If the vehicles are selected on the basis of appropriate technology, manufacture of some spare parts locally could be done. That is how it should occur in the context of a planned socialist economy.

It is not uncommon to witness oversupply of vehicles at one time and location and under supply at another. Where agricultural commodities are piled up, there are not enough trucks for the job, and elsewhere, trucks lie idle. There is a Ministry of Planning but it basically specializes in World Bank style financial estimation, allocation and projections.

The issue of keeping appropriate and accurate records tends to bring our students in conflict with the management. Having learned these techniques at NIT, they are eager to apply their knowledge to remedy the problem. But when they make a suggestion for improvement, it falls by the wayside. If they persist, they are told not to meddle in tasks they have not been assigned. It dawns upon them that there is a sound reason for not keeping accurate records. Good records expose bad deeds, an outcome no typical manager seeks. His philosophy is to let the sleeping dogs lie. The problem is not lack of knowledge but lack of good intentions. Invariably, I find dejected students with long tales of how they tried to make such and such positive contributions but failed to make any headway.

The existing management views our students as a potential threat to their status. When they graduate, they might replace the clearly inefficient fellows. Hence when our graduates join the state companies as full time employees, they regularly find themselves marginalized and frustrated. Play our game, join the club, else you will not get anywhere: that is the unmistakable message they get.

I can provide no better instance of this tendency than the case of AK. He joins our diploma program under the sponsorship of the TRC. Upon graduation in 1978, he returns to the corporation and is placed in the planning and logistics unit. At NIT, he was a bright, diligent student. With TRC, he is a dedicated employee often taking steps beyond those directed by his superiors. Subsequently, he is sent for higher studies in the UK. As a part of this study program, he does an extended internship with British Rail.

I reconnect with him in early 1989, having just returned from the USA. I find him hunched over his desk in a basement office at the TRC HQ that lies across the DSM railway station. He is quite pleased to see me. After telling each other about what we have been up to in the decade past, and the whereabouts of mutual friends, we turn the present day.

> *The TRC has got a multi-million dollar loan from the World Bank to computerize many of its operations. The project has begun, and I am involved in it on a more than full time basis.*

For Tanzania, these are the very early days of wider utilization of such technology. Pointing to the clutter of paper and printout in each corner of his room, he adds:

> *It is a demanding assignment, but my experience at British Rail has given me sufficient background to implement it.*

I am proud that my former student has developed such expertise. But, instead of sharing my expression of joy, he seems pensive.

> *Mwalimu, to tell you the truth, I am not happy.*

> *What is the problem?*

> *A World Bank expert is in charge of the project. He is my boss, yet he knows so little about computerization of a railway system. He always asks me: how do you do this and how do you do that? In practice, I run the show.*

He pauses for a second before continuing.

> *Despite the hard work I do, I do not get any credit. In the meetings with the management, I am ignored. But when he speaks, they are attentive. He presents my ideas as if they are his own. It is quite frustrating.*

> *That is terrible.*

> *And he is paid US $6,000 per month, not counting the benefits. What do I get? Just a meager US $100 per month. It is a big joke, Mwalimu.*

The outcome of such demoralization is inevitable. AK hangs on to that job for a while before throwing in the towel. Ditching the profession in which he has become one of the foremost experts in the nation, he enters politics to eventually get elected as a member of parliament for the ruling party. He serves his constituency well and is a popular, youthful MP. At times, he fall preys to infighting among those who jockey for power and position by hook or crook. But he has gained the ear of the man at the top. In the 2000s, under the Kikwete administration, he is appointed the Head of the Parastatal Reform Commission (PRC).

There is more than a touch of irony here. The mission of PRC is to privatize state owned companies and service entities. It is a policy that the World Bank and IMF have, through the financial muscle they exercise, forced all the nations of Africa to adopt. In Tanzania, as elsewhere on the continent, it is executed in a way that can only be described as grandiose daylight robbery. Valuable public assets are transferred to mostly foreign firms at ludicrously low prices; influential local businesses and senior bureaucrats also secure windfall gains. The valiant promoters of free market capitalism, from the UK to the USA, from Norway to Sweden, herald this 100% corrupt process as 'real economic reform' and lavish accolades on the leaders overseeing the demolition of their nation's ability to stand on its own feet.

I am not happy to see one of my stellar students at NIT taking charge of this nefarious project. Moreover, he does that under the Kikwete administrations which is now known beyond doubt to have been home to numerous multi-billion shillings' worth of corrupt and shady practices in all sectors of the government and the economy.

Paradoxically, it is under AK's stewardship that the TRC, his earlier home-base, is partly privatized to a company from India. It does not take long for the move to turn into a veritable disaster for the local stakeholders, namely, the users of the rail service, the employees of the TRC and the state treasury. As the foreign management prioritizes quick enrichment of the parent company in India, it neglects the task of creation of efficient, affordable railway services in Tanzania. Passengers and customers with long distance cargo face erratic schedules under rising costs, disaffected workers are perpetually on strike against an insensitive management. At times, the treasury has to bail out the loss making corporation. Like the other privatization schemes, this one has propelled the nation from the frying pan into the fire. Rail service reaches a crisis point in a few years, leaving the government no option but to repossess the corporation. A hobbled, but crucial entity has to be reconstructed from the base. And it comes at a steep cost to the public. That it was a fiasco overseen by an erstwhile nationalist with expertise in the operations of railways adds a distressful dimension to the episode.

Not that it is a unique episode. Most NIT graduates I knew faced similar conditions. They started off at their places of work with enthusiastic diligence, keen to apply what they had learned to promote company and national development. Most received a cold shoulder and were cornered into routine tasks. Sadly, only a very few stuck to their principles. The majority joined the system of bureaucratic bungling and self-enrichment.

The transport sector in Tanzania, and especially its publicly owned segment, remained in the same unsatisfactory state as if there was no NIT. Despite the well trained planners, management personnel, mechanics, drivers and bus conductors injected into them by this one-of-a-kind Institute, the large transport firms under the NTC and all the regional transport companies remained grossly inefficient entities that eventually ran aground.

+ + + + + + +

Comment: In the *Ujamaa* era, the talk was about 'Revolution by Education.' Today, it is about 'Transformation by Education.' The experience with NIT and a host of training institutions established in Tanzania demonstrates the fallacy of such talk. Transformation by education can occur only if accompanied by complimentary transformations in the social, economic and political facets of society. If the ruling party elite, senior state officials and the heads of economic enterprises lack a concrete sense of direction and if the people remain politically alienated, then an educational institution, however relevant and distinguished, can at best exercise only a marginal impact on the economic development of the nation. In fact, by producing a cadre of misemployed, underemployed or unemployed youth, it may lead to profound disharmony and social conflict.

+ + + + + + +

FAMILY AND PERSONAL AFFAIRS

When I join NIT, I am not allotted a staff quarter. We stay for a couple of months with my parents, a couple of months with Farida's mother, six weeks housewarming a comrade's flat at the UDSM campus, etc. In the midst of this instability, our family experiences two calamities. In March 1976, NIT students are on a short break. We visit my student day comrades in Moshi. After a pleasant week, we are headed home on the night bus. Around midnight, our bus collides with a truck carrying heavy logs. More than ten of our fellow passengers die on the spot. Farida sustains minor bruises. Rosa is thrown out from the back window into the bush. Yet, by some miraculous interplay of gravitational dynamics, there is not a tiny scratch on her body. I have a long gash above my forehead and am bleeding profusely. Passing vehicles ferry all passengers, alive and lifeless, to the nearby Korogwe Hospital, where my wound is stitched up. A Bohora family graciously takes us to their home in the morning, and feeds us a sumptuous breakfast. By evening, Farida's brother and a friend arrive from DSM in a car to take us home.

Barely two weeks after this accident, Farida is in the kitchen to warm up milk for Rosa. Unfortunately, the gas pipe has sprouted a leak overnight. There is a loud explosion just as she lights a match, and she sustains deep burns on both legs. Usually, Rosa runs after her mummy into the kitchen. By a miraculous operation of human behavioral dynamics, today she did not.

Farida is discharged from hospital after three days. But her wounds get infected. She is feverish; oral antibiotics do not help. It is on the verge of becoming critical. Luckily, a wise doctor prescribes application of potassium permanganate solution on the burn area. I do that twice a day after work. It is a laborious task. The solution has to be applied with a small brush between the numerous tiny bits of the crusted skin on both legs. The sting is sharp and painful. Yet, Farida bears it with a brave face for nearly ten days. Finally the germs are vanquished, the fever abates, and we breathe a sigh of relief. Complete healing takes over a year. The stretching of the skin over the burn area is at times so distressing as to keep her awake late into the night.

NIT allocates me a house in the Mikocheni area in June 1976. It is, however, too far from where my parents live. They have been taking care of Rosa much of this time. The house is in an isolated location. Safety is an issue. Farida has applied for a job. If both of us go to work, who will take care of the girl?

Just then, my father, in all his magnanimity, comes up with an ideal solution. Some three hundred meters from their place and on the same road, a two story flat is on the market for TSh 54,000, or approximately US$ 5,400. I have TSh 12,000 in the bank. He grants us the remaining amount. The deal is done and, in early July 1976, we move into our new abode. (It is in the same place that I write these words in 2018.)

Farida is employed as a secretary with the Kibo Paper Company. Our family settles into a decent routine. Kristina, our maid, clocks in early each weekday morning. A short while later, Farida boards her company bus and I ride to work on the NIT bus. On his way to his shop in Kariakoo, my father takes Rosa to a nearby nursery school. He collects her during the noon hour and takes her to his place. My mother is happy to pamper and over feed her precious granddaughter.

Rosa is brought home around two in the afternoon. Kristina gives her a bath and puts her to sleep. Farida returns from work around 4 pm, and I come home between 5 and 6 pm. Kristina cooks well. Hence on most days, a decent evening meal lies in wait. In all my five years at NIT, apart from a bout of measles and a couple of infestations with worms, Rosa remains in robust health. But we have to guard against a quirky tendency: the moment your attention is diverted, she puts whatever is in front of her straight into her mouth. And she has an affinity for small shiny or colorful things. Twice, a marble lodges in her throat. Luckily, I am right there. Both times, I hold her upside down, thump her back with vigor, whereby it is dislodged and ejected.

During these times, we host comrades from UDSM and elsewhere on Sundays. A discussion on a book we have read or on current socio-political affairs is topped by a sumptuous lunch of *pilau* and *kachumbaro*. Rosa, however, is the star attraction for the guests.

Apart from her burn injury, Farida is in a tiptop shape. At work, she is valued as a diligent, conscientious, and efficient employee. In 1979, she is sponsored by her company to pursue a Certificate in Management and Administration study program at the Mzumbe Institute of Development Management. It is a nine month program. The institute lies about 180 kilometers from DSM.

Never having been away for an extended period, she is apprehensive at first. But it does not take time for her to bond with her classmates. Water supply in the student dorms is unreliable, and cafeteria food is not too appealing. So they cook in their room now and then, and find creative ways of dealing with the other challenges. We have relatives in the nearby Morogoro town. That helps. Studies are demanding, but class friends help one another.

In those nine months, Rosa and I see her only every other weekend. That is, apart from the two short vacations, each lasting three weeks. In the final phase of her program, she has to do on-site research with an industrial firm. By a stroke of chance, she is posted to the *Urafiki Textile Mill*, which not only is in DSM, but is as well located right next to NIT. The entire family rejoices the day she is awarded a deserved certificate by none other than Mwalimu Nyerere.

In terms of health, my story purses another trajectory. In Sumbawaga, I was in stellar shape, able to endure many a trying circumstance with ease. In DSM, I am beset by a multiplicity of ailments that worsen over time. It starts in mid-1976 with acute sinusitis which leads to fever and acute bronchitis. These attacks recur, about every four months. I take antibiotics as if they are candies. A dry cough turns persistent. One doctor says I have TB, and puts me on anti-TB drugs. The side effects are not pleasant. Careful tests at the Muhimbili Hospital reveal it was a misdiagnosis. A year later, I am admitted to this hospital in order to flush out my excessively congested sinuses. It just provides a temporary respite.

Then come recurrent backaches, leading to X-ray upon X-ray, and bottle upon bottle of pain pills. Happily, this condition resolves after a good doctor, the same one who had shown us the remedy for Farida's infected burns, shows me a series of exercises to alleviate back pain. I adhere to his advice to the letter. Soon that pain is history. His wise guidance serves me well to this day.

Not that I am off the hook. In 1978, I start getting heartburn on a daily basis. It settles into an established case of duodenal ulceration. Medications only partly reduce my distress. I walk around with a pack of biscuits; the moment I feel a pang of hunger, I pop two into my mouth.

By early 1980, physically speaking, I am in the doldrums. The cumulative effect of the huge work load, in the form of a multiplicity of responsibilities, that I have been carrying since the inception of NIT is leading me to a state of physical and mental exhaustion. Yet, there is no end in sight. I need time off from the unrelenting stress.

Further, a distinctly sour atmosphere now prevails between the NIT administration and myself. In the first two years, due to my persistent stand against bureaucratic inefficiency and waste, and for making student interests a priority of the first order, the Principal had considered me a thorn to be avoided or ignored. After my investigations into the student unrest in the Department of Motor Vehicle Mechanics, I become Public Enemy No 1. He now isolates me as much as he can. If there is an out of town trip or conference, I am not chosen even if I am the ideal choice. When important visitors come to NIT, I am not invited to the table. NIT has a staff training program. Scholarships can be availed through the Ministry of Transport or the NTC. He knows that I want to get a doctoral degree in statistics. But no opportunity is sent in my direction. No doubt, it is sheer vindictiveness. I am lucky that my promotion to Senior Instructor came through just before this crisis; else he would have jockeyed to delay it. Students and staff are aware of his hostility towards me.

For reasons of poor health, excessive work stress and further education, I decide to strike out on my own. I also want my family to see the world.

Over this time, I have developed a keen interest in medical statistics. What I have read in relation to my own ailments no doubt cemented that interest. I send in an application to enroll in the Master of Science in Biostatistics at Harvard University in Boston, USA. It is a two year program, I aim for it to be a stepping stone into the doctoral degree program. I as well apply for the Harvard Agakhan scholarship. Administered by Harvard, two scholarships are available every year to eligible students of Muslim background from all over the world. Competition is stiff. But on the strength of my GRE results and educational record, I gain admission into Harvard as well as get the scholarship.

As I present this to Mr Sanga, he has no choice but to grant me study leave. Else, he knows that I will tender my resignation. He does not want to lose a useful work horse. As I leave his office, he manages to utter a barely audible word of good luck.

I am scheduled to depart for Boston in early September. I hope Farida and Rosa can join me three months later.

FAREWELL BASH

When they get the news, the NIT instructors congratulate me and wish me well. I hear the students are a bit dismayed. But they remain silent, and continue to interact with me as if nothing is afoot.

It is the final days. I pack my papers and books in my office and set aside that which I will give to the NIT library. Major Gama, the President of NITSO enters:

Mwalimu Hirji, we have organized a farewell party for you. Can you and Mrs Hirji attend?

He hands me a typed note of invitation. I am pleasantly surprised.

Of course, we will attend. This is very nice of you.

On the day of the party, Farida and I are at the NIT campus just after 6 pm. Shiraz Ramji, who has been a part-time instructor at NIT, is with us. The program indicates an elaborate three hour event (see below). Major Gama escorts us to the venue. As we enter, pleasant Taraab music delights our ears. The place is packed with NIT students. The instructors from my department sit at the front. Anthony Kondella, the head, is also present.

Senior administrators and the heads of the other departments have chosen not to attend. The Principal is to give a short speech but he has other priorities. NITSO had wanted to hold the party in the main hall of the new complex. But the facilities manager did not approve the request saying that the event lacked clearance from the Principal.

So we are in the student recreation room in the wooden block. Though congested, it is a fitting place since that is where I had held my first class in 1976. All present are in ebullient spirits, unshaken by the petty insults from a petty personality.

Program: Farewell Party for Ndugu KF Hirji
NIT Bar, 28 August 1980

TIME   EVENT
18:30 Arrival of Guests (soft Blues/Taarab Music)
19:00 A Word: Chairman of Organizing Committee
19:05 Speech: NITSO Minister for Education
19:10 Speech: Head of Department of Transport Management
19:15 Speech: NIT Principal
19:20 Soft Music

19:30 First Poem – Mr Shabani
19:35 Music – NIT Orchestra
19:45 Amusement Show
19:50 Boxing Show
20:05 Music: NIT Orchestra
20:15 Second Poem: Mr. Riwa
20:20 What NIT Students Say
20:35 Third Poem: Kichekesho
20:40 Amusement Show
20:45 Gifts Presentation
21:00 Speech: Ndugu KF Hirji
21:15 Soft Music
21:20 Shaking Hands with Ndugu Hirji
21:30 Program Closing (Official)

It unfolds as a colorful, joyous occasion with three speeches, three poems, live music, amusement episodes, presentation of gifts and handshaking (Photos in Appendix D). People dance during the musical interludes. To the delight of all, Farida joins in. The boxing match and the tummy-pillow fight are staged with a touch of hilarity. Mr Hussain enlivens the atmosphere further with his regular jocular interjections. I hear one after another student express appreciation for what I have accomplished at NIT, and several of them roundly denounce the administration for how it has treated me. I get a chance to say a few words at the end. But I am too overcome by emotion to say more than a few words. I just thank everyone for this wonderful party and wish the student success in their studies and lives. Below is one of the poems composed and recited by a student.

Farewell to Mr Hirji
by JWM Shabani, 28/8/80

Ladies, Gents, ... Let me tell you a story about a man.
He is a lecturer, ... An academician.
A friend of students, ... A simple man.
Indeed, he is a man of the people.
We love him, ... We admire him.
We enjoy his presence, ... We accept him.
He is nobody but Mr Hirji.
Come to the Institute, ... Ask for Hirji.
The transportants will show you.
The technicians will say they know him.
Mathematics for the technicians.

Transport Statistics for the transportants.
And not to forget the quantitative methods.
Mr Hirji, ... You are going back to school.
To learn more and come back with more knowledge.
We pray for you.
Your services shall be remembered.
Your dedication shall not be forgotten.
You were able to quench our thirst.
Thirst for knowledge!
Away you go, ... But we shall miss you.
Go well and come back safely.
May Allah be with you.

And this is a shortened and edited version of the speech of the President of NITSO.

Tribute to Ndugu KF Hirji
JB Gama, NITSO Chairman, 28/8/80

The students and members of staff of the National Institute of Transport are assembled here today in a reception to honor Ndugu Hirji who is soon going for further studies at Harvard University. We gather to express our appreciation for his exemplary work to further the academic and social life at NIT.

Ndugu Hirji joined this institute in October 1975. He played an essential role in the development of its academic program, enabling it to start in early 1976. He was later joined by Ndugu Hussain. They encountered many problems but managed to place the NIT onto a high academic standing. That is what we celebrate today.

Many qualified people in the nation have run away to more rewarding and satisfying jobs. He did not. Instead, he stayed and struggled. But now he is going for further studies.

His academic life here has been like a jack of all trades. His main subjects are Mathematics, Transport Statistics and Quantitative Methods. In addition, he has taught Transport Development and Planning, Transport Logistics, Economics and even Siasa. He has done all that with commendable results.

His devotion to students is equaled by his dedication to teaching. He sought to mint educated students instead of standardized robots. He is a simple man. He has helped us around the clock, in academic and social problems. Students go to him in his office, in the corridors and even to his home. We admire his intellect, sympathetic attitude and democratic approach. Even outsiders come to seek his help.

Ndugu Hirji has served the Institute in many capacities. He headed the Department of Transport Management, and served as the Librarian, Chairman of Research and Consultancy Committee, and Chief Adviser of the students' journal, The Transporter. His regular contributions to this journal are indicative of his closeness to the students.

He is not corrupted by power. He puts the interests of the majority before his own. Many times he has suffered for his defense of the truth. We cannot mention all he has done for NIT. It needs him more than he needs it. His unique scholarship, willingness to share knowledge and readiness to learn from them demands appreciation. That is why we are assembled here.

In that spirit, the students and staff of NIT would like to give him six presents that reflect his vision and spirit. They are our awards of honor to him.

The first two gifts are books on history and social analysis, the third is a Makonde carving representing a wise teacher surrounded by his students, the fourth is a pen to enable him to conduct his academic battles at Harvard University, the fifth is an NIT bag to remind him not to forget his students and the nation, and the last is a special gift for him from his close academic comrade, Ndugu Khalifa Afzal Hussein. They founded our academic program, and actively promoted it all this time. The material on our library shelves is indicative of that effort.

Finally, we all wish him a good time at Harvard University.

Farida and I are deeply touched by this grassroots expression of love, solidarity and appreciation. Students, not only from my department but also from the Department of Motor Vehicle Mechanics, have turned out in full force. The party has been organized at their own initiative and expense; the administration did not contribute even a cent. And what pains they have taken to make it a resounding success.

If I am asked to point out the foremost highlight of my four decades of teaching, I would say it was this spontaneous demonstration of love from my students. I have always regarded my students as a part of my extended family and have endeavored to do my very best for them. In the midst of the personal difficulties I had faced, I did not miss a single scheduled class at NIT. Rain or shine, the students knew that

Mr Hirji will be there. He works hard for you, so you better sweat away accordingly as well. And, with this farewell party, they are proclaiming in a loud, clear voice that they consider me as one of them. Despite the exhaustion and health effects I have endured, it has truly been worth it. There is no bigger award a teacher can aspire to.

EXIT

My arrival in Boston starts an over three decades long venture into the beguiling arena of health statistics. In that period, I will learn the subject in depth, teach it at leading universities in three countries, do extensive theoretical and applied research, and publish voluminously. My work will win a prestigious international award as well as bring me face to face with novel ethical conundrums. That tale, however, has to await another day. Here I note my final official interaction with NIT which occurred during that period.

In 1986, upon graduating with a doctorate in Biostatistics, I write a letter to Mr Sanga. I say that due to the nature of my specialization, it would be more appropriate for me to teach at a place where my training was of specific relevance. I also send a job application to the Department of Biostatistics and Epidemiology of the Faculty of Medicine of UDSM. This I do in the expectation that my earlier 'sins' matter no more. What will carry weight, I hope, is that I am the first Tanzanian with a doctoral degree in Biostatistics. And that in a nation where there are at most ten citizens with a master's level degree in that field. Hence I rate my chance of joining the Faculty of Medicine as quite high.

Mr Sanga does not wait to respond. In a strongly worded letter, he accuses me of violating the contract I had signed with NIT and absconding. Further, he tells me that if I do not return to NIT immediately, legal proceedings will be instituted against me. But he stands on shaky grounds. My subsequent reply makes three points. First, I am not absconding but seeking a transfer from one public educational institution in Tanzania to another. Second, by requesting his consent, I am following a procedure allowed by the contract. Third, according to that contract, for the first three years of my study leave, I would be paid a portion of my salary. I tell him that actually not a single cent was deposited into my bank account (This fact has been conveyed to me by my father). Turning the tables, I declare that it is NIT and not I who has violated the contract. I add that someone in the NIT finance office has pocketed the money due to me. Thus it is I who should report the matter to the police for appropriate action. After this I do not get any further communication from the venerable Principal.

Over the years, I have kept in touch with former students and colleagues from NIT. Several of them continue to visit me at home. Over a cup of tea, we muse about the good old days and damn the confounding modern times.

ON SELF-RELIANCE

It is apropos at this juncture to list the key developmental features of the National Institute of Transport during the first five years of its existence.

- It was financed through locally generated revenues.
- Its study programs, course curricula and organizational structure were formulated by local experts and stake holders.
- Reliance on foreign instructors was minimal. The two who were employed were selected on the basis of academic relevance and lower expenses.
- Local graduates in relevant disciplines were recruited and sent abroad for specialized training. By the end of 1980, the Institute had a decent number of qualified Tanzanian instructors.
- The training offered at the Institute was embedded within the national transport sector and economic policy.
- By 1980, the Diploma in Transport Management granted by the Institute had received international recognition.
- It was the only academic institution of its kind in sub-Saharan Africa and was beginning to attract students from neighboring nations.

Consider these features in the context of the national policy of Socialism and Self-Reliance. Elaboration of this policy for the educational sector was provided in the document *Education for Self-Reliance* (ESR). In Chapter 6, I presented the case that in secondary schools, ESR was implemented without appropriate plans, or practical guidance. A key shortfall was the lack of integration of ESR activities with the academic curriculum. The school system was thereby ensnared in an existential limbo, with profound dissatisfaction reigning among the students, teachers and parents.

The institutions of higher learning were as well not provided a coherent guide to implement the national policy. Each one was left to its own devices. In pedagogic and organizational aspects, each institution went on operating essentially as in the past. The occasional directive from above just made them scramble to show that what they were doing was aligned with the political mood of the day.

In this atmosphere of failure and fumbling, there were a few islands of exemplary achievement. Dedicated teachers in these schools initiated well planned and executed projects. Transparency and control over misuse and abuse of project resources sustained student enthusiasm and participation. For example, the ESR projects at the Kantalamba Secondary School in Sumbawanga were run in a reasonably successful manner. The proceeds from the school farm had enabled the opening of a student run shop on the school premises.

In the context of higher learning institutions, I hold that the noted features of NIT qualify it to be designated as an outstanding case of implementation of the policy of ESR. And this not just in terms of specific projects but together with the setup, operation and societal role of the institute. It operated in the spirit of self-reliance and, by producing skilled manpower, it served to enhance self-reliance in the national transport sector.

Yet, ultimately, it only achieved a small level of the success with respect especially the second goal. That was due to two primary factors. First, NIT functioned in a sea of trends in the transport sector and the national economy that entrenched external dependency. Second was the fact the existing management in the state transport firms and senior bureaucrats across the transport field were not receptive to the ideas and youthful enthusiasm of the graduates from NIT. Often, they were frustrated and sidelined. Be like one of us, or you will get nowhere — that was the message they got. Given the social pressures of the day, it is not surprising that many joined the system, and contributed to the eventual bankruptcy of the entire public transport. Only a few hardy NIT graduates swam against the conformist tide for quite a while and made meaningful contributions to the organizations and firms they worked for.

This type of outcome was also observed for many specialized educational establishments in the nation. You cannot create a revolution by education alone. If education, however sound and relevant, is not complemented by revolutionary trends in the key sectors of the economy, and a real transformation of the relationship between those in power and the ordinary people, it can not only lead to nowhere but can even backfire.

I end this chapter with a general remark on where NIT stands in 2018. It recently celebrated its 40th anniversary. It now has a much larger student body enrolled in a wider variety of programs and grants degrees. It trains many types of vehicle operators, and carries out vehicle inspections on behalf of the traffic police. And of recent, it has launched training programs for pilots and air services personnel. Indeed, to this day, it stands out as a unique educational establishment in sub-Saharan Africa.

Like the other higher education institutions in the nation, it underwent a marked decline in the 1980s. With the advent of the neo-liberal era, many institutions received more funds, particularly from abroad, and through student fees. Student numbers, buildings and facilities, and the variety of study programs increased. But the quality of education, as measured by a multiplicity of criteria, plummeted. Now you have graduates in literature or science who comprehend their subject at a level not that distant from that of a Form VI leaver of the 1960s.

I am not sure of the extent to which this general observation applies to the present day NIT. Has the quality of training it offers been diluted by quantity? It is not within the purview of this memoir to give a comprehensive history of the NIT. I leave that task to others who possess a much longer familiarity with it than I do.

But what I would like to say is that the lessons and features of the first five years of the life of NIT remain relevant to this day. The need to stress relevance to national requirements and promote self-reliance through usage of local manpower, funding, and creative thinking, and avoid 'donor' dependency is as crucial as ever. Self-reliance is not isolationism. It signifies resorting to external resources on our own terms, at our own pace and at our own price. It means not succumbing to the agendas and constraints set by foreign powers and the agencies they control. It means ditching policies that benefit a wealthy few and the multinational companies and adopting those that will develop the nation as a whole. And that applies to all sectors of the economy including transportation.

The fundamental message is a simple one: Either we stand and run on our own feet towards our goals, or interminably hobble about on crutches and just go round and round in a cycle of mass impoverishment.

9

THE ACADEMY TODAY

Teaching is not a lost art
But the regard for it is a lost tradition
Jacques Barzun

+ + + + + + +

I JOINED THE TEACHING PROFESSION in April 1971 and formally retired from it in July 2012. This book focuses on the first ten years of that forty one-year career. After the first decade, I entered a new field, medical statistics, obtained doctoral level training in it, and went on to teach and do research at universities in the USA and Tanzania. The story of that distinct period awaits a separate volume.

However, at this stage, I consider it appropriate to make a general comparison of how the current academic climate differs from what it was in the 1970s. That is because my final eight years of teaching occurred in a drastically altered academic environment, with the new changes being mostly deleterious in nature.

That is what I highlight in this chapter, which is divided into two sections. The first section narrates my extended encounter with an aspect of symbolism in education. Then I give specific examples of the changes I witnessed in the modern academy.

GOWNS AND GRADUATIONS

Our lives are peppered with milestones: entering a school, marriage, the birth of a child, the award of a special prize, onset of a major illness; to name a few. For the positive milestones, we celebrate, in private or public. The completion of any stage of education, especially higher education, is a key milestone generally marked by a formal graduation ceremony.

I passed my BSc degree exam in March 1971. The graduation ceremony was held three months later. The joyous occasion began with an academic procession. The graduates and academic staff were attired in academic gowns that reflected each person's academic status. Parents, friends and onlookers in the hundreds were on hand to witness the event. The Chancellor of the UDSM, President Julius Nyerere, conferred the degrees onto about four hundred candidates.

Even though I was one of a few who had a First Class Honors pass, I did not join this ceremony. While my classmates marched to the podium, I was in the crowd of onlookers selling the latest issue of a student magazine. While I was happy and proud to have overcome a major hurdle in life, I had serious reservations about how this event was organized. These were noted in a letter I had written to the editor of the main English language newspaper in Tanzania a few days earlier.

My first concern was that the nature of the ceremony reflected feudal European traditions. I understood why the University of Cambridge held such a ceremony. But should we ape them because we were colonized by the British? My outlook was not that of a blind Africanist who rejected everything foreign. There are many things of value we can and should adopt, adapt or learn from abroad. These include scientific and medical knowledge, organizational methods, literature and aspects of the education system. Feudal gowns were, in my view, not among them. We should conduct graduations in attires and in a manner reflective of local tradition. My other concern was that the ceremony reeked of elitism. In particular, it was not in line with the socialist values the nation was supposed to be promoting at that time. It symbolized a moment in the graduate's life history whereby he or she was certified as no longer one of the common folk. Though my letter was not published, I remained faithful to my words.

The stand I took at this juncture was but the beginning of an extended saga. My second chance to adorn an academic gown came in 1972, after the completion of my master's degree at the London School of Economics. But the issue was moot as I had returned to Tanzania before the graduation ceremony took place. The next occasion arose in 1982 when I was awarded the master's degree in Biostatistics at the Harvard School of Public Health in Boston. Held in the open courtyard adjacent to the main school building, it was a modestly colorful affair. Among the graduating class of about three hundred American and international students, some ten of us did not put on a gown. I was one of them. And when the graduation for my doctoral degree in Biostatistics was held at the same institution in 1986, I had left Boston.

Subsequently as a member of the academic staff of universities in the USA and Tanzania, I had numerous chances to participate in gown draped processions. I rarely attended these ceremonies, and when I did, it was as an onlooker without a gown. But there were two exceptions. While at UCLA in the 1990s, a student I had supervised was to be awarded the PhD degree in Biostatistics. It was customary that the supervisor joined the academic procession and was on the podium to confer the degree. So there I was, standing with other members of the faculty, ready to march. While everyone had put on an elegant gown that reflected his rank and alma mater, I just wore a jacket and a tie. Five minutes to the starting time, the secretary of the Dean of the School of Public Health approached me. She was concerned:

Professor Hirji, I have a right sized gown for you.

Thank you, but I do not need it.

Are you sure?

Quite sure.

She was dismayed at my response. Yet I was allowed to participate in the ceremony without any more fuss. I guess they were used to having a few oddballs around.

At the the Muhimbili University of Health and Allied Sciences (MUHAS) in Dar es Salaam, I once decided to participate in the annual graduation ceremony. It was a happy occasion for a class I had taught. A number of students had performed in an outstanding manner and I wanted to be there to celebrate the occasion with them.

The academic staff procession was to start from the main lecture hall. I was there on time, as were many of my colleagues. But I was the only one not attired in cap and gown, a fact that raised eyebrows and concerns. As we greeted one another, fellow academician and persons high up in the administration asked me why I had not been given a gown. Their first thought was that it was a bureaucratic oversight. When I said that it was my own decision and gave my reasons, some colleagues actually said:

But, professor, there is always a first time.

Most of them, including an associate dean, found my view an odd one. But no one expressed an objection to my taking part in the academic procession. There was also a lively discussion. Some colleagues agreed that graduation ceremonies had become trivialized. Our talk went on even as the academic procession began. We marched slowly to a half-way point and stopped. Here we were to wait until the guest of honor, President Jakaya Kikwete, had taken his place. After that we would march to the area reserved for the academic staff. As we waited, the Deputy Vice Chancellor for Academic Affairs approached me. With a stern face, he said he had a gown for me. When I declined the offer, he firmly told me that according to the university rules, everyone in an academic procession must put on the gown. No exceptions could be permitted.

Somewhat dismayed, I left the parade and joined the members of the public who had come to watch the event. My spirits were somewhat down, but I was glad that I had not compromised. In any case, I was getting tired under the hot sun. In fact, I did not stay on for the entire ceremony. After my students had been awarded their degrees, I slowly trekked back home.

None of my colleagues later raised the issue of my unceremonious ejection from the procession with me. I did not either. It was probably the only time in the history of the university that a senior professor had been humiliated in public. But I do not harbor ill feelings about it. It is an expression of the bureaucratic rigidity that has come to rule our academia. We pay lip service to academic freedom but clamp down on even a minor deviation from the norm. We meticulously stick to petty rules and regulations but blithely let substantive breaches of the required modes of teaching, research and professional conduct fester for years and years.

Some people adopt a symbolic stand in order to avoid positive action, or to mask misdeeds. Was my resolve to never put on an academic gown a purely symbolic stand, with no broader import? I wish it was so. Unfortunately, it is not. It is also a stand against the replacement of substance by form that has occurred throughout the education system, particularly at the top level.

Today kindergartens and primary schools have grand graduation events. What began as a trend in the USA has been copied by the nations of Africa. Tanzanian papers often carry photos of tiny tots standing and sweating in gowns under the tropical sun. It is a strange sight. What once was a mark of some sixteen years of educational achievement has lost its significance. In a nation beset with childhood poverty and malnutrition, the event expresses the vast social inequality prevailing today. Elite private schools mount fancy ceremonies while the poor students go to overcrowded schools without desks, sufficient number of teachers, books or toilets. For these schools, graduation ceremonies, with or without gowns, are but a dream. Graduating in ancient European feudal attire constitutes a sheer waste of resources that can be put to better use. No doubt, we should celebrate the fine accomplishments of our students. But let us not trivialize them. Let us have simple events that express a creative recourse to our own culture and traditions.

AN ACADEMY IN DOLDRUMS

In 1971, Tanzania had one university with the student population at less than three thousand. By 2017, there were nearly fifty public and private universities enrolling about two hundred thousand students. But this quantitative expansion has gone along with a serious qualitative decline. Accordingly, the marked rise of symbolism in the education system in Tanzania over this period has gone hand in hand with a dramatic decline in the standards of instruction and attainment. The extent of this deterioration at the university level is nothing short of astounding.

I give examples from my personal experience to illustrate the type of changes that have occurred during that period. My aim is not to cast blame on individuals but to point out the systemic nature of the problem. Hence I leave out specific identifying details but only note that what I narrate occurred at MUHAS between 2006 and 2012 while I was a Professor of Medical Statistics at this university.

Post-Graduate Students: My primary teaching assignment at MUHAS was a semester long course on Biostatistics and research methods for the class of postgraduate students pursuing specialties in public health, medicine, nursing, dentistry, pharmacy and other disciplines. It was a required first year course for them. Most other courses were taught under what is called team-teaching. I saw that at MUHAS this method lowered standards and led to inadequate coverage of the subject matter. Hence I always taught the entire course on my own.

In 1989, the number of students in my class was twelve; in 2012, it had burgeoned to one hundred and fifty! In itself, this is not a problem. Giving a lecture to ten or two hundred students requires more or less the same effort. But there are tasks like providing individual guidance, grading homework, continuous assessment tests, the final exam and the supplementary exam, and preparing the class report. At MUHAS, all this has to be done without any tutorial assistants.

A major difference between a postgraduate and an undergraduate course is that in the latter, the students are expected to take more initiative and tackle journal articles on their own. The instructor follows each student's progress through close interaction. But following that scheme is impossible for a huge class. Furthermore, as compared to the 1980s, the level of comprehension of the subject matter and the ability to express oneself in the English language among the recent students had declined precipitously. It was now common to give an article from say, a pediatrics journal, to a doctor now training to be a specialist in that field only to be told *Mwalimu, sielewi* (Teacher, I do not understand it).

These postgraduates had to be first taught what they should have learned at the undergraduate level. And despite all my efforts, half the class remained in the dark. The rule was that each course should have two continuous assessment tests. But to make the students aware of their weak points and improve the understanding of the topics, I set four tests, even though it entailed double the work on my part. The students did better if the test had questions that required purely memorization. But if there were questions that required reasoning and explaining the answer, the majority wrote down ungrammatical and incorrect answers that did not make any sense. Sometimes I wondered whether I was teaching a postgraduate class or a Form VI class.

Unethical Conduct: When, after a long absence, I restarted teaching this course in 2006, I found out that in the previous years, all the students had been sailing well through it. This was because it had covered undergraduate type of material and the exams were of a routine type and easy. Furthermore, there was quite a bit of cheating going on during the tests and final exam.

In order to prevent that I always set 10 different minor varieties of each test, and warned the students that it was risky to copy from the neighbors because they may not be doing the same test. Yet, each time, two to four students were foolish enough to copy. During marking, I would be able to catch them and also find out the persons they had copied from. All of them would get the score of zero points, a stern warning and their names were announced in class. Some students were also caught copying during a final exam. I made sure that it was reported to the higher university officials. Unfortunately, no action was taken against them, thus setting a bad precedent.

The academic staff were aware of such dishonest practices yet, apart from grumbling to each other, they did nothing to control it. When it was uncovered, they simply turned a blind eye. On one occasion, a group of diligent postgraduates wrote an open letter to the Vice Chancellor complaining about how copying in tests was easy for other courses and citing my course as the one where such a thing was not possible. They also noted an instance when the class had been left without an invigilator and rampant cheating had occurred. But apart from making me unpopular among my colleagues, the letter had no impact.

In the case of student research, unethical conduct in a variety of forms including plagiarism, using made up data and getting some other party to write the report has become widespread in the recent years. As a result of meticulous auditing of the research material of a postgraduate student project I was co-supervising, I was able to prove beyond doubt that most of the data had been concocted. I alerted the other supervisor and the Director of Postgraduate Studies about this problem. They agreed with my finding. The least that should have been done was to make the student redo the project. Yet no action was taken. The student got a passing grade and the degree. The authorities were afraid of opening a veritable can of worms and, in particular, of being accused of engaging in selective persecution. All the academic staff are aware of rampant dishonesty that affects student research today. However nothing is done to fight the situation.

Study Abroad: The Department of Epidemiology and Biostatistics at MUHAS was contemplating recruiting two tutorial assistants in Biostatistics who would be sent for master's and doctoral level training, possibly at the Harvard University.

Candidates with an upper class bachelor's degree in mathematics or statistics are needed. The relevant departments at UDSM are requested to send us recent graduates with high credentials. With twelve eager persons at our door, I am assigned the responsibility to evaluate them and recommend who is suitable. I often get the tasks for which there is no *bahasha* (envelope with cash). But I am happy to oblige.

The Travails of a Tanzanian Teacher

I interview the candidates one by one, spending one and a half hours with each. The academic transcript of everyone shines with A and A+ grades in a variety of basic and advanced courses in mathematics and/or statistics. At face value, each has an impressive record. So I begin:

What was your favorite subject?

Most say Multivariate Analysis or Data Analysis; a few mention Multivariate Calculus or Vector Analysis.

What was the textbook for this course?

The invariable reply is:

Oh, we did not have a textbook.

This is a major revelation. In my time at the same university, each course in the Faculty of Science had one or two required textbooks and one or two optional books, all of which were available at reasonable prices in the university bookstore.

So what did you have?

The lecturer gave us electronic or hard copies of the power point slides.

How many homework exercises did you do per semester?

One.

Then I ask specific questions about the favorite subject. For Multivariate Analysis, I ask:

Please write down the formula for the bivariate normal distribution.

He thinks for a while and replies:

Sorry, I do not recall that one.

What about the univariate normal distribution?

That too, I have forgotten.

I write the formula for the Poisson distribution on the blackboard and ask:

What is this?

It is the poison distribution.

The name is mispronounced.

Please derive the mean value of this distribution.

It is a task suitable for a Form VI class in statistics or applied mathematics. Yet this fellow with his honors level first degree fumbles for five minutes and gets nowhere. And that is how it went with all the candidates. All except one were total washouts. The one who stood out demonstrated Form VI level of competence and not much more.

After I submitted my report, our department selected, despite my reservations, this 'exceptional' candidate as a potential recruit. But since the administration did not make available the funds needed to hire him, the entire effort came to naught.

I narrated this episode in a public forum some time later. A professor from Ethiopia who has been teaching multivariate analysis at UDSM for over two decades was in the audience. He approached me when the session was over and made a frank confession:

> *Professor Hirji, you are quite right. I am the one who taught multivariate analysis to those students. We do not have textbooks. The background of the students is so poor these days. And the classes these days are huge. It is difficult to manage them. You literally have to spoon feed them. What can we do? Everyone teaches in that style now. In the end, basically everyone gets a passing grade. There is no point in giving supplementary exams. It is too much work and, in any case, they will fail again.*

When I applied to Stanford University, Oxford University and London University to pursue master's and/or doctoral study in mathematics in 1971, they requested the syllabuses for the courses I had done at UDSM. Upon receipt, I was accepted by all the three universities. It was up to me to choose where I wanted to go. In those years, the quality of education offered at UDSM in basically all fields was at par with education at leading international universities, and was recognized as such.

In 1974, a student I had taught at UDSM joined a program for the master's degree in mathematics at a leading Canadian university. Three months into his studies, he sent me a postcard:

> *Mr. Hirji, I am so grateful for what I was taught at UDSM. In comparison, the courses here are quite easy.*

When I joined the Harvard School of Public Health in 1980, I requested my academic adviser to exempt me from most of the first year courses because I had covered such material in my undergraduate years at UDSM. He granted my request but warned me that there was a qualifying exam for the doctoral program. I passed that exam despite the fact that I spent most of those two years in the medical school doing courses like anatomy and microbiology.

Today such things do not happen. Today a bachelor's degree in mathematics or statistics from UDSM does not enable one to pass the undergraduate courses in that field at any good university outside Africa. And it is a wide ranging problem. All fields are afflicted by the pathetic quantity and quality of knowledge displayed by the graduates of Tanzanian universities. Complaints about it are commonplace in our newspapers.

Symbolic Seminars: Just as the new academic year is about to start, we get a circular from the Dean of the School of Public Health. A week long seminar for the academic staff will be held from Monday onward. We are asked to attend and make presentations. The topic: Improvement of the student research being done at the school. From experience, I know that most seminars are not worth attending. They just distract us from paying due attention to teaching. But the topic of this seminar is an important one. So I not only plan to attend but also make a presentation on how to evaluate the quality of a research report. It is an area in which I have published papers in peer reviewed journals. My weekend is spent preparing my presentation and photocopying the material I plan to distribute.

On Monday morning, the Director of Postgraduate Studies opens the sessions by urging us to delve deeply into the issues and come up with viable solutions to a critical problem. His remarks are off-the-cuff, casual remarks that lack guidance in terms of what needs to be done. But he sets the ball rolling for what is going to become the main theme of the week: blame the students.

A short discussion later, it is time for a break. There is tea and coffee with warmed *samosa*, *mandazi*, *kabab* and fried bananas. In the next session, a senior professor makes his presentation. Other than snippets from his personal experiences, it is done in the same casual style and does not add new substance to what has already been said. A sumptuous lunch is then served. The attendance in the afternoon session falls dramatically.

And that is how it goes each day: vacuous presentations, superficial discussion but excellent meals. Thus, the Head of the Master of Public Health degree program thunders on about irresponsible students who do not want to put in the effort needed to conduct a valid research study and who take unethical short cuts. Yet he has zero information on the number and type of research projects annually being done in that program or the trend he has seen in terms of their quality.

There were, however, two exceptions. An invited lecturer from the Department of Education at UDSM formally summarized, using PowerPoint slides, the situation of the quality of student research at his institution and the steps being taken to raise it. My presentation as well used an overhead projector to explain how research quality is assessed in the context of systematic reviews and details a case study from my own published investigations. I am the only one to give out a handout of papers. From the third day onward, the afternoon sessions are curtailed altogether, and the seminar soon comes to a dribbling halt.

Other than taking us away from crucial tasks associated with teaching, what did this week long exercise achieve? No formal steps of binding nature were spelled out at the end. Though there had been a note taker from the Dean's office, no report of the seminar was circulated among the academic staff. In the following months and years, they go on with business as usual. No discernible improvement in the quality of student research being done at the School of Public Health was seen.

So, why was it held? For one thing, the academic and administrative staff got delicious free meals for a week. And we got attendance allowance. No wonder, such seminars are occasions whereby academics who otherwise are supposedly busy doing important research make an appearance. But probably there was another underlying consideration. Possibly an unspent grant of say US $20,000 from the Clinton Foundation or some such organization needed to be utilized by a deadline. What better way to spend it than on the issue of improving student research in the arena of public health?

Later, a glossy report to the funding agency would contain the seminar program, daily lists of attendees, a summary of the issues discussed and a breakdown of the associated expenses. The auditors from the agency would be satisfied that the money had been well spent for a good cause.

Yet what had transpired was a symbolic endeavor devoid of academic value, truly a waste of time and money. And it had occurred in an institution lacking funds in critical areas. How the conduct of the academic supervisors was contributing to the persistently high prevalence of substandard student research was an important issue completely neglected in the proceedings. Of recent, I regularly encountered final reports with vague or flawed objectives, an inappropriate study design given the objectives, faulty mode of data collection and in which the compilation, analysis and interpretation of the data had been done in rigid, erroneous style. Yet, all had been approved by the supervisor concerned.

Surprisingly, in our seminar no one complained about the high number of the candidates he or she had to supervise. Unlike in the 1970s, these days one gets the allowance of TSh 100,000 per project supervised. If you supervise five or more projects, you collect a handsome amount with minimal effort. Often the supervisor pays cursory attention to the research proposal and the final report, and the student gets away with shoddy work.

Once I was asked to chair the final defense of a student in the Norwegian financed and assisted Master of Health Policy and Management program. His topic related to the user experience with private health insurance schemes in Tanzania. Upon reading the thesis, I detected many major flaws. Basic information like the number of private insurance companies in the country, the size of their client base and their growth over time was missing. The number of subjects interviewed was too small. The questionnaire had sixty lengthy items but only twenty had been utilized in the report, and the conclusions drawn were questionable. I was convinced that this thesis was deficient to the extent that the entire project needed to redone. I was surprised to note the supervisor was the most senior health economist at MUHAS.

Besides the candidate and myself, the others at the defense were the supervisor, the internal examiner and the external examiner. The latter was a senior professor from the Ardhi University. I began the session by introducing all present and posing two questions of a general nature to the candidate. Then I gave the floor over to the internal examiner. He started by congratulating the candidate for tackling an important issue and doing a good job. He only had three questions of a superficial type for the candidate. Then it was the external examiner's turn. He too proceeded in an identical manner. It was apparent that each of them had probably taken a hasty look at the thesis this morning. So I began by outlining my principal concerns and posing a series of questions. The candidate was unable to give an acceptable reply to any of them. Thus, he said that only twenty questions had been used for data analysis because during the interviews, the subjects generally declined to proceed further. They had other things to do. Vital information was thereby not collected. Clearly he had not been given good guidance in terms of questionnaire design and the need for a pilot exercise.

My conclusion was that the whole exercise needed to be redone. The supervisor conceded that there were a few minor problems but not much more. In the end, I was outvoted. The candidate was given a passing grade subject to minor revision. This was the one and only time I was given the task of chairing a thesis defense. Reputation spreads; better leave this troublemaker out. Unless you fall in line and become a team player, no more *bahashas* for you.

Now and then, as I sat with my colleagues for morning tea in the common room, the clerk from the Dean's office would come with a bundle of envelopes in hand. Many of those present would get one. In formal terms, I outranked almost all of them. But I never got a *bahasha*. Even the junior staff knew: no *bahasha* for Professor Hirji. The message was clear: Attempt to do a decent job in the modern academy, and that is the price you will pay.

I was well liked by the students. They were regularly at my door for guidance on the design and analysis of their research. But it was always on an informal basis. While they valued my assistance, with one exception, no one requested me to be the supervisor or co-supervisor. I was known to be a no-nonsense fellow, and no wanted to risk a failing grade.

Dubious Foreign Experts: From the early days when it was a part of the UDSM, foreign academics and health experts working for long or short term basis have been a part of the MUHAS life. Up to the mid-1980s, they were of two different persuasions: a number expressed commitment towards the socialistic goats the nation had set for itself while the others had a liberal Western orientation. In any case, they were usually knowledgeable and experienced in their respective fields, and generally contributed well towards enhancing the scholarship standards at the university.

In the recent times, the situation has changed. Nowadays, it is common to find foreign experts who have a paternalistic or condescending outlook towards Africa. They come here mainly to further their own standing at the home institution. For many it is a chance to get a tropical holiday at the same time. And many among them possess questionable qualifications for the work they are supposed to be doing here.

Once I met two economists from Norway who were at MUHAS for a week to give lectures to the Master of Health Policy and Management degree students. When I asked them about the research they had done on health economics in developing nations, their reply was that their job was to teach basic economic theory which was universal. Not only is that a flawed conceptualization of economics but it also betrayed their paucity of knowledge about Africa. But there were here to guide us on managing our health system.

An incident: The announcement on the noticeboard says that a two-hour seminar on special methods teaching for public health disciplines is to be conducted by a professor from Boston University. She is part of a team from that has come here to assist us on such matters. Sounds interesting, I tell myself.

I sit in the front row to catch her every word. I expect she will enlighten us on how to inject new topics like evidence based public health, systematic reviews, genetics and participatory strategies for rural primary health into our teaching. Yet she does no such thing. There is hardly anything in her presentation that specifically deals with public health. She is a Professor of Education, not a Professor of Public Health! And her talk focuses on using participatory techniques of the type taught to school teachers.

I am thoroughly annoyed. At question time, I am the first one to speak up. I tell her frankly that I did not come to this session to be treated as a trainee primary school teacher. I mention the key issues that ought to have been covered but were not, noting especially the need to integrate relevant papers from health journals in an instructional style that oscillated between the theoretical and practical dimensions of the subject being taught. Careful selection of the papers by the instructor and giving electronic copies to the students at the outset was thus a central part of the teaching effort.

She was visibly disturbed by what I had said but was gracious enough to concede that the issues I had raised were quite important. The others in the audience, my colleagues, were also annoyed but at me, not her. This delegation from Boston University represented another pot of gold from America for the academics at the MUHAS School of Public Health. There were research grants, international travel funds and other perks. Insulting them was a risky, undiplomatic proposition. In order to reverse the damage I had inflicted, one after another of them rose up to praise the distinguished speaker and pose a distracting type of query.

The next day, the Boston University professor came to my office. With a friendly demeanor, she asked for concrete examples of a teaching style that oscillated between theory and application. I suggested that she attend some sessions of the postgraduate class I was teaching. To her credit, she came to two lectures and later thanked me for the opportunity.

In contrast, I note that during my time at MUHAS, I often requested the tutorial assistants and junior academics in my department to attend my lectures in order to learn how to integrate in an organic manner articles from the health literature into the teaching of medical statistics and epidemiology. Despite undertaking to do so, no one ever did.

I can give more examples of how dubious foreign experts and their projects only serve narrow agendas, and in the long run, harm the standing of local universities. The efforts of lecturers and professors are sidelined in the pursuit of easy dollars and vital pedagogic activities are neglected. Consequently, a vicious dependency syndrome based on questionable priorities comes to dominate our academic and research institutions.

Academic Irresponsibility: A picture similar to that painted above emerges from talking with academics from other universities in the nation. The local media features numerous stories about the low levels of knowledge and skill demonstrated by graduates from Tanzanian higher education institutions. At the newer universities, the malady is more serious. At MUHAS and UDSM, there are qualified and experienced academic staff but the essential pedagogic tasks are being neglected. At other places, an acute shortage of well trained staff is the norm. The senior most rank in an entire department may be assistant lecturer. And the publication record for the academics in such places is often shockingly poor.

The fundamental problem may be labeled an epidemic of academic irresponsibility. By and large, our academics do not uphold the primary tenets of the academy. They operate in ways that compromise academic integrity, and dilute the required standards of scholarship in instructional and research endeavors. Instead, they resort to shortcuts and put in the minimal effort required to maintain appearances. Often they overlook even egregious conduct of some colleagues.

In 1971, a professor at UDSM earned the equivalent of US$ 400 per month. By 1989, it had dwindled to half that amount. But the recent years witnessed a big rise. In the year 2012, the salaries of professors at UDSM and MUHAS exceeded US$ 2000. If you add in the multiplicity of allowances, payments from research projects, consultancy and private practice earnings, the professor can easily rake in over US$ 5000 on a monthly basis. No wonder many senior academics now own substantive real estate and commercial enterprises. The astounding fact is that the steep decline of university education has occurred at the same time as the academics have prospered.

On the one hand, with humongous class sizes and resource shortages, they have genuine complaints about the difficulties they face. The administrations regard the academy as a business. The more study programs and the more students there are, the greater the inflow of funds. In their eyes, having strict academic standards spoils the reputation of their institution. Students will be attracted to places where it is easier to get a degree. So unless they come under intense external pressure, they do not inquire too deeply into the issue of academic standards.

Yet the academic staff often use the constraints they face to avoid taking steps that can be undertaken in these conditions. For example, the lack of affordable textbooks is a common complaint. Yet, in this electronic age, many alternative solutions exit. For many disciplines, free textbooks can be downloaded from a variety of websites. But the instructor has to read them first and recommend a suitable one. In this day and age, even that is too much to ask. In my recent years at MUHAS, I never came across a professor with a book in his or her hands, or discussing a book in conversation with colleagues.

Another concern is the students of today have an aversion towards in-depth learning. Lecturers who teach only the basic material and set easy examinations are popular. Those who adhere to the required standards and make them work hard are not. But this is not the fundamental problem. If the teachers acted in a cooperative and concerted manner, it can be quickly turned around.

Many steps in that direction are available. For example, at MUHAS, we could use the WHO provided portal to access, download and print out papers from a large number of international journals that relate to the varied health and medical specialties. In that respect, the situation is much better than it was in the 1970s. Nonetheless, the academic staff use this facility only for writing their research and consultancy reports. Using it to enhance classroom instruction was a rare event.

For my postgraduate course, I would download about twenty relevant articles. I also had a detailed series of lecture notes and other material. All this stuff would be placed on a flash drive and given to the class representative at the beginning of the semester. While the students did not have books, each had a laptop computer. Copying the flash drive gave all of them a ready access to the material that would keep them busy for the duration of the course.

Adopting this teaching strategy required quite a bit of effort at the outset. In the subsequent years, that was not the case. Each year I made minor modifications to the notes and changed a couple of articles. During meetings and in person, I often mentioned what I was doing. But no one in the School of Public Health ever took a step in that direction.

There is a minority of academics who are dedicated to their profession and seek to teach at the level required for the course in question. But they are not encouraged or rewarded for their efforts. In fact, they are often placed in a disadvantageous position. A number of young assistant lecturers who begin by doing things as they should be done find themselves frustrated and embrace the practices of the easygoing majority.

The availability of external funds and presence of foreign experts has created a diversionary environment. The core academic activities thereby get much less attention than they deserve. The key thing is not to reject external assistance but to have our own primary agenda and to ensure that it is provided on our own terms and not terms set from outside.

Of recent, the academic standards at Tanzanian universities had become so low that it promoted the Tanzania Commission on Universities to stop about half of them from enrolling new students. But the remedial steps being taken only scratch the surface. But the rot is too deep and ingrained and affects the so-called top tier universities as well.

Without a gigantic, concerted discipline by discipline effort jointly undertaken by all the universities and regulatory bodies spanning over several years, we are bound to essentially remain where we are now. We have the qualified manpower and the intellectual wherewithal to successfully perform this major task. The question is to initiate it on a national scale in a fully transparent and participatory manner with parliamentary and civil society oversight.

Instead, the blame game prevails. Politicians blame teachers, who in turn blame students and work conditions. While there is a grain of truth in these assertions, the solution lies not in blame but in struggle; struggle on all fronts – educational, social, political and economic. And the teachers have to be the primary actors in this struggle to fundamentally transform education. For, in the final analysis, we, the teachers, must bear in mind that:

When our students have failed,
We, as teachers, too, have failed.
Marva Collins

10

FUNDAMENTALS OF TEACHING

―――――――

Teachers have three loves:
Love of learning, love of learners, and
Love of bringing the first two loves together.
Scott Hayden

+ + + + + + +

THERE IS NO UNIVERSAL recipe for the ideal teaching method. Yet, anyone who has stood in front of students for decades tends to develop what he or she deems as the key principles of effective teaching. While the recipe will vary from teacher to teacher, there will be common principles on critical aspects.

After teaching over four decades, I too have come to formulate what I consider to be the fundamental principles of good teaching. Six in number, I lay them down in this chapter. I do not expect universal agreement with them, or with the relative stress I put on them. I simply offer them as my contribution to the dialog about teaching and teachers that continually goes on among educators, students, parents and citizens. Teaching, it must be said, is an ever evolving profession.

LOVE YOUR SUBJECT

A teacher who is fondly remembered usually has a strong attraction towards his or her subject. Students can easily sense whether you teach because you have to or because you really want to. Your demeanor in the classroom will reveal to them how enamored you are with the topic. And that spirit will also infect your students.

The love of what you teach will keep you learning about it for as long as you teach, and later on as well. It will lead you to avoid teaching in a routine fashion. You will be driven to introduce fresh perspectives as you go along. And occasionally you will point to material beyond the curriculum and stray into novel realms.

I always strove to keep up with the developments in the field of theoretical and applied medical statistics and, during the long vacation every year, upgraded my lecture notes and changed the reading material. It never seemed like a burden but just a part of who I was. I can thereby confidently affirm that:

> *I was still learning when I taught my last class.*
> Claude Moore Fuess

RESPECT YOUR STUDENTS

As a teacher, you have a grave responsibility to play your part in the process of the development of your students as human beings. Your noble job is to shape their knowledge base and skills and mold their attitudes towards their profession and the world at large.

Your students are your second family. You have to be attentive to their educational and personal problems, and be flexible when it is warranted. They should know that you care, and are always willing to listen and act appropriately. A teacher who just comes to class, says what he has to say and disappears neglects a basic part of his job, namely, to engage with the students after class. It is only through such interaction that you can come to know your students well, monitor their progress and modify your pace and style accordingly. Each group of students has its own characteristics and you should not assume that what worked last year will suffice this year as well.

I told my students that I was there to facilitate their learning and designated two hours every week when they could come to my office for individual or group consultation. Those who could not make it during those times because of clinical duties or other reasons made separate appointments. It was an unusual thing at MUHAS. Because of the large class size, a line of students would form at my door. If a student was unable to do a test because of family emergency or illness, I would set a separate test for him or her. Overall, I agree that:

> *The secret in education lies*
> *In respecting the student.*
> Ralph Waldo Emerson

ADHERE TO HIGH ACADEMIC STANDARDS

Being helpful to the students as much as possible does not, however, imply compromising on the academic standards. While you go the extra mile, at the end of the day, they have to demonstrate that they have put in the effort needed to learn the subject. If they have not, they have to bear the consequences. There can be no exceptions on this issue.

At MUHAS, there was a distinct long term effect in not setting easy tests and exams. After the initial year, students began to realize that in my course, it was possible to fail the second supplementary final exam, and be disbarred from the degree program. It was an unheard of phenomenon at MUHAS. Word filtered down to the incoming batches. Attendance in lectures in the following years rose to 100%, and the students took the course material much more seriously than in the past when passing this course was a guaranteed thing. A few lecturers were heard complaining that the students were paying excessive attention to my course and neglecting other courses.

At the outset, many students, at UCLA as well as MUHAS tended to be unhappy at my demanding requirements. They would complain but to no avail! But once the course was over, quite a number would thank me for making them go through the arduous drill: 'Professor, we really learned something.'

At both universities, I saw instructors who only taught the easier material and gave substandard exams. It lessened their work and earned them cheap popularity. Because of the breakdown of the system of external examiners at MUHAS, they got away with doing a poor job. Many of today's students prefer such instructors, and those who make them sweat become unpopular.

Once a group of students approached me to complain about the final exam given for a course I was not involved in. They claimed that it did not reflect the material that was taught and wanted me to raise the issue in the meeting of the Examiner's Board. My reply was:

> *I know that nearly a third of the lectures in this course were not given. At that time, none of you complained. Now that the exam was not to your liking, you are upset. I am doubtful about your seriousness towards education. Sorry, I cannot help you.*

In comparison, the issue of standard of instruction was a critical one at UDSM in the 1960s and 1970s. In all the faculties and disciplines, the instructors demanded a lot from their students. It was the norm. There was no grade inflation. Though the pass level was just 40%, getting a passing mark required hours of backbreaking work on a daily basis. A first class pass was a rare event. With a bachelor's degree from UDSM, you could compete with graduates from the best global universities. Sadly, that is no more. Today even a person with a doctoral degree from UDSM or MUHAS generally demonstrates a level of intellectual attainment and maturity that is more deficient than an honors level undergraduate of the earlier era. I thereby strongly concur that:

> *What all good teachers have in common, however,*

*is that they set high standards for their students
and do not settle for anything less.*
Marva Collins

PRACTICE AND REQUIRE ETHICAL CONDUCT

It is your fundamental obligation to advocate and practice the highest standards of ethical behavior. You should never engage in favoritism for financial, personal or other reasons. And you should never cut corners or misrepresent your work. Your conduct inside and out of class has to be guided by uncompromising intellectual integrity.

Sad to say, breakdown of ethical norms is a common affliction in the modern academy. Not just the students but the academic staff too fall prey to that pernicious bug. I have given some examples earlier. I note one more.

In the year 2000, a student in the Master of Public Health program approached me to help in relation to her research project. It concerned people receiving anti-retroviral drugs for HIV infection. I do not lecture in this program and was not her supervisor. But I usually do not decline to help a student. I soon realized that though she was one of the top students in her cohort, her knowledge of research methods and data analysis was poor. Given the number and type of lectures they had been given, one could not expect more. Thus I spent many hours instructing her on the basics and improving her research proposal. Of course, there was no *bahasha* for this work; that would go to her designated supervisor.

Then she went off into the field to do the research. Three months later, she was back in my office, now with a thick research report in hand. She wanted me to look it over and give comments before it was finalized. As I perused it, I was astonished. It was a first class, well organized report on a fairly large number of subjects. Data analysis, illustration and interpretation had all been done in an appropriate manner. A novice had accomplished in three months what it would take a team of qualified professionals a year or more to do so.

I was not fooled. It was not her work. She had obtained outside help. Perhaps the data were in large measure manufactured. So I politely told her that I had already provided sufficient assistance and it was the responsibility of her supervisor to comment on and approve her report. She passed with flying colors and I never heard from her again. As for myself, I was quite demoralized and dejected. All that effort ground to dust. As I walked home that evening, I wondered if the leadership of public health efforts in our nation is coming under the hands of experts who have been educated in this style. Where are we going?

INTEGRATE THEORY WITH PRACTICE

When teaching any subject at any level, it is essential to maintain a balance between ideas and facts, between the general and the specific, between theory and practice. This precept applies whether you are teaching carpentry or surgery, mathematics, history or biology. And the balance has to be maintained in a dynamic fashion from beginning to end.

The manner in which a discipline or craft is visualized or practiced by professionals in the field does not represent the ideal way through which newcomers should be taught. Both for slow learners and the bright students, a one-sided emphasis on one aspect or the other of the subject interferes with the learning process. It can even be counterproductive.

Applied statistics (medical statistics, transport statistics, education statistics, agriculture statistics, etc.) is typically taught as a series of techniques for handling a set of numbers. The instructor demonstrates a procedure with an example, and then goes on to another. You waddle through one form of drudgery to another. Most examples are routine and contrived. Your job is to memorize the procedures and apply them when needed. For most students, the subject is banished from the mind as soon as the exams are over.

Unfortunately, this is the alienating approach by which medical statistics is taught in all the study programs at MUHAS, and in general, across the world. Alternatively, it can be taught by organically integrating it into the applied field. Both at UCLA and MUHAS, I taught this subject using a content article based approach. Each lecture took off from one or two health related papers, electronic copies of which had been distributed to the students beforehand. These required readings had reports of research on conditions like polio, malaria, childhood diarrhea, ear infection and so on. A key criterion for selecting an article was that it had in some fashion utilized the statistical tool or method I wanted to cover in class on that day.

I did not begin a lecture with formulas or numbers but would start discussing the substantive issues in the article. With their medical or health related background, the students would be readily drawn into the discourse. The statistical issues and numbers would naturally arise in the process, with the students hopefully realizing that they were essential for a complete understanding of the article and the health questions at hand. And often I would critically analyze it to indicate how the study and data interpretation could be improved. My ultimate goal in the course was to convince the class that a basic grasp of the major principles of statistical thinking is a prerequisite for the sound and effective practice of their respective professions. On this matter, most students were skeptical at the outset. But, by the end of the course, I felt that many had changed their attitude towards statistics.

INJECT EXTRANEOUS MATERIAL

While study subjects are taught separately, reality is not compartmentalized. The biological and physical realms, including human life at the individual and social levels, exist and develop as integrated processes. Human health also embodies physics, chemistry, biology, numbers, psychology, economics and sociology as a complex, dynamic entity.

When teaching any subject, especially at the university level, it is imperative to make the students aware of its wider ramifications, even though doing so may entail stepping beyond the formal curriculum. I firmly hold that such digressions are a necessary part of understanding the subject and it contributes towards their evolution as socially responsible and competent professionals.

My courses on medical statistics at UCLA and MUHAS integrated the actuality of statistics in the real world. I would inform the class about the numerous instances of the misuse and abuse of statistics in medical research and published papers, how conflict of interest, drive for promotion and commercial motivation contributed to compromising the quality of research even in the industrialized nations. I would tell them that statistics focuses on uncovering the truth about a usually complex reality. Without strict adherence to the ethical norms in research and reporting, the ensuing numbers are not just worthless but potentially harmful to human health too. Dealing with such issues tends to engage the students in a more solid manner in the course and improve their critical thinking skills. Quite a number of students I meet years later thank me for making them aware of the deeper realities of health research.

In addition, I would talk about the history of medical research and the contribution of statisticians to the development and refinement of the methodology and dealing with ethical matters like fairness, balancing risk and benefit and consent. The central role played by statisticians in uncovering the importance of the placebo effect in medicine was covered. Once in a while doses of humor and fascinating episodes from the history of medicine would punctuate a technical presentation. Well selected and timed digressions contribute to a richer learning process. I enjoyed them and the students did too.

The best teachers are the best story tellers.
We learn in the form of stories.
Frank Smith

II

THE BLACKBOARD SAGA

Unthinking respect for authority
Is the greatest enemy of truth
Albert Einstein

+ + + + + + +

UP UNTIL THIS ELECTRONIC ERA, the blackboard was an enduring companion for a teacher. From the age of five or six, she faced it regularly as a student for some two decades. Then, in her work life, she stood beside it for hours on end almost on a daily basis.

The blackboard is unique as a communication device. It allows the instructor to convey the unfolding pattern of her thoughts in a dynamic and flexible style. What she writes, and her pace of writing, are adjustable to the perceived receptivity of the class. To the student, it clarifies the logic employed by the teacher. They as well come to know her personality from how she uses it to interact with them.

I rank the blackboard as one of the most important pedagogic innovations. Sadly, it is being replaced by the PowerPoint screen that seems more useful but is basically a sterile device that permits an intellectually shallow presentation to be viewed as something grand. At MUHAS, I observed many instructors using the same set of PowerPoint slides from one course to another, and for years on. It decreased the amount of time they devoted to teaching and converted the learning process to the rote memorization of the slides.

I remained a devotee of the blackboard to the last day of my teaching. I never used PowerPoint slides for any regular course, be it at UCLA or MUHAS. It was not that I was opposed to the use of electronic technology. I judiciously employed it when it served a purpose, for example, to distribute notes and reading material to the students. Yet, I always felt that without the blackboard, my performance in the classroom would not be as effective as it ought to be.

There was another advantage to relying on the blackboard. In those years, power outages were common in the city and at the university. If you were a devotee of PowerPoint, ten minutes into the lecture you could find the screen go dark and dead. Many lecturers then found themselves in a bind, and would stumble through the rest of the class. In my case, I just had the students open all the shutters and windows and carried on as usual.

Yet, in the final six years of my teaching career, it became increasingly arduous to link up with my favorite teaching device. How this situation arose casts a distinctive light on the pedagogic trends and priorities in the Tanzanian academia. Thus I find it fitting to end this book with this curious tale.

CLASSROOM ALLOCATION

Lecturing in a Lab: The increase in the number of degree programs at MUHAS in the 2000s did not simultaneously occur with a corresponding increase in the number of classrooms. My Biostatistics class in the year 2006 was held in a laboratory of the School of Medicine. It was not an ideal teaching environment. Some students sat on stools and others on benches. They had trouble taking notes. But there was a large blackboard at one end of the lab that was regularly wiped before lecture time. Writing chalk was in good supply and a large new duster was at hand as well. I taught in this place for two years.

A Contested Classroom: Since the number of students in my course was rising every year, a bigger and better lecture room was needed. At that time, someone in the administration realized what should have been obvious long ago. The so-called shortage of classrooms was actually the result of an inefficient and irrational system of allocation of the teaching rooms. Under it, each group and subgroup had its own dedicated classroom. Others could not use the place even if there was no scheduled teaching activity going on there. An appropriate system in the early days of the university, it had outlived its utility.

After spending two years in a laboratory, my course and related courses for the postgraduates were allocated a decent lecture theater right under the office of the Vice Chancellor. Students could sit in comfort and take notes as I spoke and wrote on the large blackboard.

Though there was one major snag: communication with the student group that had traditionally occupied this room had been poor. No one in the administration had sat down with them to explain the new system of allocation of the teaching rooms. The students had developed a strong attachment to their traditional rooms and felt that they were being deprived of some inalienable right!

When I conducted my first lecture in this place, I encountered a large group of students not belonging to my class occupying nearly half the seats and doing their own work. My students had to squeeze in to find a seat. The recalcitrant students would also talk among themselves and walk in and out while my lecture was going on.

It was the strangest teaching situation I had ever encountered. It needed immediate change. I immediately lodged a strong complaint with the head of my department and the university administration. But no action was taken for two weeks. Exasperated and angry, in the third week, I took an unprecedented step. There was a large mango tree adjacent to the administration building with a few cement benches under it. The shade and a cool breeze gave protection from the tropical sun. Standing on a bench, I lectured under the tree. A few students sat on the other benches, some sat on the ground, and others just stood. Though there was no blackboard, I was able to communicate a fair amount of the material to the class.

Around that time, Tanzanian newspapers often carried photos of primary school children in the rural areas being taught under a tree. At times, there would be a small blackboard leaning against the trunk. In higher education institutions, biology teachers take students out in the bush for practical sessions. But that specific day represented the first and only time a lecture in a major Tanzanian university was of necessity conducted under a tree.

In the staff common room, it elicited chuckles from my colleagues. Faced with a similar situation, some of them had either truncated or canceled their classes. But my unusual action had an immediate effect. The following week, I was placed in a larger lecture theater right next to the administration building.

A Hazardous Classroom: Despite the change, the problem of students clinging on to their traditional study room had not been resolved. In the new place, I had to confront it as well. But here the number of stubborn students who chose to remain during my lecture was smaller. Further, they sat at the back, did not walk in and out, and remained silent. In the first session, I told them that so long as they behaved themselves, I had no objections to their attending my lecture. My students sat comfortably in the front rows, and things went well at the start.

There was, however, one nuisance I had to deal with. The blackboard was always hidden by a large projection screen. The rarely used board was usually not clean, and to use it, I had to raise the screen. On the first day, I did that and proceeded in my unusual style. But on the second day, this procedure occasioned an almost lethal catastrophe. A few minutes into the lecture, after a brief rumble above my head, the metal casing holding the projection screen came crashing down in its entirety.

The heavy object passed barely six inches from my body. Had I been standing slightly in front, it would have landed squarely on my head, and in all likelihood, I would not be writing these words. My luck had it that only one sharp edge grazed my forehead, making a small, superficial cut in the skin. The class, though mostly composed of medical doctors, was too stunned to take immediate action. I simply took out my handkerchief, pressed it against the wound and the bleeding stopped instantly. After pausing for a minute to catch my breath, I carried on as if nothing had happened.

At tea time, my colleagues wondered why there were drops of blood on my shirt. Upon hearing my tale, they were sympathetic, blaming the administration for not adequately maintaining university facilities. But I think some also felt that it was time I discarded my old fashioned ways and use PowerPoint as everyone else did.

Falling objects constitute a serious occupational risk for construction workers, not academics. I do not know if there are relevant statistics. Based on my experience, perhaps teachers in higher education institutions should also consider wearing hard hats on the job.

Word of the almost catastrophic event must have reached the administration. But no one from their exalted offices came to me to inquire about it, or offer a word of sympathy. However, it did have a singular positive effect. In a couple of weeks, my class and a related course offered by our department finally secured a satisfactory teaching space.

A Good Classroom: The new location was the main lecture theater of the School of Dentistry. Near the entrance of Muhimbili Hospital area and two hundred meters from the School of Public Health, it entailed a pleasant early morning walk.

With sitting space for over a hundred and fifty students, it had everything I desired. It was airy and well lit. The giant sized blackboard was always clean. Once in a while, chalk ran low. But it was my habit to have a couple of pieces with me.

Why did my class have to go through years of inconvenience to land in this place? The solution to the problem was just a matter of administration-initiated negotiation between the School of Dentistry and the School of Medicine. The fact that all the postgraduate students from the School of Dentistry had to take my course was a sufficient justification to make the dental lecture theater available. Yet until now no bureaucrat had taken the trouble to initiate this elementary step to resolve a major problem affecting all the first year postgraduate students at MUHAS.

This is the place where I blissfully and uneventfully lectured for two years. I have but positive memories about that time. I recall often stopping by the fruit stand next to the hospital entrance on the way back to my office and buying some delights to take home.

A Classroom Without A Blackboard: Good things do not, as they say, last forever. The two gigantic lecture theaters and a new office block that had been under construction for some years were finally ready for use. The undergraduate classes, numbering over three hundred students, were accordingly sent there. Since that move freed up the lecture theater they had used previously, the postgraduate classes, including mine were relocated there.

This theater, with a slightly larger capacity than the one in the dental school, was narrower and longer. It had a good sound system that worked most of the time. There was as well a modern projection system with the projection screen, I was pleased to note, securely attached to the wall.

It nonetheless had a surprise in store for me—there was no blackboard, absolutely none, kaput. One could write on the projection board with a marker pen. But the pens ran dry fast, and the writing was troublesome to erase, needing a solvent at hand. Moreover, using the pens was an expensive proposition. I wanted the good old chalkboard. Yet this was the first time in my four decades of teaching that I was placed to teach a semester long course in a room that was lacking one.

Since classroom allocations were announced, like most things, at the last minute, I became aware of this deficiency just two days prior to my first session. I marched immediately to the office of the Dean of the School of Medicine to see if something could be done. I was promised that a writing board would be installed the next day. But what I found in the first class was a small, slanting board stand with a two feet by three feet plain paper writing pad placed on it. A box of marker pens was nearby. As far as I was concerned, it was a most unsatisfactory solution to the problem. Because of its size and placement, the visibility was poor for the students in the back rows and first two front rows. If you wrote in large letters, the pages filled up in no time. Plus referring back was cumbersome. The Dean's secretary probably thought she was doing me a favor by providing me with a contraption that was suitable for executive presentations!

By the next lecture, I managed to have a slightly larger chalkboard installed on the stand. An eraser and chalk were also provided. Yet, it was too small for the amount of stuff I usually write in a lecture. The issue of poor visibility remained. But I was told that this was the best that could be done.

The office of the Dean of the School of Public Health was unhelpful, as the lecture theater was in a building under the control of the School of Medicine. So I went to a senior administration official, the Director of Postgraduate Studies, for assistance. He was sympathetic and said he would find a satisfactory solution. But nothing was done for a week. I was thoroughly frustrated. At the start of the next lecture, I went to the Director's office and literally dragged him to the lecture hall. Upon seeing the problem first hand, he promised in the presence of the students to deal with it immediately. In two days, two mid-sized boards were installed, one on each side of the projector screen. I was elated; other instructors used the boards as well. And it was in the august company of these indispensable tools of pedagogy that I formally ended my teaching career in July 2012.

INVERTED PRIORITIES

Wherever the staff or students at MUHAS raised the issue of inadequate facilities the standard reply from the administration in those years was to be patient. New lecture theaters and offices were under construction. The administration put all its efforts on large, expensive, prestige projects. The simple steps that could be taken to alleviate the problem including better coordination between the different schools were sidelined. Long term plans for training new academic staff were deficient. For the students and staff, the administration functioned like an entity high in the sky. Effective communication was but a distant dream.

The dire situation in the Tanzanian higher education sector became a matter of public concern in the year 2017 when the Tanzania Commission on Universities (TUC) ordered nineteen universities not to enroll new students for the current academic year. Another twenty two universities were prohibited from enrolling students in seventy five study programs. The affected institutions had not fulfilled minimal requirements like adequate numbers of qualified academic staff and appropriate teaching facilities and supplies. Nearly three quarters of the universities in the nation were affected by the ban (Kamagi 2017).

Fundamental matters like quality of instruction and standards of assessment, which need prolonged, in-depth, discipline by discipline evaluation, were not probed by the TUC inspection. A university can have qualified staff but the quality of teaching can nonetheless be sub-standard. Thus, if the standards prevailing at UDSM in 1975 had been employed as the current required standards, I do not think any current university would have made the grade. The education provided in Tanzanian universities today does not deserve to be called university education.

PARTING THOUGHTS

Teaching has been a true love of my life. It gave me a second family and provided meaning to it. Like for all families, it had ups and downs; good apples and bad apples. Overall, it was a decent family. My dedication to it is reflected in the fact that throughout those four decades, I missed a regularly scheduled class only twice and was late to class also only twice.

What pains me now is the current state of the academy in Tanzania. I am sad to see that most professors and lecturers have abandoned their responsibility to provide high quality and relevant education. Only a few hardy ones among them are keeping the flame alive. This has to change, for the sake of our national dignity and welfare of our people. It can be done. Please play your part.

APPENDIX A
AKIVAGA CRISIS TIMELINE

THIS APPENDIX PROVIDES a chronological summary of the pro-democracy uprising, commonly called the Akivaga Crisis, that began at the UDSM in July 1971.

Date	Event
July 1970	Pius Msekwa becomes the first VC of UDSM.
October 1970	Symonds Akivaga elected President of DUSO.
November 1970	USARF and *Cheche* banned.
7 July 1971	First UDSM graduation ceremony. Speech of the VC disliked by students. DUSO cabinet drafts open letter to VC.
8 July 1971	Open letter, signed by Akivaga, delivered. Akivaga summoned by the Disciplinary Committee.
9 July 1971	Akivaga rusticated, arrested by the FFU and deported to Kenya. Students boycott classes. Academic staff meet.
10 July 1971	General academic staff meeting, attended by the VC. Daily student *baraza*s commence.
12 July 1971	University Council meets. Calls upon students to end class boycott.
13 July 1971	VC, Chairman of Council, Minister of Education and two student representatives visit Mwalimu Nyerere. Class boycott ends.
14 July 1971	The student representatives report to the Student *Baraza*.
25 July 1971	Mungai committee appointed to probe the university crisis. DUSO rejects its composition.
26 July 1971	DUSO submits appeal against Akivaga's rustication.

Date	Event
3 August 1971	Mungai Committee begins work.
3 August 1971	DUSO withdraws from Mungai Committee.
15 August 1971	Akivaga allowed to return to DSM for his appeal.
19 August 1971	Appeals Committee expels Akivaga from UDSM.
23 August 1971	DUSO cabinet resigns. Student representatives withdraw from all university bodies.
8 September 1971	University TANU branch passes a resolution calling for the return of Akivaga.
27 November 1971	Mungai Report released.
28 November 1971	University TYL branch rejects Mungai Report.
July 1972	Akivaga allowed to return to UDSM for his final year of studies.
August 1972	Akivaga-led student government overthrown by pro-establishment students.

APPENDIX B
AKIVAGA CRISIS IN HISTORY

THE JULY 1971 PRO-DEMOCRACY UPRISING at UDSM, commonly called the Akivaga Crisis, was described at length in Chapter 5. The features of this student led movement included formation of bonds solidarity between students, academic staff and the campus workers; grassroots discussion and decision making on a daily basis; the progressive nature of the demands; the special role played by female students; and its long term impact. Such features make it a unique and one of the historically most important occurrences at this university.

After 1972, many authors of varied social and political persuasions have written about this event. My review of this historical record shows that it is filled with errors and misrepresentations. Not a single writer has given an accurate and balanced picture. This type of historical record needs to be corrected. Hence the aim of this appendix is to review and critique these writings and investigate the sources of their flaws.

It is logical to begin with the voices of the two principals in the crisis, Symonds Akivaga, the student leader and Pius Msekwa, the university Vice Chancellor. The student leader subsequently lectured at the Department of Education of the University of Nairobi before retiring around 2010. My attempts to contact him through several channels, however, did not bear fruit. I learned with sadness that he passed away in 2017.

The former VC has been a prominent political personality in Tanzania. Interviewed by my research assistant in February 2017, he at first denied that there had been a class boycott during his time at UDSM. When he was shown the documentary evidence, he declared that the media had a tendency to distort and exaggerate. He terminated the interview shortly thereafter. More details about his version of the Akivaga Crisis are fortunately available in Msekwa (2014). On pages 107–109 of this book, the following points are noted:

1. Msekwa's arrival at UDSM was associated with the University coming under the purview of the ruling party, TANU. Some people, especially foreigners, disliked this and began to work for his ouster.
2. Recognizing the rebellious nature of students, Mwalimu Nyerere had advised him to have sound reasons for his administrative decisions. Because he followed this advice faithfully, no major problem or unrest had occurred during his tenure at UDSM.
3. After Akivaga, a Kenyan, had issued a statement calling for his removal, he held a meeting with the student government. He saw that there was

no substantive problem. The statement reflected plain political intrigue. That was why Akivaga was suspended for a year.
4. The move generated politically motivated student unrest, demanding his return to the campus. He attended the meeting of the academic staff and explained his reasons. Yet the staff meeting supported Akivaga's return.
5. At this juncture, the Chairman of the University Council called a meeting of the Council. His aim was to make the Council support the return of Akivaga to the university. During the course of the meeting, the Chairman received a call from Mwalimu Nyerere. He was told that the immediate return of the student leader was out of the question. Akivaga had to serve his suspension first.
6. Throughout this period, a tranquil atmosphere prevailed at the university. There was no incident that could have led to suspension of classes or closure of the university. An FFU unit had come to the campus. After ascertaining that everything was orderly and peaceful, it had left.
7. Patriotic Tanzanian students, led by George Mkuchika and Ahmed Kivanuka, were disturbed by the political machinations behind this event. After Akivaga's return, they made a plan to disband his student government. When he was informed about their plan, he assured them that the university administration would recognize and work with the new government. Thus a new student government led by Tanzanians came into being, and started work without any hitches.
8. Throughout this crisis, he had the full backing of Mwalimu Nyerere.

+ + + + + + +

Comment: Pius Msekwa's account hides many key aspects of the crisis and is replete with errors and distortions. According to him, the basic problem was a conflict between Tanzanians and outsiders. His account serves to portray his tenure at UDSM in a favorable light. Nonetheless, it is revealing in two aspects: the role of Mwalimu Nyerere in this episode and the part played by his administration in the overthrow of a democratically elected student government.

+ + + + + + +

Next, consider the official history of the University of Dar es Salaam, as presented by Kimambo, Mapunda and Lawi (2008). Three chapters in this book touch on the Akivaga Crisis.

Kimambo (2008) traces the roots of the Akivaga Crisis to the entry of 'new, non-academic bureaucrats' at UDSM. However, his case is based on the words of the first two vice chancellors of UDSM. The conflict at the university is reduced to a conflict between patriotic Tanzanians, on the one hand, and non-Tanzanians and Marxists, on the other.

Itandala (2008) just makes two brief points about the Akivaga Crisis: Democracy at the university was the key issue in the crisis, and that it generated the momentum towards the establishment of an organization of the academic staff.

Of the three chapters, Mihanjo (2008) has the most coverage of the Akivaga Crisis. The main points in that regard are:

1. DUSO under Akivaga was a militant student organization.
2. 'Lack of effective communication' fueled the conflict between the administration and the students.
3. Rustication of Akivaga led to a four-day class boycott.
4. Students accepted the call by the University Council to resume classes.
5. Akivaga's rustication was endorsed by the Executive Committee of the Council.
6. The Council set up a commission to look into the crisis. DUSO did not cooperate with the commission.
7. DUSO cabinet resigned on 23 August 1971.
8. Akivaga was reinstated on 1 July 1972.
9. A 'revolutionary' student government displaced Akivaga and his DUSO cabinet, and ruled for fifty four days.

+++++++

Comment: The version of the Akivaga Crisis in Kimambo (2008) is too one-sided and unsubstantiated to deserve attention. The comments in Itandala (2008) are too brief. Scrutiny reveals that almost all the material in given in Mihanjo (2008) relating to the Akivaga Crisis is extracted from two official annual university reports (UDSM 1973; 1974). But the page citations are incorrect and several sentences are reproduced almost verbatim without using quotation marks. A few sentences are arbitrarily truncated, distorting the meaning of the original. The pro-administration biases in the annual reports are thereby reproduced and compounded.

Consider the role of the university TYL branch: 'The TANU Youth League University District, during the year under review, was somewhat dormant because of the student unrest.' (UDSM 1973, page 225). Itandala (2008) converts this to: 'Students' absence during the crisis between 1971 and 1972 made the TYL University Branch dormant.' (page 213). The annual report lists in part the activities of the TYL Branch, which gives the contrary impression, that the branch was quite active during that academic year. Itandala (2008) doesn't have the list but goes on to claim that 'The (TYL) Branch tried to intervene so as to solve the student crisis but the efforts were unsuccessful.' (page 213). The source of this assertion is unknown, as it is not present in the annual report.

The fact of the matter is that the University TYL Branch played a prominent role in the Akivaga Crisis. It consistently sided with DUSO and strongly castigated the administration. It held meetings and issued a detailed statement analyzing the roots of the crisis and branding the university administrators as 'Hitlerite fascists.' This statement, written in English and Swahili, was widely circulated on the campus and beyond. The branch later held discussions of the Mungai Report and wrote a critical analysis. In sum, Itandala (2008) is replete with factual and conceptual errors, and tends to favor the administration's account of the crisis.

None of these three chapters in this book refer to any document or newspaper report of the time. With such distorted and restrictive accounts, the official history of UDSM does a poor job in documenting the development of the Akivaga Crisis, one of the most important episodes in its history.

+ + + + + + +

Next I look at the publications of scholars who have written about the Akivaga Crisis. First I consider the traditional scholars whose works reflect an implicit or explicit pro-capitalist orientation.

In general, these scholars mention the crisis briefly and note a few basic points: (i) The crisis was caused by the authoritarian nature of the new administration, (ii) It led to the democratization of the governance of the university, and (iii) It catalyzed the efforts to establish an organization of the academic staff (see Mkude, Cooksey and Levey (2003); Ngirwa, Euwema, Babyegeya and Stouten (2014); and Mbwete and Ishumi (1996)).

One exception is Omari and Mihyo (1991). It stands out in three aspects: (i) It is based on documents and on newspaper reports of the time, (ii) It gives a fairly accurate day by day account of how the crisis progressed, and (iii) It presents a perceptive picture of the multifaceted nature of the crisis.

+ + + + + + +

Comment: Nonetheless, I place this book together with the previous three publications because their common underlying message is that the crisis emanated from the attempts by the new administration to inject the ruling party's socialist policies into the academia. It is a simplistic narrative that permeates most convectional writings on Tanzania. All the problems in Tanzania of that era are attributed, in a formula like manner, to socialism. Yet, the practical contents of this socialism are not examined in depth.

To elaborate this point, consider Table 2 'Causes of Student Unrest' in Omari and Mihyo (1991). It groups the causes of the Akivaga Crisis into four categories: (i) Political, namely, 'protest against banning of student' publications and independent associations, introduction of military training at university, introduction of Party Youth Wingers [?] as the official student union, and bureaucracy and corruption'; (ii) Academic, namely, 'protest against lengthening of academic year from 31 to 40 weeks'; (iii) Welfare, namely, 'use of and bylaws passed by Parents Association opposed, consultations on university governance wanted'; and (iv) Managerial, namely, 'students disagree with Vice Chancellor's graduation speech' (page 31).

On the political causes, note that only one student association (USARF) was banned. Further it and its publication *Cheche* had a staunchly socialist orientation. The membership of USARF did not exceed five percent of the student body. Its radical stance often brought it into conflict with the main student organization. Though the students and academic staff in general did not approve the banning of these entities, the disapproval did not rise to the extent of becoming a major grievance of the student body.

The military training started at UDSM during the 1970/71 academic year was for Tanzanian students only. Conducted for a week during vacation time, it was a part of the National Service scheme in which the students were already enrolled. By this time it was no longer controversial. Many students took it as a welcome break from demanding mental work. What the students took exception to was the fact that the VC bragged about it as if it was a major achievement on his part.

The existing official student union, DUSO, was enshrined in the act of parliament establishing UDSM, and the question of replacing it with the Party youth wing, TYL, did not arise during the academic year preceding the Akivaga Crisis. Even the university branch of TYL did not forward such a demand. Actually during this period the university TYL was regularly at odds with the administration. During the crisis, it expressed strong opposition to the stand taken by the administration.

The students did take exception to the bureaucratic behavior of the administration. One arena of potential corruption they were concerned about was the cooperative shop. Yet, they were not opposed to this socialistic move. The idea was welcomed by the staff and students as it would provide an accessible venue for purchasing essential supplies at reasonable prices. What was not accepted was the lack of transparency associated with the project. It was felt that senior administration officials would use it for their personal benefit.

The extension of the academic year was opposed both by students and lectures because the decision was taken in haste without due consideration for implications on research and teaching, and without consultations with the affected parties. The bylaws relating to the residence halls took the students by surprise. When asked why the students were not involved in the decision, the VC claimed that he had consulted the Tanzania Parents Association. But the bylaws were formulated by the administration and not by the said association.

All the segments of the university community were alienated by the actions of a bungling, authoritarian administration that lacked a vision or plan for how to govern and develop either a traditional university or a socialist university. Apart from a few lackeys, everyone, from leftists to rightists, had problems with how the university was run by Mr Msekwa. The process of reorienting the university curricula towards a more Africanist, socialistic direction had begun long before he arrived at the university. It was an internally generated endeavor deriving from protracted efforts of progressive students and staff. If anything, the steps taken by the Msekwa administration worked to undermine and reverse those pioneering initiatives.

To view the Akivaga Crisis as a conflict between socialism and capitalism, or that arising from the attempts by a nationalistic bureaucracy to make the university education relevant to national needs is to obfuscate the reality. It is indicative of unwillingness to explore the complexity of the situation and ideological bias.

+ + + + + + +

Finally, I turn to the scholars whose writings generally display a clear socialist orientation.

John Saul, an internationally renowned left wing analyst, portrays the Akivaga Crisis in a dramatic fashion:

> [The] student president Akivaga [was] whisked away from the campus and summarily dispatched home in a waiting plane: his crime, apparently having been to invoke 'Mwongozo' in criticism of the university's hierarchy! Saul (2011).

A paragraph on, he continues:

> Here I refer to the invasion of the campus of the University of Dar es Salaam by the Field Force Unit in 1970. Standing in the nearby coffee area next to the central administration building, straining to see what the soldiers were upto, I saw my own student Simon Akivaga, the Kenyan leader of the University Student Council, having been summoned to a meeting with the principal, being dragged, at gun-point, down the cement stairs at the front of the building, tossed like a sack of old clothes into a waiting army vehicle and sped away to his aforementioned expulsion from the university and the country. Saul (2011).

For him, this crisis was an instance of the stark contrast between the rhetoric of grassroots empowerment enunciated in a ruling party policy document and the harsh suppression of the people who attempted to puts its message into practice.

+ + + + + + +

Comment: This essentially is the sum total of the description of this crisis from Saul. Parts of the same description appear almost verbatim in a number of his writings, for example, Saul (2009). It is a firsthand account. He was at the scene of Akivaga's arrest, he attended staff and student meetings during the crisis, and signed the staff petition supporting the students. All that make his report a particularly important one.

Yet, almost every sentence he writes has errors. One, the TANU Guidelines is correctly dated to the year 1971, but the Akivaga Crisis is wrongly placed in 1970, a year earlier. How could Akivaga have invoked a document that had yet to be issued? Two, the student organization is given an incorrect name. Three, the Field Force Unit was not an army unit but a branch of the police. This is a critical point in the context of what was happening in Africa in that era. Four, his student's first name was Symonds, not Simon. Five, Akivaga had been summoned not to a meeting with the 'principal' but to appear before a disciplinary hearing. Six, the formal title of the head of the university administration was not the principal but the Vice Chancellor. Seven, Akivaga was marched out, not dragged out; he was not tossed into the vehicle but was made to climb in. Eight, Akivaga was standing on a small six-step stairway when he was arrested. He was pulled by a policeman, not dragged down. Nine, at that point in time, Akivaga was not expelled but 'rusticated' (suspended) from the university.

In a sense, these are minor errors. That so many are packed within a single paragraph that constitutes his main description of the crisis is disconcerting. A tendency to exaggerate and play around with facts is on display here. John Saul had earlier written a perceptive paper on student radicalism at UDSM to his credit (Saul 1973). Yet, in relation to the Akivaga Crisis, he has no further comments of the causes, actuality and consequences. The sole thing he notes about this is the dismissal of Arnold Temu of the History Department that occurred later on.

+ + + + + + +

Next, I look at an article by Haroub Othman, a veteran, prominent socialist scholar (Othman 2005). I quote his description and comments pertaining to Akivaga Crisis in full:

> *In July of [1971] the University held a graduation ceremony where the*

Vice-Chancellor, Mr Pius Msekwa (now the Speaker of the National Assembly) made a speech. The students' union, known then as the Dar es Salaam University Students Organization (DUSO) took strong exception to the Vice-Chancellor's speech and this was expressed in an open letter signed by the DUSO President, Mr Symonds Akivaga. The University authorities decided to rusticate the student leader, and since he was from Kenya, it meant also deporting him back to Kenya. The students reacted by boycotting classes and staging a sit-in at the entrance to the Administration Block, demanding the rescinding of the rustication order. Riot police, known as the FFU, were called in and with their fingers on the trigger, surrounded the students.

In those days, my office was in the Law Faculty Building, and on that morning, I was walking to the Senior Common Room to have my morning tea. I came face to face with the students and saw the riot police forcefully taking away Symonds Akivaga. My immediate reaction was to rush to Walter Rodney's office which was in the building next to the Administration Block. Walter was busy writing his How Europe Underdeveloped Africa. After telling him what was happening, we rushed out to the Administration Building. On arrival there, Walter went straight into the crowd and stood on the stairs of the building and addressed the crowd. He urged them to be calm and not to destroy any property.

The students' boycott was total, and the next morning academic staff held a meeting, in this very lecture theater where we are today holding Rodney's commemorative meeting, and called on the university authorities to rescind the rustication order. Later on Akivaga was allowed to return to the campus, DUSO was dissolved and a new students union was established. But what was interesting were the stories that followed, no doubt put forth by the university authorities and disseminated by politicians in town, that the Left, headed by Rodney, had engineered the world episode! Othman (2005), pages 301–302.*

+ + + + + + +

Comment: The first paragraph above is an accurate account of the central episode of the Akivaga Crisis. But the second one has a major error: Walter Rodney did not climb up the stairs and talk to the assembled students. If he was around, he maintained a distance from the center of action. The two people who calmed the enraged students were fellow students: the Vice President of DUSO and the Speaker of the Student *Baraza*.

The errors continue in the third paragraph. The first meeting of the academic staff took place that same afternoon. As indicated from the names of those who were present, Walter Rodney was there. In the staff meeting held the next day, the VC and student representatives were also invited. Rodney did not play a prominent role in these meetings. Additional comments on the role of Walter Rodney in the Akivaga Crisis will be given later. Another misstatement concerns the dissolution of DUSO. This did not occur during, or in the immediate aftermath of, the Akivaga Crisis. It happened years later, in connection with another student demonstration.

Othman does not talk about the unity that developed between students, academic staff and campus workers in this period, the outstanding part played by female students, the broader political dimensions or the long term consequences — issues one would expect a socialist scholar to highlight.

+ + + + + + +

Now consider the words of Professor Issa Shivji, a prominent Tanzanian socialist scholar, on this crisis. In one article, he wrote:

> *The traditional student body at the university, the Dar es Salaam University Student Organization (DUSO), under Akivaga, a former member of USARF, raised some fundamental questions which culminated in what came to be known as the 'Akivaga Crisis'. In 1971, in response to the Vice Chancellor's graduation day speech, Akivaga, in an open letter, accused the University administration of bureaucracy, high-handedness and undemocratic behavior. Students boycotted classes and staged sit-ins. The show of commitment, solidarity and firm-ness on the part of the student body was unprecedented. Once again the state could not tolerate such 'insolence', similar to those of the workers. The FFU was dispatched post-haste to round-up Akivaga and shove him off to the airport wherefrom he was deported to Kenya, his home country.* Shivji (1987), page 137.

On the following page, he adds:

> *Student struggles everywhere revealed the impatience and spontaneity of its petty-bourgeois social base as it indeed did in the Akivaga crisis. In that episode, an excellent opportunity [??] with the striking workers was missed, nay never even considered. While a few elements called for a protracted, public debate on the place of the University outside the Campus involving broad sections of the population, the large majority of*

> *the student population was only interested in getting Akivaga back to the Campus. When the university administration cleverly conceded by flying Akivaga back to the Hill, the wind was taken out of the sail. Students returned to classes and settled down on getting their certificates, marking an end of an important period in the history of student struggles and ideological debates at the University.* Shivji (1987), page 138.

+ + + + + + +

Comment: First note the obvious errors. The students had resumed classes by the middle of July but Akivaga was allowed to temporarily return in the middle of August in connection with his appeal. No concession, clever or otherwise, was offered by the administration. The appeal was summarily rejected and he was served with an expulsion order. Though the class boycott did not resume, the DUSO cabinet resigned, an atmosphere of noncooperation with the administration prevailed, and the struggle continued in other forms. For the rest of the academic year, the demands for Akivaga's return and democratization of the university remained in the forefront.

Following the acute phase of the Akivaga Crisis, ideological classes and public lectures by progressive personalities continued on the campus. Many issues of the radical student journal *MajiMaji* with well researched papers (including those by Shivji) and informative debates were published. Progressive students worked in *Ujamaa* villages and distributed socialist material in schools. It is thereby inaccurate to call the ending of this crisis as a point denoting the end of student and ideological struggles at UDSM. Historically, it is more valid to call the fratricidal ideological tussles of the mid-1970s between leftist academics at UDSM, which demoralized the entire progressive community, as the turning point in that respect.

Shivji does not give a reference for his assertion about the call for 'a protracted, public debate' during the Akivaga crisis. What and who he refers to are unclear. In actuality, that had been a long standing demand of the socialists among the staff and students at UDSM. There is no evidence that it garnered enhanced attention during this crisis.

On the key issue of worker-student relationship, elsewhere, Shivji adds:

> *Though the students showed remarkable unity [during the Akivaga Crisis], they failed to mobilize fully the staff and workers who labored under the same debilitating bureaucracy. They paid scant attention to the grievances of their natural allies.* Shivji (1980)

To buttress his depiction of this as an anti-worker episode, he quotes the English translation of a statement written by some campus workers that was published *in MajiMaji* No. 13, of January 1974. In part, it reads:

> *In the University [Akivaga] crisis of 1971 which resulted in the rustication of the students' leader (which was preceded by the banning of the most revolutionary organization to have existed in the history of the University—U.S.A.R.F.) one of the most important things the radical students did was to shout in the name of workers and peasants. But not a single worker answered their call even though some of us—the workers—were fighting the same enemy.* Source: Shivji (1980).

All these assertions are factually flawed and highly misleading. The Akivaga Crisis was the only event in the history of UDSM in which solid bonds of cooperation between students, staff and campus workers were formed. Student representatives attended staff meetings, and staff and worker representatives attended the student *barazas*. Important student statements were translated into Swahili and disseminated among the workers. The campus Workers Committee issued a statement in support of the students that was read out in a *baraza* amid much applause. Students held discussions with workers, conducted literacy classes for them and joined them in work activities in the cafeteria and the halls of residence. Female students played a leading role in those endeavors. But DUSO never claimed to be shouting 'in the name of workers.'

In contrast, USARF, 'the most revolutionary organization,' which did shout 'in the name of workers [and peasants]', never concerned itself with issues affecting the campus workers. Not a single one of the numerous statements it issued during its lifetime reflected their concerns. While it can be lauded for its Pan-Africanist and socialist stand and activities, it had a noteworthy shortfall on the domestic front.

Shivji and the worker statement he quotes, written two years after the Akivaga Crisis, conflate the actions of the (few) radical students (under USARF) with those of the main student body. Earlier, the general student organization at UDSM had restricted itself to student bread-and -butter matters. During this crisis it, for the first, and thus far the last, time formed a solid alliance with the campus workers.

A crucial thing Shivji does not bear in mind is that when the Akivaga Crisis began, the post-*Mwongozo* struggles against heavy handed, irresponsible leaders in work places and educational establishments were in their infancy. The open letter signed by Akivaga, which explicitly cited this important policy document, was a pioneering step on that front. It stimulated and energized this struggle, and thus deserves to be given due credit.

Another observation made by Shivji is:

> *Walter Rodney was once again one of the most prominent participants in staff and joint student/staff meetings during the [Akivaga] crisis, which lasted for fairly long.* Shivji (1980).

What he notes on this score is consistent with the words of Othman (2005). As will be shown later, this is not just a matter of detail but has important methodological implications.

When it comes to considering the long term consequences of the Akivaga Crisis, Shivji sets a different tone.

> *The first cry against incipient bureaucratization process on the campus was raised by the Akivaga episode. Once again, it involved mainly the student body, although eventually members of staff were also drawn in. It was through their participation in the so-called 'Akivaga crisis' that the staff for the first time realized that they lacked an organization and a forum of their own; hence their demand for an academic staff assembly, which took a whole decade to materialize. (It has not been said for nothing that the struggle is a process for self-education.)*

> *Following the Akivaga Crisis and the Mungai Report, formal democratic structures were installed at the University. This took the form of a proliferation of committees on which staff and students were variously represented. To that extent, the demands of the 1968–71 student struggles were partially met.* Shivji (1981).

+ + + + + + +

Comment: Here, Shivji is right on the mark. Yet, he fails to explain the manner by which an event he otherwise disparages had such positive consequences.

+ + + + + + +

Finally, we look at a paper by Chris Peter and Sengodo Mvungi, two former law students and later, members of the academic staff at UDSM (Peter and Mvungi 1985). It contains an apt rendition of how the initial phase of the Akivaga Crisis unfolded. The deficiency of democracy at UDSM is placed as the central issue in this crisis. Affecting both students and staff, it formed the basis for their united stand. The furtherance of democratic structures and initiation of the drive to form an academic staff association are declared as the two major achievements of the crisis. But otherwise, their verdict on the crisis is not a salutary one:

> *The Akivaga Crisis, for example, was the best example of the deterioration in the content of the student struggle. .... [The students] failed to involved [sic] in their struggle the workers and members of staff who had similar grievances against the university bureaucracy. Their resistance had no articulate and deep going analysis of the events.* Peter and Mvungi (1985).

+ + + + + + +

Comment: The general take on the Akivaga Crisis of these authors is almost identical to that presented by their professor. It appears that the summary of the initial days of the crisis in Shivji (1987) was based on their article. Both reflect the same type of errors. Hence my critique of Shivji on this matter applies equally to their work. Also, what they say about the staff student relationship at this juncture is not consistent with what they write elsewhere.

+ + + + + + +

Overall Comment: To put it mildly, the presentations of the Akivaga Crisis by these progressive intellectuals are hardly satisfactory. They are limited, distorted and flawed. Since they write about their natural constituencies, workers and students, we expect them to give faithful, comprehensive accounts of their struggles. Yet, they do a shockingly poor job.

The question is: How come? Is it a shortcoming confined to this particular event, or does it have broader ramifications? And what are its methodological roots? We pursue these issues next.

SCIENCE AND ERROR

Science is more than a body of knowledge. Primarily, it is a method of acquiring knowledge. Its evolution was spurred by a growing realization that what we think is the truth often is not, a realization that was frequently contemporaneous with emergent practical needs in society.

A proposition that is patently false, factually and conceptually, is held as the gospel truth by the multitude even today. Science aims to uncover such misperceptions of nature and society, understand their character and origins, and design methods of collecting, collating, analyzing and interpreting information that will give us an as accurate and valid a picture of a usually complex reality that can be had with the technical and conceptual means at hand.

Scientists categorize the errors skewing our understanding of the reality into two basic types: systematic error and random error. Take the case of measuring blood pressure. If the nurse performs the task in a hurried manner, she can overestimate or underestimate its true value. Better training and an unhurried setting will reduce such an error. But it cannot be avoided altogether. As long as no pattern exists and provided they are small, such errors do not skew the doctor's judgment about the patient's condition.

On the other hand, suppose we are looking at two different drugs for treatment of high blood pressure. Most of the patients getting the new drug are obese while most on the old drug are of normal weight. This dissimilarity in the patient groups can produce readings that give a deceptive picture of the comparative efficacy of the two drugs. An error of this form is called a systematic error, or bias. To counter such bias, study designs that generate patient groups that are similar according to key features that effect disease status and outcome of treatment are necessary.

Biomedical researchers have identified more than two hundred different types of systematic errors, and have devised varied ingenuous strategies to control them (Mullane and Williams 2013). Yet, bias remains an entrenched feature of health research. Critical external factors influence why it is persistent. Many investigators have inadequate training in research methods, and do not consult research method specialists at the stage of designing their study. Seeking to fatten their cvs, they compromise the quality of published papers. Conflicts of interest, commercial and other, intrude onto the health research arena as well (Angell 2005; Editorial 2004; Editorial 2006; Kassirer 2000; Mayer 2005).

I note two examples from my own work. I conducted critical, in-depth analyses of two highly regarded, award winning papers published in prominent British medical journals. One dealt with the treatment of ear infections in children, the other, with the initial treatment of children with severe malaria. Each paper was seen to have serious methodological, practical, analytic and interpretative errors and biases (Hirji 2009; Hirji and Premji 2011).

In the social sciences, including history, the scope for such errors is greater. Material from the past gets damaged over the years; memories become hazier. Existent documents reflect the biases of the recorders, both in observation and opinion. Lives of the upper strata of society get more detailed, gentle treatment while the material on the lower strata often is scant and unfairly presented.

> *No history can be a faithful mirror. If it were, it would be as long and dull as life itself. It must be a selection and, being a selection, must inevitably be biased.* T E Hulme.

The almost cavalier treatment of truth found in the works of prominent authors writing about East Africa is disconcerting. For instance, the memoir of the acclaimed Asian-Tanzanian-Canadian author Moez G Vassanji, *And Home Was Kariakoo: A Memoir of East Africa* (Vassanji 2014), has a plethora of elementary errors of fact, and pervasive methodological, economic and racial biases (Hirji 2016).

While the elucidation and control of systematic and random errors has secured extensive attention, consideration of one overarching source of error has been sidelined. This error, of central importance to history and the social sciences, derives from the framework for the analysis of human society consciously or subconsciously adhered to by the researcher. While its character differs, it affects both conservative and progressive scholars.

Every historian operates under a particular world view, an overall framework for visualizing the structure and functioning human society. She does not collect information about the past in a random fashion. Rather, she focuses on types information and relationships deemed relevant by her world view, and disregards or pays scant attention to items not regarded as critical or relevant by it. Because a vast ocean of information exists, every historian has to select. The young historian engaged in research becomes ensnared into a particular, dominant world view because almost all the historians around her employ the same approach. It is held that it is an objective, fair minded approach. The minority who take issue with it are viewed with suspicion. They are called the biased scholars who introduce politics in the academy.

Bias of this form is internalized subconscious bias. It promotes ideologically driven selectivity and affects historians of all social, political, economic and cultural spectra. The operation of this type of bias is encapsulated in the following quote:

> *Born with blue spectacles, you would think the world was blue and never be conscious of the existence of the distorting glass.* T E Hulme.

The paper 'Maoism in Tanzania' by Priya Lal is an instructive instance (Lal 2014). Based on a Cold War era driven conceptualization of Tanzania and China, utilizing an extreme degree of selectivity of events and data, employing an inconsistent manner of citation of sources, and resorting to numerous superficial analogies, it solemnly arrives at the acceptable conclusion for the US academia that Maoism exercised a major influence on the policy and practice of *Ujamaa* under Nyerere. The author claims to be countering negative perceptions of Africa. But if you subject this work to a systematic, fact-by-fact scrutiny, its premises, method, analogies and conclusions begin to unravel in no time.

Purely objective history does not exist. Those who profess such objectivity are deluding both themselves and their readers. Instead of striving for a mythological form of objectivity, every historian should declare her basic premises and overall framework in a transparent manner. Having done that, she must approach her task with scrupulous eyes on the control of random and systematic error of all forms, and strive to render an as valid an account of history as she can. While ideological bias is unavoidable, it is not a license to compromise the truth.

This is what Walter Rodney does in his majestic work, *How Europe Underdeveloped Africa*. At the time he began his work, the approaches toward the history of the continent masked the depth and structural scope of the impact of imperialism on Africa. When the struggles against colonial and racist rule gained traction, a new generation of African and expatriate historians began a massive empirical and theoretical project to present a more authentic view of African history. Standing in the forefront of this effort, Walter Rodney's two principal works exemplify meticulous research and astute socio-economic analyses enjoined with novel interpretation of the past.

Establishment historians branded him as a politically minded, shallow scholar. His approach, which integrated economics and class analysis into historical analysis, was anathema to those who focused mainly on cultural and political analysis, and that with a bourgeois slant. A major crime in their eyes was that Rodney combined the struggle for social justice with scholarship. Today, while the hostility of the mainstream scholars remains unabated, Rodney's works are regarded as indispensable to a comprehensive understanding of Africa's past. Key elements of his methodology are integrated, but in an unacknowledged form, into most of the major writings on African history nowadays (Hirji 2017).

Rodney declared the framework of his analysis in a comprehensive and clear manner. While his major work can be corrected in terms of some errors of fact, he cannot be accused of disguising his methodological principles and predilections.

MISREPRESENTATIONS OF THE AKIVAGA CRISIS

With these introductory remarks, and bearing in mind that all the accounts we have seen of the Akivaga Crisis were, in one way or another, seriously flawed, let us pose the question: Were the noted flaws instances of random error, or do they signify forms of bias?

In one case, the answer is apparent: The bias in the one-sided accounts from the university administration stems from a tendency to defend the socio-political system of that era as well as the desire to rationalize the actions of prominent personalities. In the case of the mainstream scholars, the limited nature of their accounts originate from a subtle form of bias, namely, their unwillingness to transcend the confines of the capitalist world view. That reduced their capacity to present an in-depth and balanced account of the crisis. For, such an account would call into question their simplistic view the policy of *Ujamaa* in Tanzania.

The main enigma arises for the accounts of the left wing writers. How come the pictures they painted were full of major errors and gave impressions the opposite of what would be expected from them? Were some forms of bias at work here? To help us tackle these questions, we consider the case of Walter Rodney, now not as a historian, but as a subject of history.

Rodney spent approximately eight years at UDSM. His life and work have been described in a number of biographies (See Hirji (2017) for an almost complete list). But a thorough account of his life, writings, teaching and politics at UDSM does not exist. Issa Shivji deserves the most credit for keeping the memory of Walter Rodney alive in Tanzania. Yet, there are some aspects of his work that can assist us in addressing the question of bias posed above.

Let us begin with the Rag Day, an event of British origin some African universities emulated in the 1960s. On a designated day, students dress up in rags to march around the city to raise funds for charity. For the year 1968, the Rag Day at the Dar es Salaam University College was scheduled for 9 November 1968. Viewed as an opportunity for fun by the student body, many eagerly awaited it. However, members of USARF felt that it was a hypocritical gesture that mocked the poor, and embodied a counterproductive approach to combating poverty. On the morning of the scheduled event, they mounted an action that led to its demise at this university for good. Rag Day was replaced by voluntary farm work done by students on a regular basis. The proceeds went to worthy causes including the African liberation movements based in Dar es Salaam.

What role did Walter Rodney play in this battle against the Rag Day? On this issue, we have four sources; three by one author, and one by two of his students:

> *Some of the members of USARF could not stomach this out-right mockery of the masses. They called a meeting on the eve of the so-called Rag Day. At this meeting of USARF the whole question of the role of charity and philanthropy in a bourgeois society was analyzed. Comrades, among whom was Rodney, discussed issues at great length ....* (Shivji 1980).

> *USARF called a public meeting on the eve of the rag day to discuss the rag day. The role of philanthropy and charity in capitalist society was discussed at great length. As Rodney, summed it up, 'Charity is giving by the ounces and taking by the tons.'* (Shivji 1992).

In the text of Shivji (2016), we read

> *[USARF's] view of charity was summed up as a 'euphemism for those who plunder by the ton and give by the ounce.'* (Shivji 1992).

In an accompanying footnote, the source of the phrase under quotation marks is declared:

> *Quoted in Peter C and Mvungi S, 'The state and the student struggles' in Shivji IG (ed.) The state and the working people in Tanzania, CODESRIA, Dakar, 1986. I believe the phrase was originally coined by Walter Rodney during the meeting on the eve of the Rag Day.* (Shivji 2016).

Peter and Mvungi (1986) cite that phrase but do not give a source or attribute it to any person. It is likely that they obtained it from their professor. But in the process, they modify it but nonetheless place it in quotation marks. As Shivji (2016) then repeats the second quote, we do not know what Rodney exactly said on that day.

The bigger question is: Did Rodney make any statement on that day? I was present at the meeting in question and took part in the sabotage of the Rag Day the next morning. My diary, though, says that I first met Rodney in early July 1969, eight months after the Rag Day. How could I have not met him on that day? Are my memory and my diary leading me astray?

It is an indisputable fact that in the middle of October 1968, Rodney, based at the University of Jamaica, was at a conference in Canada. He was then barred by the government of Jamaica from returning to the island. Was it possible that he subsequently flew to Tanzania in time to participate in the Rag Day debacle? I wrote to Patricia Rodney and inquired as to when she and Walter had returned to DSM after he was expelled from Jamaica. Her reply:

> *I returned to Dar in December 1968 with Shaka and pregnant with Kanini. Walter stayed in Cuba until June 1969 when he returned to Dar. Kanini was three months old when he saw her for the first time.* (email from Patricia Rodney, 2016).

Rodney surely did not take part in those Rag Day actions as it was physically impossible for him to have done so. To locate and quote him in that context is pure fictionalized history.

Consider another milestone in the history of student activism at UDSM, namely, the ban on USARF and its organ *Cheche*. The fundamental reason was that USARF and *Cheche* championed socialism and Pan-Africanism in an uncompromising manner, and exposed the shortcomings and contradictory tendencies of TANU and the state on these issues. Thus, its special issue featuring *Tanzania: The Silent Class Struggle* by Issa Shivji exposed the pseudo-socialist nature of the nationalizations of banks and other firms done in 1967. What role did Rodney play in the prelude to the ban? We read:

> *The issue [of Cheche] that followed carried commentary on my long essay. One of the comments was by Walter Rodney, and after that the journal was banned and the organization [USARF] deregistered.* (Shivji 2013)

But if you look at 'the issue that followed,' namely, *Cheche* No. 4, you find that it does not include Rodney's commentary. *Cheche* was banned in November 1970, while this commentary appeared in January 1971, in the inaugural issue of a new magazine called *MajiMaji*. So, as is implied, Rodney's commentary could not have been one of the factors that triggered the ban.

Besides being factually flawed, Shivji's declaration is also conceptually contentious. Rodney's commentary (together with that by John Saul) was presented at a regional social science conference in December 1970. Shivji was in London at that time. On his behalf, I presented his long essay in a session in which Rodney and Saul gave their comments. I recall a sharp exchange with both. What they said, and published, was more conciliatory towards Tanzania's socialistic endeavors than the take home message from *Tanzania: The Silent Class Struggle*. It can be argued that had Rodney and Saul's articles appeared in *Cheche*, it would have been a mitigating factor for not imposing the ban on the magazine.

Let us return to the Akivaga Crisis. The question of relevance is: What was Rodney's involvement in the crisis? As we noted earlier, the answers to this question emanate from Haroub Othman and Issa Shivji.

Othman's depiction of the role of Rodney in this crisis, written more than 35 years later, does not reference any supportive documents. While it is a firsthand account, it is purely a memory based one. The major flaws it contains have been described earlier.

Issa Shivji, on the other hand, was in London at this time. Chris Peter and Sengondo Mvungi came to UDSM much later. None of them cite any relevant documents of that period. Did Shivji acquire his perceptions of the crisis from subsequent discussions with students and academic staff, including Walter Rodney? We do not know.

The names of academic staff who played a prominent role in supporting the students are found in the newspaper reports and documents of that period. Rodney is not one of them. Rodney kept a low public profile during this crisis. The radical students held private talks with him and progressive academics. But that did not make him 'one of the most prominent participants' in the gatherings held. Rodney's name appears in the first academic staff memorandum issued during the crisis. But it is one among sixty four names, the majority whom are non-Tanzanians. I retain a copy of this document. The names of the academic staff who actively backed the students and addressed the student *baraazas* appear in the newspaper reports and documents of the crisis. None of them bears Rodney's name. Had he been publicly and prominently active, it would have been reported by Naijuka Kashivaki, the former chairman of USARF, who wrote a series of excellent reports of the crisis for the main English language daily, *The Standard*, and in the stellar summary of the crisis in Njagi (1971).

Rodney's stand of keeping a distance was consistent with two key aspects of his conduct at UDSM. He held that at times, the right to self-determination outweighed the possibility that it may lead to a faulty course of action. Tanzanians needed the space to decide their own future without an external 'expert' telling them all the time that this was good and this was not. They would learn from their mistakes. Secondly, he was aware that the bogey of foreign agents could be employed by the authorities to suppress a genuinely internal movement. Such a call was indeed issued by some reactionary academics, the administration, the Chairman of the University Council and politicians who wanted to derail the unity generated by the crisis. The students did not buy into this propaganda, but it did permeate the national media.

I have two photos taken at the time of Akivaga's arrest by the FFU. They are 8×10 inch photos (Appendix D). There was a time when, with the help of a magnifying glass, I could identify many students and students in them. But now I can pinpoint just three persons among them with any degree of confidence, one of them being George Hadjivayanis. What I can affirm is that Rodney (or Haroub Othman, for that matter) was never in my identifiable group. But John Saul was.

During his time at UDSM, Rodney worked closely with the radical student groups but was not involved in the activities or affairs of the main student union. That was also the case during the year leading up to the Akivaga Crisis. Furthermore, he had had major tussles with the state authorities just a short while back. It is unlikely that he was in the frame of mind to initiate another one. In practical terms, he was, as noted by Othman, in the final stages of completing his major work, *How Europe Underdeveloped Africa*.

+ + + + + + +

My assistant and I interviewed, by email and in person, over 15 people who were at UDSM during the Akivaga Crisis. One thing that stood out was the extremely varied nature of their recall. The fickleness of human memory makes an exclusive reliance on it for writing history fraught with danger. It is generally affected by not only the biases one had in the past, but critically, one's present day biases as well. Excessive dependence on memory magnifies the operation of **confirmation bias**, namely, the tendency to collect, select, recall, present information in ways that favor one's prior beliefs or conclusions on the issue.

The distortions and exaggerations found in the accounts of the Akivaga Crisis in general and in some actions ascribed to Walter Rodney by the left wing scholars can largely be attributed to confirmation bias. Rodney was a principled activist intellectual who got involved in grassroots struggles wherever he was. Thereby, reliance on memory alone would lead you to stipulate that most probably he was intimately involved in these episodes. No other research is done, and a stipulation is converted into a fact of history. Rodney's stellar accomplishments, however, do not need embellishment. As a meticulous historian, he would have frowned upon such deviant renditions of the actuality of his life.

Saul's exaggerated rendition of an episode from the Akivaga Crisis exemplifies a tendency to enhance the brutal and arbitrary nature of the actions taken by the state authorities in that era. Indeed, numerous actions of this type did take place. But there is no need to magnify any to make that point. And he gets so carried away by these enhancements as to omit from his writings the exemplary features of the Akivaga Crisis he witnessed in person.

The progressive scholars on this crisis have given us accounts and verdicts that seriously misrepresent one of the most important episodes in the history of UDSM. And because those accounts are accepted widely and quoted by other scholars, these misrepresentations persist to this day. Here we observe the operation of **bias towards authority**, namely, the tendency to uncritically accept statements made by a person regarded as an authority expert in the field. If the premier progressive writer in the nation has drawn such a picture of the Akivaga Crisis, who will see the need to question it?

Another form of bias emerging here is **citation bias**, that is, the bias generated by inappropriate citation. One instance of this is circular citation. Thus, scholar A presents a supposition; then B cites it as an observation; and C converts it into an established fact; which later is cited by A to back up his initial supposition. In the biomedical literature, such practices lead to the persistence of scientifically dubious propositions. In the case of Rodney's role in the 1968 Rag Day event, Shivji made a memory based claim. Peter and Mvungi, relying on him, repeated it. In his subsequent work, Shivji cited these authors as his source, thereby giving greater credence to it.

Another important matter is that of apportioning blame. For Saul, it lies with the university authorities. But Shivji and his students go a step further. They blame the victims, the students, for not mobilizing their 'natural allies.' Their accusatory tone is predicated on the assumption that students are the sole agents of social change. The issue of how these natural allies acted is not raised. Did the academic staff or the leadership of the workers contemplate undertaking a go-slow or non-cooperation type of action? Did they directly raise demands of their own, as fellow workers in the nation were doing? While expressing solidarity with the students, they did not take a concrete step that would have sustained the momentum of the struggle. Had that been done, a potential opportunity to examine the substance and function of the university in a society aiming to build socialism could have materialized. Objectively, it was a general failure among the three disenfranchised and aggrieved campus groups to form a solid coalition and struggle for change. To solely the blame the students is not historically accurate.

An important issue they avoid is the role of the Chancellor, Mwalimu Nyerere, in this crisis. First, he appointed a man lacking vision, knowhow or experience to lead UDSM towards lofty academic, socialistic heights. And when that man's high level of ineptitude was revealed beyond doubt, he backed him to the hilt. It was this crucial act on his part that downgraded the morale of the campus community.

The student uprising of 1971 had many ideological and practical limitations. But it also had unprecedented and singularly laudatory features from which many lessons relevant for our day and age can be drawn. It was a short lived episode. History rarely marches in a linear way. Ups and downs, some of a transient variety, are the general norm. The Paris Commune, which laid the basis for a modern day socialist state, was crushed in a matter of weeks. Yet, it served as an inspiration for generations that followed.

Those who desire social change must strive to keep the authentic memories of the past alive. The activists of the future will be inspired and educated by them. More work thus needs to be done in relation to the Akivaga Crisis. An accurate picture of what went on during a time when grassroots democracy, tripartite solidarity and hope bloomed on the UDSM campus, and how and why all that was quashed, is required. And it has to be done before the records of the era and the persons who were involved in it are no longer accessible.

APPENDIX C
DEMOCRACY AND EDUCATION

Explanatory Note: This is an edited version of an article I wrote for the student magazine published at the National Institute of Transport. It appeared in 1980 under the pseudonym A Correspondent. (Hirji 1980). It is included here because it provides further insight into the state of higher education in Tanzania in the 1970s.

+ + + + + + +

NEWSPAPERS ARE LIKE THE TIP OF AN ICEBERG. What they reveal is only a small fraction of what there is. And that too may not be in a proper perspective. But if they are anything to go by, they indicate that many places of learning in Tanzania today are in a state of crisis.

The *Daily News* of 29 August 1979 reported that around 1,000 students of the Dar es Salaam Technical College had marched the day before to the office of the Ilala District Party Secretary to present complaints about intolerable conditions at the college. To quote the report:

> *The students' complaints included allegations of food shortage, bad food, bad accommodation, academic problems, bad services and bad leadership at the school.*

On 16 August of last year, the same paper had carried a story about a scandal at the National Institute of Transport. A large number of students who had been told to resit their examination had actually passed in the first place. Thirty students were asked to supplement when only eight should have done it. Attributing this to administrative negligence, the report went on as follows:

> *Among the many complaints students listed included shortage of books, science laboratory, minimal practical training and general lack of organization.*

Recently, eight students of the Nyegezi Social Training Center were expelled for leading a protest against one of the lecturers. Eighteen other students were issued with warning letters for boycotting the classes of the lecturer who, they claimed, was not competent (*Daily News*, 16 November 979). Just a few months age there were reports of serious disturbances at the Mtwara Technical School when students went on rampage, stoning teachers' houses.

Besides expulsions and suspensions, absenteeism also prevails in schools and colleges. Even mass punishments are heard about. In some secondary schools, students get severe thrashings. For example, a Radio Tanzania broadcast on 22 October 1979 mentioned the case of three pupils of the Ifunda Technical School who had been hospitalized after being caned at school.

Many examples can be cited but the above suffice to raise serious questions regarding the situation in our educational establishments. Schools and colleges are being transformed from a battle-field of ideas into an arena of chaos. What is the cause? Students, teachers, parents, administrators — indeed all concerned with social progress — need to tackle these issues with seriousness they deserve.

THE CLASSROOM

The interaction between teachers and students is the core of the education process. Any tension or hitches in this relationship will reverberate throughout the entire system. What is the nature of this interaction these days?

Learning has to be cooperative endeavor between teachers and students. Now it has become like a competitive tug of war. Both groups are pitted against each other in a condition which is not favorable for appropriate education to take place. Both are victims of circumstances beyond their control. The students see the teachers as just interested in dumping a mass of complex material on them. So they struggle, by means foul or fair, to score a grade, which will enable them to get the coveted certificate or diploma on which their future depends.

Under the guise of removing excessive reliance upon examinations a new system called continuous assessment has been introduced in schools and institutions of higher learning (IHL). It is supposed to be a progressive system as compared to the inherited British system of assessing someone's ability and knowledge through end of the year three hour memory testing exercises. But this system has only recreated in a continuous form miniature exercises in the same old fashion. Emphasis is a still on examinations, the difference being that instead of once a year, you have them once a month or once a week. This has become a nightmare for both the students and the teacher alike. Only administrators, with their preference for methodical drabness, draw satisfaction from the mass of reports filled in. The students are justified in calling it a system of continuous harassment.

Education becomes an assembly line process, tailored to produce standardized robots. Creativity is being banished to a dark corner. Any flexibility in teaching or evaluation is viewed with horror as leading to lowering of standards. Emphasis is on weekly tests with multiple choice questions to facilitate marking. The talk is of combination of theory with practice. The snag is that either the theory is impractical or the practice is just a formal one.

While students are supposed to undertake project work, teachers lack experience to guide them well. The students are besieged with so many tasks that they hardly have time to think about and digest anything well, let alone engage in creative work which projects demand. They just memorize current topics only to forget them as soon as they have got the required units. Project reports turn out to be an odd assortment of data gathered from here and there interspersed with diffuse ideas from textbooks. For the teacher the system has become a spine wreaking burden he or she has to bear day by day and from year to year.

Schools and colleges had shortages of teachers before continuous evaluation was introduced. The teachers were already overburdened. Now their load has increased to an extent that their life has come to resemble that of the fully jammed UDA buses which groan as they crawl along the road, sagging completely on one side and liable to breakdown at any time. Teachers are similarly occupied all the time correcting a pile of papers and filling in progress reports. Given the trends, one can forecast that in future, teachers will be spending more time filling forms and reports than preparing lessons.

Many teachers supported the new system at its inception, unaware of what lay in store for them. Now that it is here to stay, they respond by not completing the syllabus, superficially carrying out the assessments, and in some cases, manufacturing the marks. The purpose of continuous evaluation is to ensure that the students' heads are immersed in books and the teachers are on their toes all the time. But whether a better education is being imparted is something which is yet to be established.

The syllabuses of various subjects being taught at schools and colleges give the impression that we are aiming to set exalted standards for the whole universe to emulate. They contain topics too difficult for the level at which they are taught and in any case, there are too many topics per subject. A teacher who wishes to complete them has to rush through it like a hurricane. In setting the syllabus, the officials tend to include what they found from an advanced course here or abroad, or whatever their learned professor had lectured them about. It is not uncommon to see teachers issuing to students the same handouts and books they got at the university.

Part of the problem is the high turnover in the teaching profession. Most local teachers are inexperienced ones, fresh from college or university. After a few years of teaching they seek other jobs which are better rewarded and more satisfying. There are only a few experienced and qualified local teachers who take their work seriously and stick to their profession. Consequently there is the ongoing reliance on expatriates. But these are here today and away tomorrow. One cannot expect long term improvements by relying on transient elements. Besides, many of them tend to be timid yes-men, who, in the hope of renewing their contracts, will just follow, perhaps conscientiously, the system as it is rather than struggle for a better one.

Moreover, teachers and students have to work in the face of numerous material constraints. Books and stationery are in short supply. And so are typing and duplicating facilities. Orders are misplaced or delayed; suppliers are not paid in time, etc. Priorities are reversed. An air conditioner for the main office is more important than a duplicating machine, teachers handouts are set aside when office correspondence has to be typed, etc.

In spite of the high standards set (or may be because of them) the quality of the students emerging from the education system from the schools to the university is nothing one can boast about. In places, when faced with the projects of mass failures, the teachers become lenient and simply pass everyone. This means that at the next stage of the educational ladder, the students will have to be taught what they are already supposed to have mastered.

This state of affairs causes frustration among students and teachers alike. The dissatisfaction of the students spills over into other areas and causes the type of disturbances we hear about now and again. The academic drudgery they are subjected to is reflected in the fury with which they react.

THE INSTITUTIONAL ENVIRONMENT

Teacher and students are the two major pillars of education. The workers and administrators are employed to assist the learning process. The situation in many places of learning gives the impression that the teachers, students and workers are there to serve the administrators. The resources and facilities in education are prioritized for the convenience of the administrators.

Some examples have been cited above. Take the utilization of vehicles. Many IHLs have one or more vehicles sat their disposal; some have a whole fleet of cars, vans, lorries and buses. If one investigates their usage, all sorts of revelations emerge as vehicle meant for academic usage are diverted for other purposes. A van may be bought for research but the sole research it may end up doing is around brothels on Saturday nights.

If it is a question of getting a vehicle for collecting external tutors, sending students on field trips, sending teachers to supervise students' projects etc., none seems to be available. It takes a major effort to procure a vehicle. But if it is a question of sending the principal's wife for shopping or a bag of cement to the bursar's house, there is no problem. There is a clear inversion of priorities. In some cases college vehicles are found near the bars at night, being used for private business purposes. Such practices contribute towards the mounting grievances in these institutions.

The general services provided to the students and teachers also tend to be poor. In many cases it is due to lack of organization and sheer neglect by the authorities. Class rooms lack simple things as dusters and teachers have to bring their own rags to clean the blackboard. The purchase of supplies for schools and institutes is riddled with scandals. Food is bought at inflated price and someone pockets the difference. The same story prevails in the purchase of books, stationery, laboratory and workshop equipment. Most schools and some IHLs have a shortage of funds. But instead of trying to make the best of it, a few individuals try to make the most of it. Students end up eating rotten beans and maize purchased at high prices and when they complain they are told it is a national problem.

Favoritism is also rampant in these places. Be it the question of recruiting students, employing cleaners or promoting teachers, the role of *ndugunization* is critical. Students know about their fellows who are there not through their know-how but know-who. Teachers are not surprised when one of them rises fast up the ladder without any achievements to his credit. There is favoritism in giving scholarships. Many IHLs get scholarships from international organizations for the purpose of training their teaching staff but members of the administration often are the first ones to taste the cake. The teachers get left over after the bosses have taken their share.

In many places, the administration lacks the necessary foresight and competence to run the places well and plan its long-term development. Shortsightedness and narrow horizons govern their decision making which in most cases is done on a day to day basis. Instead of emphasizing academic excellence, they stress loyalty. Many fear to recruit qualified and competent local staff in the fear of being replaced or exposed. Local staff are frustrated through insufficient incentives, lack of fringe benefits and facilities, and too strict a promotion policy. Some administrators prefer expatriates or local staff with dubious qualification who are content with being their yes-men.

Administrators tend to run their colleges or institutes like primary schools, with emphasis on petty issues. They want to exercise a strict control on everything that goes on. Some go to the dining hall at meal times to ensure that the students do not get more than the specified share. They emphasize attendance, obedience, and punctuality, and are very strict towards any student who show any signs of violating the rules. In some IHLs teachers are required to report on duty at 8:00 in the morning daily and be on the premises for the entire working time irrespective of whether they have classes to teach or not. A teacher is turned into an office clerk. His efficiency inevitably declines because of the lack of flexibility which his work demands.

BUREAUCRACY OR DEMOCRACY

Bookish drudgery makes students less involved in extracurricular activities. This also affects their outlook and awareness. Participation in sports, students clubs, discussion groups, student organization affairs, and student magazines becomes restricted as most students are permanently buried under an avalanche of tests and assignments. These activities are an important a component of education. The aim of education is not to produce stunted robots. Without such activities, the outlook of the students will be shallow and careerist and they will be unable to play their full role in social development.

A sound education must be based on democratic foundations. The old fashioned bureaucrat who dismisses students as an unruly lot has no place in the modern education system. The lack of participation of students in decision making is one of the fundamental causes of the present crisis in the system. Even teachers often have little say in what goes on in their places.

Absence of participation and control from below enables some individuals in key positions to take advantage of existing problems and magnify them into gigantic ones. Numerous wanton practices proliferate when bureaucracy has the upper hand and lead to mounting frustrations among students, teachers and workers. To prevent such explosions and to improve the situation in schools and institutes there is a need to strengthen participatory democracy, institute grassroot control and promote freedom of information.

WHAT IS TO BE DONE?

The long term solution to the existing impasse in education is to organize the system on a firm democratic footing. With the involvement of all parties, solutions to different specific problems can be worked out. Participation of the students in decision making relating to the affairs of the school or college community is crucial.

The present situation of academic drudgery for students and over work for the teachers must be remedied, and a more rational system of learning and evaluation has to be worked out.

There is a need for an independent and democratic student organization through which the students will channel their contributions. The recent announcement of the establishment of National Union of Students is a welcome one. But it should not be loaded with bureaucratic controls that would turn it into a student organ in name only. And the students need to elect their leaders with care. Some student leaders are only interested in prestige and running bars, and do not look after the interests of their constituents. Students should elect committed and bold leaders who exhibit a deep understanding of the society in which they live.

In a similar fashion there is need for a National Union of Teachers with branches at all the places of learning. It should be a democratic, autonomous organization which would promote the interests of the teaching profession and higher academic standards. It should work to attract and retain competent and committed teachers by struggling for the improvements of the terms and conditions of work for teachers.

And there is a need to promote freedom of ideas through free flow of information and discussion. All members of the school or college community should have a right of access to information regarding the affairs of the school or the college. The present bureaucratic system of locking up even the pettiest detail leads to small problems being undetected or dealt with until they assume mammoth proportions. Students and teachers, through their elected representatives, must be informed about all community affairs and how the community resources and finance are used. In case of misuse, they must be empowered to take appropriate measures.

In order to promote debate through which different problems can be discussed and resolved, students and teachers must establish their own magazines, journals or newsletters to voice their opinions on academic, institutional and national issues.

The problems of the educational system cannot be solved without the participation of the students and the teachers. The reforms suggested here intended to ensure that this participation occurs on a free and democratic basis.

+ + + + + + +

Comment: From the above article we see that in the 1970s, the Tanzanian higher education system was beset with a myriad of major problems. Nonetheless, the quality of education imparted in those days was superior compared with what prevails in our colleges and universities today. The typical graduate of that era had a reasonably good command, in theory and practice, of his discipline. In contrast, most current graduates display a shallow and confused understanding of even the subjects in which they obtained a high grade.

APPENDIX D
PHOTOS

Photo 2.1 UDSM Supervisor and Trainees, Tanga: 1969

Photo 3.1 Departure for London: 1971

Photo 5.0 FFU Arrests Student Leader: 1971 (The Standard, 9 July 1971)

Photo 5.1 FFU Confronts Students, UDSM: 1971

Photo 5.2 FFU Takes Away Student Leader, UDSM: 1971

Photo 6.1 Lecturing at UDSM: 1973

Photo 7.1 Initial Family Residence, Sumbawanga: 1974

Photo 7.2 Visiting a Fishery Project, Lake Tanganyika: 1975

Photo 8.1 *Short Course Participants and Instructors, NIT: 1979*

Photo 8.2 *Farewell Party, NIT: 1980*

Photo 8.3 Farewell Party, NIT: 1980

Photo 8.4 Farewell Party, NIT: 1980

Photo 8.5 Farewell Party, NIT: 1980

Photo 8.6 Farewell Party, NIT: 1980

Photo 8.7 Farewell Party, NIT: 1980

Photo 9.1 Graduation at Harvard, Boston: 1982

ACKNOWLEDGMENTS

MANY PEOPLE provided relevant information and useful comments for this book. I list them in a chapter-wise manner.

Chapter 2: Elizabeth Jones, Shiraz Ramji

Chapters 3 & 6: Noorally Jiwaji, Clifford DaCosta

Chapter 4: Abdul Sheriff, Fatma Alloo

Chapter 5 & Appendix B: George Hadjivayanis, Jenerali Ulimwengu, Iqbal Dewji, Andrew Lyall, Joe Shengena, Peter Lawrence, Patricia Rodney, JL Kanywanyi, Marjorie Mbilinyi, Saida Othman, Ramesh Chauhan and Hon. Pius Msekwa

Chapter 8: Khalid Kachenje

Others who assisted me are:

Research, Interview & Typing: Yusuf Ahmad, Farida Hirji

Typing, Checking Typographic Errors, Communication & General Support: Farida Hirji

Comments & Editing: Peter Lawrence

Organization of Records, Detailed Comments, Formatting, Editing, Communication & Copy Editing : Rosa Hirji

General Support: Firoze Manji

All of them have my profound gratitude.

REFERENCES AND READINGS

General References

Akers DS and Bagader AA (editiors) (2008) *Oranges in the Sun: Short Stories from the Arabian Gulf*, Lynne Rienner Publishers, Inc., Boulder, Colorado.
Ali T (2005) *Street Fighting Years: An Autobiography of the Sixties*, Verso, New York.
Angell M (2005) *The Truth About the Drug Companies: How They Deceive Us and What To Do About It*, Random House, New York.
Babu AM (1991) The 1964 Revolution: Lumpen or vanguard? In A Sheriff and E Ferguson (editors) (1991), pages 220–247.
Bagdikian B (2004) *The New Media Monopoly*, Beacon Press, Boston, MA.
Berman DM (1979) *Death on the Job*, Monthly Review Press, New York.
Braithwaite ER (1977) *To Sir With Love*, Penguin Books, New York (first published in 1959).
Chomsky N et al. (1998) *The Cold War & the University: Toward an Intellectual History of the Postwar Years*, The New Press, New York.
Coulson A (1982) *Tanzania: A Political Economy*, Clarendon Press, Oxford.
Derber C, Schwartz WA and Magrass Y (1990) *Power in the Highest Degree*, Oxford University Press, New York.
Editorial (2004) Depressing research, *The Lancet*, 363:1335.
Editorial (2006) Unravelling industry bias in clinical trials, *Pain*, 121:175–176.
Ferguson CH (2012) *Predator Nation: Corporate Criminals, Political Corruption, and the Hijacking of America*, Crown Business, New York.
Fanon F (1965) *The Wretched of the Earth*, Grove Press, London.
Fanon F (1967) *Black Skins, White Masks*, Grove Press, London.
Harrison GP (2013) *Think: Why You Should Question Everything*, Prometheus Books, New York.
Hinton W and Magdoff F (2008) *Fanshen: A Documentary of Revolution in a Chinese Village*, Monthly Review Press, New York.
Hirji KF (1973) School education and underdevelopment in Tanzania, *MajiMaji*, No. 12:1–23.
Hirji KF and NIT Students (1980) *Accidents at Work: The Case of Motor Vehicle Workshops*, Research Report No. 1, National Institute of Transport, Dar es Salaam.
Hirji KF (1980) The Political Economy of Transport, in Mrema TK (Ed), *Transport in East Africa: Part II*, The National Institute of Transport, Dar es Salaam.
Hirji KF (1980a) (A Correspondent), Democracy and Education, *The Transporter*, No. 4:11–17.
Hirji KF (1980b) Colonial Ideological Apparatuses in Tanganyika under the Germans, in HY Kaniki (Ed), *Tanganyika Under Colonial Rule*, Longmans: London.
Hirji KF (1990) Academic pursuits under the link, *CODESRIA Bulletin* (Senegal), No. 2:9–16. (New version in CB Mwaria, S Federici and J McLaren (editors) (2000), Chapter 6.)
Hirji KF (2009) No short-cut in assessing trial quality: A case study, *Trials*, 10:1, Paper with editorial comment in *Trials*, 10:2, www.trialsjournal.com.
Hirji KF and Premji Z (2011) Pre-referral rectal artesunate in severe malaria: A flawed trial, *Trials*, 12:188, www.trialsjournal.com.

Hirji KF (2011) *Cheche: Reminiscences of a Radical Magazine*, Mkuki na Nyota Publishers, Dar es Salaam.

Hirji (2016) Adios Kariakoo: An assessment of *And Home Was Kariakoo: A Memoir of East Africa* by MG Vassanji, *AwaaZ Magazine*, Volume 13, Issue 1, July 2016, http://www.awaazmagazine.com/volume-13-issue-1

Hirji KF (2017) *The Enduring Relevance of Walter Rodney's How Europe Underdeveloped Africa*, Daraja Press, Canada.

Hussain KA (1973) *The Development of Roads and Road Transport in Pakistan*, Transport Consultant Corporation, Lahore, Pakistan.

Kassirer J (2000) Financial indigestion, *Journal of the American Medical Association*, 284:2156–2157.

Komagi D (2017) Ban on 19 universities remains in force, as academic year opens, *The Citizen*, 20 October 2017.

Lal P (2014) Maoism in Tanzania, in AC Cook (editor) *Mao's Little Red Book: A Global History*, Cambridge University Press, Cambridge, UK, pages 96–116.

Lee–Potter E (2015) I dropped out of teaching after six months – so I'm not surprised other teachers are leaving in their droves, *The Independent* (UK), 3 January 2016, www.independent.co.uk/voices.

Legum C (1972) *Africa: The Year of the Students*, Rex Collings Ltd., London.

Mayer M (2005) When clinical trials are compromised: A perspective from a patient advocate, *PLoS Medicine*, 2:e358.

Mullane K and Williams M (2013) Bias in research: the rule rather than the exception, *Biochemical Pharmacology*, www.elsevier.com/editors-update/story /publishing-ethics/ bias-in-research.html.

Nkrumah K (1966) *Neo-Colonialism: The Last Stage of Imperialism*, International Publishers, London.

Nyerere JK (1967) *Education for Self-Reliance*, in JK Nyerere (1968), pp. 267–290.

Nyerere JK (1968) *Freedom and Socialism: A Selection of Writings and Speeches, 1965–1967*, Oxford University Press, Dar es Salaam & Oxford.

Nyerere JK (1970) Relevance and Dar es Salaam University, in JK Nyerere (1973): 192–203.

Nyerere JK (1973) *Freedom and Development: A Selection of Writings and Speeches, 1968–1973*, Oxford University Press, Dar es Salaam & Oxford.

Parenti C (2000) *Lockdown America: Police and Prisons in the Age of Crisis*, Verso Press, New York.

Phillips CJ (2015) *The New Math: A Political History*, The University of Chicago Press, Chicago and London.

Rodney W (1972a) *How Europe Underdeveloped Africa*, Bogle-'LOuveture and Tanzania Publishing House, Dar es Salaam.

Rodney W (1971) Some implications of the question of disengagement from imperialism, *MajiMaji* January 1971, No. 1:3–8.

Salaam al-Mundhri YB (2008) Oranges in the sun, in DS Akers and AA Bagader (editors), (2008), pages 103–105.

Saul JS (1971) Who is the immediate enemy? *Majimaji*, January 1971, No. 1:9–15.

Sawyer WW (1962) Abstract and concrete, www.marco-learningsystems.com /pages/ sawyer, accessed 29 April 2016.

Sawyer WW (2001) Modern Math and its critics, www.marco-learningsystems.com /pages/ sawyer, accessed 29 April 2016.
Schalk DL (1991) *War and the Ivory Tower*, Oxford University Press, New York.
Sheriff A (1991) Conclusion, in A Sheriff and E Ferguson (editors) (1991), pages 249–261.
Sheriff A and Ferguson E (editors) (1991) *Zanzibar Under Colonial Rule*, James Currey, London.
Stuart A, Ord K and Kendall M (1987) *Kendall's Advanced Theory of Statistics: Volume 1: Distribution Theory*, fifth edition, Oxford University Press, Oxford.
TANU (1967) *The Arusha Declaration and TANU's Policy of Socialism and Self-Reliance*, TANU Publicity Section, Dar es Salaam.
Vassanji MG (2014) *And Home Was Kariakoo: A Memoir of East Africa*, Doubleday, Canada.
von Freyhold M (1979) *Ujamaa Villages in Tanzania: Analysis of a Social Experiment*, Monthly Review Press, New York.
Western B (2007) *Punishment and Inequality in America*, Russel Sage Foundation, New York.
Whitaker R (2010) *Mad in America: Bad Science, Bad Medicine, and the Enduring Mistreatment of the Mentally Ill* Basic Books, New York.
Whitaker R (2011) *Anatomy of an Epidemic: Magic Bullets, Psychiatric Drugs, and the Astonishing Rise of Mental Illness in America*, Broadway Books, New York.

Akivaga Crisis – Documents

ACD-00: Nsekela AJ (1971) Speech by AJ Nsekela, Chairman of the Council of the University of Dar es Salaam at the graduation ceremony on 7th July 1971, 7 July 1971.
ACD-01: Akivaga S (DUSO President) (1971) Open letter to the Vice Chancellor, Dar es Salaam University Students' Organization, 8 July 1971.
ACD-02: Mwingira AC (Chief Administrative Officer) (1971) Charges of disciplinary offenses against Symonds Akivaga, University of Dar es Salaam, 8 July 1971.
ACD-03: Muwowo JAT (Dean of Students) (1971) Rustication letter: Symonds Akivaga, University of Dar es Salaam, 9 July 1971.
ACD-04: Kanywanyi JL, Malima KA and Mbilinyi M (Ad Hoc Committee of Academic Staff) (1971) Call for a general staff meeting (endorsed by 64 staff members), University of Dar es Salaam, 9 July 1971.
ACD-05: Moshi EA (DUSO Vice President) (1971a) Letter to all students on the rustication of the DUSO president, Dar es Salaam University Students' Organization, 10 July 1971.
ACD-06: TYL (1971) Statement of UDSM TYL branch (in Swahili and English), University of Dar es Salaam TYL Branch, 10 July 1971.
ACD-07: Materu FM (Hall Chairman) (1971) Resolutions of members of Residence Hall III, University of Dar es Salaam, 10 July 1971.
ACD-08: Moshi EA (DUSO Vice President) (1971) Letter of explanation to campus workers regarding events of 9 July 1971 (in Swahili and English), Dar es Salaam University Students' Organization, 10 July 1971.
ACD-09: Kanywanyi JL and Malima KA (Ad Hoc Committee of Academic Staff) (1971) Recommendations of the university teaching and research staff, University of Dar es Salaam, 10 July 1971.

ACD-10: Moshi EA (DUSO Vice President) (1971) Letter to all students explaining the stand of the Academic Staff, Dar es Salaam University Students' Organization, 10 July 1971.

ACD-11: Chenge A and Lyall A (Student and Lecturer, Faculty of Law) (1971) Memorandum on the legality of the recent actions taken by the Administration of the University of Dar es Salaam, UDSM Faculty of Law, 11 July 1971.

ACD-12: UDSM Academic Staff (1971) Memorandum to the Special Committee of the Council of the University of Dar es Salaam, University of Dar es Salaam, 11 July 1971.

ACD-13: Nsekela AJ (Chairman, Council of the University of Dar es Salaam) (1971) Council Resolutions, University of Dar es Salaam, 12 July 1971.

ACD-14: DUSO (1971) Letter to the Chancellor: An explanation of the students' views, Dar es Salaam University Students' Organization, 12 July 1971.

ACD-15: Swai FS (Speaker, DUSO) (1971) Letter to the Chancellor: *Baraza* resolutions, Dar es Salaam University Students' Organization, 13 July 1971.

ACD-16: Moshi EA (Vice President, DUSO) and Dewji IM (DUSO Representative to the Council) (1971) Report of the Student Delegation to the Chancellor, Dar es Salaam University Students' Organization, 14 July 1971.

ACD-17: DUSO (1971) *DUSO News Bulletin – The University Echo*, Dar es Salaam University Students Organization, 16 July 1971.

ACD-19: UDSM Workers' Committee (1971) Grievances of the workers on the Hill (in Swahili), 12 July 1971, reported in summarized form in DUSO (1971), University of Dar es Salaam, 16 July 1971.

ACD-20: Moshi EA (Vice President, DUSO) (1971) Letter to all students: The situation at the moment, Dar es Salaam University Students' Organization, 23 July 1971.

ACD-21: Wanyandeh AA (DUSO Minister for Campus Affairs) (1971) Letter to all students: Acute shortage of chairs and utensils, Dar es Salaam University Students Organization, 24 July 1971.

ACD-22: Kanywanyi JL and Malima KA (Academic Staff Ad Hoc Committee) (1971) A background to the Academic Staff Resolution of 10th July 1971, University of Dar es Salaam, 10 August 1971.

ACD-23: TYL (1971) *MajiMaji*, Issue No 3, August 1971 (with editorial and two reports on the Akivaga Crisis.

ACD-24: Mutalemwa CAK (DUSO Minister for Academic Affairs) (1972) Letter to students: Election of Student Representatives for Faculty Boards, Dar es Salaam University Students' Organization, 10 November 1972.

Akivaga Crisis – Newspaper Reports

ACNR-01: Students boycott classes at the Hill, *The Standard*, 10 July 1971.
ACNR-02: University council to meet tomorrow, *Sunday News*, 11 July 1971.
ACNR-03: Staff want student back, *Sunday News*, 11 July 1971.
ACNR-04: Msekwa explains rustication, *Sunday News*, 11 July 1971.
ACNR-05: Editorial Opinion: University row, *Sunday News*, 11 July 1971.
ACNR-06: Varsity students stick to their resolutions, *The Nationalist*, 12 July 1971.
ACNR-07: Students discuss crisis at Hill, *The Standard*, 12 July 1971.
ACNR-08: University Council meets, *The Standard*, 13 July 1971.

ACNR-09: Varsity students told to go back to classes, *The Nationalist*, 13 July 1971.
ACNR-10: Five off to see Mwalimu on University crisis, *The Standard*, 14 July 1971.
ACNR-11: Editorial Comment, *The Standard*, 14 July 1971.
ACNR-12: Varsity students resume classes, *The Nationalist*, 14 July 1971.
ACNR-13: University team returns after talk with Mwalimu Nyerere, *The Standard*, 15 July 1971.
ACNR-14: Varsity delegates back from Dodoma, *The Nationalist*, 15 July 1971.
ACNR-15: DUSO reports back, *The Standard*, 16 July 1971.
ACNR-16: Nairobi students rap Dar 'varsity, *Daily Nation*, 16 July 1971.
ACNR-17: Varsity probe team, *The Nationalist*, 26 July 1971.
ACNR-18: DUSO drafts appeal for Akivaga, *The Standard*, 27 July 1971.
ACNR-19: DUSO appeals against Akivaga's suspension, *The Nationalist*, 27 July 1971.
ACNR-20: Committee on varsity crisis meets Tuesday, *The Nationalist*, 29 July 1971.
ACNR-21: Probe into Varsity crisis starts, *The Nationalist*, 4 August 1971.
ACNR-22: DUSO explains why students boycotted probe team, *The Nationalist*, 5 August 1971.
ACNR-23: Varsity Council c'ttee adopts procedure, *The Nationalist*, 6 August 1971.
ACNR-24: University committee making progress, *The Standard*, 10 August 1971.
ACNR-25: University expels Akivaga, *The Standard*, 20 August 1971.
ACNR-26: University student cabinet resigns, *The Standard*, 25 August 1971.
ACNR-27: TYL branch rejects Hill report recommendations by University probe team, *The Standard*, 29 November 1971.
ACNR-28: Hill TYL team to study report, *The Standard*, 30 November 1971.
ACNR-29: *Tawi la vijana lapinga ripoti ya Mlimani*, *Uhuru*, 11 December 1971.
ACNR-30: Why Hill TYL rejects Mungai report, *The Standard*, 16 December 1971.
ACNR-31: Missing features from the Mungai report, *The Standard*, 21 December 1971.
ACNR-32: University crisis, searching for compromise, *The Standard*, 22 December 1971.

Akivaga Crisis – Articles and Book Chapters

Chauhan R, Kavishe W and Minja F (1971) Editorial, *MajiMaji*, No. 3, August 1971:i–iii.
Douglas T (2007) *The History of the University of Dar es Salaam: Chronicling the Importance of the Student Voice*, Unpublished undergraduate thesis, Georgetown College, Washington, DC.
FouéréMA (editor) *Remembering Nyerere in Tanzania: History, Memory, Legacy*, Mkuki na Nyota Publishers, Dar es Salaam.
Hirji KF (1971) Crisis on the campus: Diagnosis and implications, *MajiMaji*, No. 3, August 1971:7–12.
Itandala B (2008) University of Dar es Salaam's immediate response to Musoma Resolution, in IN Kimambo, BBB Mapunda and YQ Lawi (editors) (2008), pages 193–205.
Kimambo IN (2008) Establishment of the University of Dar es Salaam, in IN Kimambo, BBB Mapunda and YQ Lawi (editors) (2008), pages 152–169.
Kimambo IN, Mapunda BBB and Lawi YQ (editors) (2008) *In Search of Relevance: A History of the University of Dar es Salaam*, Dar es Salaam University Press, Dar es Salaam.

Lueshcher TM, Klemencic M and Jowi JO (editors) (2016), *Student Politics in Africa: Representation and Activism*, African Minds, Cape Town.

Mbwete TSA and Ishumi AGM (2000) *Managing University Crises*, Dar es Salaam University Press, Dar es Salaam.

Mihanjo EP (2008) Student and staff organizations, in IN Kimambo, BBB Mapunda and YQ Lawi (editors) (2008), pages 206–226.

Mkude D, Cooksey B and Levey L (2003) *Higher Education in Tanzania*, Dar es Salaam University Press, Dar es Salaam.

Msekwa P (2014) *Uongozi na Utawala wa Mwalimu Julius Kambarage Nyerere*, Nyambari Nyangwine Publishers, Dar es Salaam, Tanzania.

Ngirwa CC, Euwema M, Babyegeya E and Stouten J (2014) Managing change in higher education in Tanzania: A historical perspective, *Higher Education Management and Policy*, Volume 24/3, 127–144.

Njagi M (1971) The upheaval against bureaucratic arrogance, *MajiMaji*, No. 3, August 1971:1–6.

Oanda I (2016) The evolving nature of student participation in university governance in Africa: An overview of policies, trends and emerging issues, in TM Lueshcher, M Klemencic and JO Jowi (editors) (2016), chapter 4.

Omari JM and Mihyo PB (1991) *The Roots of Student Unrest in African Universities*, Man Graphics Limited, Nairobi.

Othman H (2005) Walter Rodney – A revolutionary intellectual, In SY Othman (editor) (2014), pages 299–302.

Othman SY (editor) (2014) *Yes, in My Life Time: Selected Works of Haroub Othman*, Mkuki na Nyota & CODESRIA, Dar es Salaam & Dakar.

Peter C and Mvungi S (1985) The state and student struggles, in IG Shivji (editor) (1985), pages 157–198.

Provini O (2015) The University of Dar es Salaam: A post-Nyerere institution of higher education? Legacies, continuation and changes, in MA Fouéré(editor) (2015), chapter 11.

Saul JS (1973) Radicalism and the Hill, in L Cliffe and JS Saul (editors) (1973), Volume II:289–292.

Saul JS (2009) *Revolutionary Traveler: Freeze-Frames From a Life*, Arbeiter Ring Publishing, Winnipeg, Canada.

Saul J (2011) Tanzanian socialism and Africa's future: Mere footnote or first step on a long march, http://carleton.ca/africanstudies/wp-content/uploads/Saul-Nyerere-Carleton-2011.pdf.

Shivji IG (1980) Rodney and radicalism on the Hill, 1966–1974, in IG Shivji (1993), pages 32–40.

Shivji IG (1981) Freedom, democracy and apathy at the University, in IG Shivji (1993), pages 62–70.

Shivji IG (editor) (1985) *The State and the Working People in Tanzania*, CODESRIA Book Series, Dakar.

Shivji IG (1987) Debates at the Hill? In IG Shivji (1993), pages 129–155.

Shivji IG (1992) What is left of the left intellectual at 'The Hill'? In IG Shivji (1993), pages 200–219.

Shivji IG (1993), *Intellectuals at the Hill: Essays and Talks, 1969–1993*, Dar es Salaam University Press, Dar es Salaam.

Shivji IG (2013) Chapter 8, in C Chung (editor) (2013) *Walter A Rodney: A Promise of Revolution*, Monthly Review Press, New York.

TANU (1971) *Mwongozo: TANU Guidelines*, National Printing Company, Dar es Salaam.

UDSM (1973) *A Report on the Activities of UDSM for the Year 1971/72*, University of Dar es Salaam, Dar es Salaam.

UDSM (1974) *A Report on the Activities of UDSM for the Year 1972/73*, University of Dar es Salaam, Dar es Salaam.

Quotations

Note: The quotations given throughout the book are available at many websites on the Internet. Thus, I do not provide specific sources.

Photo and Image Credits

With the exception of Photo 5.0, all photos in this book belong to the author. Photo 5.0 is from *The Standard*, 9 July 1971.

AUTHOR PROFILE

Karim F Hirji is a retired Professor of Medical Statistics and a Fellow of the Tanzania Academy of Sciences. A recognized authority on statistical analysis of small sample discrete data, the author of the only book on the subject, he received the Snedecor Prize for Best Publication in Biometry from the American Statistical Association and International Biometrics Society for the year 1989. He has published many papers in the areas of statistical methodology, applied biomedical research, the history and practice of education in Tanzania, and written numerous essays on varied topics for the mass media and popular magazines.

He is the author of *Exact Analysis of Discrete Data* (Chapman and Hall/CRC Press, Boca Raton, 2005), *Statistics in the Media: Learning from Practice* (Media Council of Tanzania, Dar es Salaam, 2012) and *Growing Up With Tanzania: Memories, Musings and Maths* (Mkuki na Nyota Publishers, Dar es Salaam, 2014). He also edited and is the main author of *Cheche: Reminiscences of a Radical Magazine* (Mkuki na Nyota Publishers, Dar es Salaam, 2011). His most recent books are *The Enduring Relevance of Walter Rodney's How Europe Underdeveloped Africa* (Daraja Press, Montreal, 2017) and *The Banana Girls* (Mkuki na Nyota Publishers, Dar es Salaam, 2017).

He resides in Dar es Salaam, Tanzania, and may be contacted at kfhirji@aol.com.

www.ingramcontent.com/pod-product-compliance
Lightning Source LLC
Chambersburg PA
CBHW070133080526
44586CB00015B/1674